MARGARET MEAD
Some Personal Views

MARGARET MEAD

Some Personal Views

Edited by Rhoda Metraux

ANGUS AND ROBERTSON • PUBLISHERS

ANGUS & ROBERTSON • PUBLISHERS
London • Sydney • Melbourne • Singapore • Manila

First published in the United States of America in 1979 by the Walker Publishing Company, Inc.

Published in the United Kingdom by Angus & Robertson (UK) Ltd, 10 Earlham Street, London, WC2, in 1979.

ISBN 0 207 95893 9

To all the people who asked her questions

CONTENTS

FOREWORD

Margaret Mead's most winning gift was surely her capacity for immediate, zestful response. Whenever she went away from home, she looked, listened and asked questions. And on her lecture trips and travels around the world, whether to London or Sydney or Peri Village in the Admiralty Islands, she accepted with grace the fact that her fellow travelers and the people in her audiences wanted to ask questions too. She made a point of answering each query thoughtfully and concisely—sometimes with a single word, sometimes sharply and most often with humor. She took for granted that a sophisticated question required a sophisticated answer, but she never rebuffed the person who had to struggle to find words. One thing exasperated her: without hesitation she pricked the balloon of the pompous, pretentious questioner.

Looking and listening, asking and answering questions— these are the indispensable tools of the anthropologist, which Margaret Mead used with consummate skill. It was also her conviction that the freedom to ask questions and the obligation to listen and to answer fully and responsibly are the marks of an open society and are critically important in a period when change, coming upon all of us so swiftly, continually forces each of us to ask: Who else thinks—and feels—as I do?

Almost all the questions and answers gathered in this volume were first published in *Redbook Magazine* over a sixteen-year period, from 1963 to January 1979. A handful of them, published here for the first time, had been prepared for publication at the time of her death in November 1978. Very often when she lectured, Margaret Mead asked the members of her audience to write out their questions, so that whether or not she could answer all of them that very day, she still would have some record of what was on their minds. A great many of the questions answered in *Redbook*'s columns were chosen from the fat stacks of cards and little slips of paper she brought home from her talks with college and university students or women's groups or teachers or psychiatrists or politicians or business people—or any of the other groups and diverse organizations that claimed her time and interest. Other questions were raised by the young members of the *Redbook* staff. They were in touch with their readers and, no less than others, hoped to find out what she thought about problems that concerned and often troubled them.

Over the years a relationship that combined a lively friendship with mutual professional admiration and trust grew up between Margaret Mead and the people with whom she worked most closely at *Redbook*. Every author knows what it means to have a copy editor who will check every date and the spelling of every difficult name and, even more important, who will not hesitate to say, with tact: This sentence doesn't seem to me quite clear as yet! For eleven years, since 1967, Helene Pleasants shepherded Margaret Mead's columns into press at *Redbook*, providing a kind of consistency over time which one may hope for but seldom attains. This is reflected in the organization of this volume as well.

Here each question and answer is given with the date of its first publication or, in the case of the few unpublished ones, with the date of their completion. It is possible, therefore, to relate each one to the events then taking place, as you remember them, and to the mood of that period. Especially in the earlier years, people wondered what an anthropologist might have to say about some current problem, and through all the years there ran the bright thread of curiosity about Margaret Mead herself: who were her role models, who were her favorite storytellers?

In spite of changes in the kinds of questions, there is a congruence in the answers that reflects a consistent, human view of the world and of our shared lives, past and still to come. Margaret Mead took in the world around her as a whole person. Asked what she thought or felt or believed, she replied, as she felt she must, with a lively expression of her own, her personal views.

—Rhoda Metraux
New York City
January 29, 1979

ৰ্থ 1 ৯

MEN AND
WOMEN

How would you explain the fact that the most outstanding creative people in all fields have been predominantly men? MARCH 1963

Throughout history it has been men, for the most part, who have engaged in public life. Men have sought for public achievement and recognition, while women have obtained their main satisfactions by bearing and rearing children and making homes for men and children. In women's eyes, public achievement makes a man more attractive as a marriage partner. But for men the situation is reversed; the more a woman achieves publicly, the less desirable she seems as a wife.

There are, of course, certain exceptions. Women have made distinguished careers on the stage, where a man can take pride in the acclaim given a woman for feminine qualities of beauty or charm, and in those professions which are regarded as extensions of woman's domestic role and which depend on womanly virtues of compassion and care—nursing, teaching and social work. But in general, creative women are exposed to a constant pull between a desire for and enjoyment of children and home and a desire to do creative work.

There are three possible positions one can take about male and female creativity. The first is that males are inherently more creative in all fields. The second is that if it were not for the greater appeal of creating and cherishing young human beings, females would be as creative as males. If this were the case, then if men were permitted the enjoyment women

13

have always had in rearing young children, male creativity might be reduced also. (There is some indication in the United States today that this is so.) The third possible position is that certain forms of creativity are more congenial to one sex than to the other and that the great creative acts will therefore come from only one sex in a given field.

There is some reason to believe that males may always excel—by just the small degree that makes the difference between a good capacity and great talent—in such fields as music and mathematics, where creativity involves imposing form rather than finding it. There is also reason to believe that women have a slightly greater potential in those fields in which it is necessary to listen and learn, to find forms in nature or in their own hearts rather than to make entirely new ones; these fields could include certain areas of literature, and some forms of science that depend on observation and recognition of pattern, such as the study of living creatures or children or societies.

It can always be argued, however, that though women have done good work in fields that fit this formula, the greatest work has been done by men. Here we run into a new problem. When women work in a creative field, even one that is particularly congenial to them, they must generally work with forms that were created by men, or else struggle against special odds to develop new forms. Until we have an educational system that permits enough women to work within any field—music, mathematics, painting, literature, biology and so on—so that forms which are equally congenial to both sexes are developed, we shall not have a fair test of this third possibility.

We do know that what one sex has developed, members of the other sex can learn—from cookery to calculus. In those countries of the Eastern bloc in which women are expected to play an equal part with men in the sciences, great numbers of women have shown a previously unsuspected ability. We run a great risk of squandering half our human gifts by arbitrarily denying any field to either sex or by penalizing women who try to use their gifts creatively.

How do you feel about our alimony laws? MAY 1963

We are caught in an interim period when our beliefs about the sanctity and permanence of marriage are confused and contradictory. On the one hand we have our traditional Christian inheritance in which marriage is treated as a sacrament and the marriage pair assume the awesome responsibility, in the words of the Book of Common Prayer, ". . . to have and to hold from this day forward, for better for worse, for richer for poorer, in sickness and in health, to love and to cherish, till death us do part. . . ." But this vow contains one promise that human beings have never known how to make themselves keep—the promise to love. And the institution of divorce has grown in the modern world with the increased emphasis upon the individual as a person in his or her own right who cannot be forced to feel prescribed emotions. In permitting divorce, however, we seem to have confused the obligations that a husband and wife hold only during marriage and those which are more enduring.

If marriage were regarded as the most solemn contract any two adults can make—a contract which can always be kept at least *in part*—some of the more degrading aspects of divorce might be eliminated. Unfortunately, we treat the tragedy of a broken marriage, begun with such high hopes, not as we treat other tragic human experiences, like illness, failure or separation, in which both partners need support and help, but as a civil dogfight, a breach of contract in which it is damages, rather than honor, that one partner demands of the other.

I believe that the institution of alimony should be a continuation of the husband's obligation to his vow to "love her, comfort her, honor and keep her in sickness and in health," an obligation that endures insofar as the wife, in leaving the marriage, is not as able as she was when she entered it to earn her own living and manage her own life. (One idea that could be encouraged is the obligation of a man to help his estranged wife, if she interrupted her education when she married him, to acquire a skill or a profession so that she will be able to support herself.) Equally, but this is seldom recognized, we need further acknowledgment of the *wife's* obligation, if she is the more able, to "keep him in sickness and in health," or to support herself if she is perfectly well equipped to do so.

Alimony so conceived would be part of an obligation one to another, contracted by two adults, and honored even after the ability to love and to live together has vanished.

Since Soviet cosmonaut Valentina Tereshkova's flight in space there has been a lot of talk about how much better the status of women is in the Soviet Union than in the United States. From your own observation would you say that Soviet women actually do enjoy greater respect and equality?
DECEMBER 1963

The Russians are far less concerned with sex differences than Americans are. Russian men do not regard their identity as being dependent on doing something that women cannot do or on making more money than women do; and Russian women do not include in their sense of identity the idea of being somehow less successful than men. While a great many women work in both Russia and the United States, a far larger proportion of women in the Soviet Union work at higher-status jobs—for example, in medicine, science and engineering, even as heads of great research institutes—and Russians accept the presence of women in responsible positions as a matter of course. It may even be said that women are achieving more than their share in the Soviet Union, because with the tremendous death rate in World War II the Russians have had to depend on womanpower in a way we have not had to do. In fact, a succession of events—the original attempt to attract women into revolutionary activity by promises of equality, the tremendous need for labor in the early days of the Soviet Union and the events during and after World War II—all have contributed to an intensive use of womanpower.

In the United States, in contrast, there has been no comparable deficit of manpower; mechanization and automation have proceeded much more rapidly, and women's work has increasingly been related to the supplementation of income rather than to the consideration of their service to society. Indeed, most public institutions have rules that prevent women from working where their husbands work, and this situation seriously limits the use of educated women in many fields where they are badly needed—for example, in teaching. As a result, while women work outside the home in both countries, American women (especially educated American women) tend to work below their level of education.

But while the Soviet Union has used womanpower more extensively than the United States has, it has been no more successful than this country in solving the problem of how women are to hold jobs and still care for their homes and children. The same difficulties occur in both countries: How to get a child into a nursery school. How to get a small child to school and home again. How to help an older child with his lessons. How to get the shopping done—a difficulty compounded in the Soviet Union by shortages and long queues. For one generation these problems have been partially alleviated by grandmothers, but no one knows what will happen in the next generation.

On the question of woman cosmonauts, the Russians have been able to be realistic and practical. If we are going to do anything important with space, especially with space colonization, then we need to know at once how well women can withstand the new conditions. The American tendency to protect men's sense of masculinity by keeping women out of things results—as does our handling of race—simply in an American loss. The Russians will know how women react to outer space; we will not.

I read much about women finding their "identity" outside their purely feminine role, yet I know women who have dedicated themselves with impressive success to the feminine arts: they look beautiful at all times, can charm any man they care to and live for giving and going to parties. **Would you care to make a guess as to whether these women, with these limited but high accomplishments, are happy and fulfilled?** NOVEMBER 1965

The arts about which you speak are not intrinsically "feminine." In the last two centuries in Western society these accomplishments happen to have been assigned to women. At most times and in most places, however, men have worn the finest feathers, the most splendid jewels, the handsomest robes and even the most elaborate hairdresses or wigs. And generally speaking, men have given and attended the elaborate feasts and parties, men have strolled in public places, men have been the charmers. The cultivation of social graces, the prerogatives of those who have wealth, power and leisure, may be assigned to either sex or to a few members of both sexes.

Where women are expected to be beauties, those who learn their role well certainly will delight the eye of the beholder. Equally, where men are expected to cut a fine figure, they will delight the eye. The cultivation of the social graces may be limited to what the French call the *haut monde*, the small group of those who devote full time to elaborating on this one basic pattern of behavior. From their point of view, the rest of the population may be mere spectators watching the pageant. Or one small group—for example, the royal family of England and its entourage—may be the epitome of what a whole people desires and live out a people's daydreams. Or the cultivation of the social graces may become the part-time occupation of a great many members of a whole population. Then, in a country like France or the United States, every woman may aspire to beauty and fashion, every woman may devote some time to party-giving and party-going and many women may succeed in setting styles for other women's clothes and hairdos—and charm.

Is this, in fact, a good idea? The belief that any woman can succeed in making herself beautiful and charming gives every American girl, even the poorest and least schooled, the most graceless and lonely, the hope that she may yet go to the ball and win Prince Charming. It disperses effort over a very wide field. But it also narrows effort down to a very small part of living.

It is probable that far more women can achieve lasting contentment where femininity is linked to the qualities that help a woman be a warm wife and mother, a devoted sister and daughter, a loyal friend, a good grandmother, and where a woman can be honored as a person because she has borne and cared for children, has taught in a school or cared for the sick, has managed a business, has practiced a profession, has written poems.

I would characterize as most feminine the arts that women have practiced longest and most often. These are, mainly, the arts that have to do with attending to other individuals. Caring for infants and children, listening to the ambitions of an adolescent, comforting a husband, teaching a child, nursing the sick, cherishing the confidences of a friend, and as an artist or a performer gladdening the eyes and the ears of those who admire and love a woman as an individual—all these are feminine arts. Of course, men must and do practice all these arts too. But they tend to practice them less well, perhaps because they are called upon to do so less often.

The identity of an unmarried woman with a job to do encompasses not only who she is but also what she does. But the identity of a married woman—that is to say, most women—is defined by who her husband is and what he does. When marriage was for life and when death was likely to come early, a woman's career as wife and mother was often completely circumscribed by her husband's career as provider and achiever.

Today, however, this is no longer true. We educate girls so that they are capable of greater intellectual accomplishment than our form of marriage and housekeeping permits them to use. Marriages are not always for life. And child rearing takes up only part of a woman's adult life. These three major changes have refocused our attention on the question of woman's identity and the relationship between feminine arts and feminine accomplishments.

19

Psychologist Ernest van den Haag has said that marriage and romantic love don't mix. The one, he writes, "is primed for a lifelong journey" and the other for "an ardent improvisation" that must necessarily end unhappily. Do you believe this is true? NOVEMBER 1965

Romantic love in its purest form is experienced by relatively few individuals anywhere. If this were not so, the activities that keep a society going would soon grind to a halt. The individual who is immersed in extreme romantic love is obsessed by the beloved person, desperately unhappy in his or her absence and wholly unconcerned with the activities of everyday life. It is a state of mind that requires a vast overestimation of the loved one, who is visualized as flawless and incomparable. Separation is felt to be a kind of death, and the death of both lovers is preferable to permanent separation.

Mythmakers, poets, playwrights and novelists portraying high romantic love treat it as an unalterable state that is as disruptive of other relationships as it is engrossing for the lovers. In romantic stories in the great tradition, the paths to lovers' meetings are beset by terrible obstacles. Where the outcome is fortunate, the united lovers "live happily ever after"—but this is the end of the story. More often the lovers are united only in death or, as in an ancient Chinese tale of lovers who ascend to the sky, they live on separated from each other forever.

Significantly, in the period in European history in which our conception of romantic love took shape, there was no idea that this kind of love should be consummated. Such ecstatic concentration on the beloved person could be maintained only where the celebration of the state of being in love was an end in itself and the two lovers remained beyond each other's reach. But where actuality had somehow to come to terms with the ideal, the outcome was inevitably comedy or tragedy—*Love's Labour's Lost* or *Romeo and Juliet*. Keats, who in his life suffered the agonies of romantic love, epitomized the ideal in his picture of lovers portrayed on a Grecian urn: "For ever wilt thou love, and she be fair!"

Even in those societies that have exalted romantic love, people's expectations about actual love relationships are necessarily far less demanding. A readiness to fall in love is, then, a state of mind that is cultivated, especially in adolescents whose inexperience gives them a heightened capacity for dreaming and falling in love with someone. That "someone" need not have the peculiar likeness of some deep, unconscious image that is the basis of extreme romantic love. It is more likely to be one of the boys or girls who is a socially appropriate mate. And the two who find each other are acting out the cultural expectation that people will fall in love and the belief that being in love is a desirable state that leads to a happy marriage. In other words, society has domesticated what is essentially a very antisocial ideal. For what the world needs is not romantic lovers who are sufficient unto themselves, but husbands and wives who live in communities, relate to other people, carry on useful work and willingly give time and attention to their children.

At best, in some societies mild romantic love is a form of behavior cultivated within the accepted bounds of courtship. In many countries the relations between boys and girls are conventionalized in ways that allow them to experience something like romantic love—for a brief period. But here romantic courtship makes little allowance for "improvisation." Virtually every song the lover sings has been written for him, every response by the girl has been pictured for her, every sign and occasion for a stolen kiss is prescribed, and the exact distance between a lover and the girl he is serenading is fixed by custom. And later the memory of the obstacles that were overcome—the love song heard from a balcony, the long night journey to catch a glimpse of the beloved, the evasion of the chaperone who carefully closed her eyes—provides a dreamlike backdrop for marriages that have become companionable partnerships.

In certain societies, including some where arranged marriage is the custom, there is also a romantic ideal of marriage itself. The young couple, facing each other alone, fall in love at first sight, or their love grows through the long years of their joined lives. Another version assumes that even many

21

years of facing each other across the breakfast table—he un-shaven and she with her hair uncombed—cannot dim the en-thusiasm of the best days of courtship. Where the dream of Darby and Joan is part of a living tradition, this may actually happen.

In modern American life, the extreme forms of romantic love can still occur, but the modified romantic love that is re-lated to courtship is becoming very rare. Without real obsta-cles to the most continuous intimacy, romantic love has noth-ing to feed upon. Only a few social obstacles (differences in age, class or ethnic background) and the heated opposition of parents, school principals and deans (invoked at an increas-ingly early age) give some sense of tension and excitement, some feeling of a distance that must be traversed. Young Americans, set on immediate possession of the body of the chosen person in the hope of establishing an immediate and yet viable marriage, may sing love songs. But their chances of experiencing romantic love in courtship are very poor.

Overestimation of a person chosen from among possible mates and a period of waiting during which full possession of the loved person is denied are compatible with happiness in marriages that are meant to last a lifetime. But overestimation of a state of mind, instead of a person, leads to frustration and unhappiness. We use the words and phrases descriptive of the all-absorbing romantic passion that occurs only rarely and consumes those who experience it. But our courtship be-havior no longer is styled so that even a modified but appro-priate "falling in love" can occur. It is not a tradition of romantic courtship that makes marriage difficult. Rather, it is the lack of a real relationship between ideal and reality, word and deed, that leads to self-delusion, unrealizable expecta-tion and bitter disappointment.

In his book *The Flight from Woman* psychiatrist Karl Stern says that a "defeminization" of society is taking place be-cause our mechanized world puts a premium on "masculine"

thinking. Accordingly, Stern believes, women take a more aggressive (i.e., masculine) role when they participate in human affairs, and he concludes that a dehumanization of society results. What is your evaluation of these ideas?

MARCH 1966

"Defeminization" can mean many different things. It may refer to changes in costume, manners and posture previously regarded as characteristically feminine. For example, when women at various periods have given up wearing long skirts, stays, bonnets, veils, shawls, laces or elaborately dressed curls, when they have given up blushing and fainting, high-pitched fluting speech tones or a tripping step, they have become—from this viewpoint—defeminized. But such changes go on continually in all societies where fashions and habits shift and fluctuate.

Defeminization may also refer to role. Where men have been the traditional breadwinners, initially it seems defeminizing when women go out to earn their living. Where all secretaries were men, as at one time they were in the English-speaking world, it was defeminizing for a woman to take a position as a secretary. Most roles of this kind are a matter of convention in a particular society at a given time. Their specific definitions as "masculine" or "feminine" often have very little to do with the capacities of men and women.

There is a sense, however, in which certain changes in women's roles may be regarded as dehumanizing. Traditionally women have had to consider their children's long-time protection and well-being to be their central goal. Where a society, by its moral conventions and standards of living or by various coercive rules and regulations, forces women to neglect any of the necessary forms of prenatal and maternal behavior, there may be a dehumanizing effect on the members of that society—both men and women.

Several comparatively recent developments in our society can make it all but impossible for women to perform their maternal humanizing role: too early marriage, for instance, before girls are able to make discriminating judgments about the men they marry; too easy acceptance of the idea that

23

women can work and bring up children simultaneously without special help; insistence on a standard of living that obliges the mother to add to the family income.

It may also be dehumanizing to require women to adopt modes of behavior that have been defined as very competitive, hostile and aggressive, as in some types of business, in commercial sport or in marginal activities of crime. Where "dog eat dog" is the expected behavior for men, women who engage in the same behavior may become more aggressive than men. Among animal species, males struggle to defend their territory and to win mates, but they seldom destroy a member of their own species. Females, however, guarding their young, usually fight to kill. As biological beings women may fight in too deadly earnest. Over millenniums it has been exceptional for women to handle actual weapons, and so in their rearing they are not subjected to the ancient, traditional controls that set limits on a great deal of masculine aggression.

Whenever women become part of an organization or an activity that is defined as aggressively and ruthlessly competitive, they must develop a style of behavior different from that of men in the same occupation if they are not to become "defeminized." In Israel both young men and women serve in the army, but only men are trained in offensive maneuvers. And in American life, in the conference room, women do better to insist on high standards of courtesy, comfort and consideration in a mixed group of which they are an integral part. In the long run it is the complex interplay of different capacities, feminine and masculine, that protects the humanity of human beings.

Will you comment on *Human Sexual Response*, the recent study by Dr. William H. Masters and Virginia E. Johnson on the physiology of sex? OCTOBER 1966

Many aspects of human experience, especially those involving deep emotions like love, anger or grief, are almost inaccessible to scientific study. Yet a science of human behavior must be based on an understanding of *all* aspects of life.

Psychosomatic medicine is one branch of science that especially takes these deep emotions into account. It is grounded in a recognition of the interconnections between physiological processes and emotional states; of the relationship between specific physical conditions, such as stomach ulcers or high blood pressure, and the person's experience of frustration, tension, anger and so on.

The problem is that the clinician in his ordinary practice seldom has direct access to people while they are caught up in emotional turmoil. Only later, when the individual becomes ill—obsessed by his own anger or prostrated by grief—is he likely to seek the help of a physician. The clinical account elicited from the patient, therefore, usually is a retrospective one, in which he tries to describe past events or to avoid reliving an unbearable experience.

Besides, he is always the exceptional case—the particularly vulnerable individual. Most people, most of the time, live through their life experiences without ever putting them fully into words. They are happy or they are hurt, they suffer defeat or enjoy success, without analyzing their own feelings. They quarrel with their parents and children, their husbands or wives, their friends and colleagues and bosses, the tax collector and the telephone company. Or they suffer through weeks and months of agonizing bereavement without asking for help. Often they do not describe in detail how they feel even to their closest friends. One result is that much of what we know about the physiology of aroused states is based not on normal but on extreme and pathological experience.

We know much less about the range of normal behavior, and we have few ways of measuring strength of response except on the basis of verbal reports. One thing we do know is that a relative lack of self-consciousness and a resistance to self-study are characteristic of normal behavior. Few people willingly wear electroencephalographic equipment or blood pressure bands to bed, or to the boss's office when they demand a raise, or when they are getting ready to punch the nose of an aggressive drunk in a bar, or when they are kneeling in grief beside the coffin of a dead parent. At such moments normal men and women characteristically reject introspection and cut themselves off from outsiders. People who would welcome the apparatus of measurement already are somewhat apart. They may be scientists, artists with unusual powers of self-observation or individuals with some special investment in exhibitionism.

Since this is so, the scientist's only recourse is to create laboratory situations that echo, even though they are different from, the whole experience of real life. The scientist attempts to study rivalry by inventing short-term situations that rouse rivalrous feelings. Or he studies fear by showing subjects films about terrifying events, real or imagined. But the simulation of sex experience—as in the work of Masters and Johnson—is particularly difficult because it requires such specific involvement of the participants in a laboratory.

Most Americans find accounts of such laboratory experiments cold-blooded, and therefore repellent. It is always disturbing and repellent to watch extreme behavior in which one is in no way involved. A well-fed, satisfied onlooker can be deeply repelled if he is forced to watch a very hungry person eat. One longs to turn away from grief one does not share. We have carefully instilled taboos against peeping and staring, and stimulation that comes from others' activities tends to rouse repulsion and disgust.

The Masters study obtained a little not very exciting data on such matters as the circulatory and respiratory effects of sex arousal and the subsidence of sex excitement. In circumstances in which material from the Masters study can be presented with complete objectivity, they provide useful data, data that can be combined with other kinds of information on the physiology of the human body to enlarge our potential knowledge of how to control and prevent illness. However, we live in a society in which cultural taboos against knowledge about the human body have been very strong. It is also a society in which many people are forced to look for vicarious sex satisfaction. On many grounds, therefore, it is difficult for readers to be objective about the purpose of the Masters study. As in the case of the Kinsey reports, this study will often be treated as if the intent were a pornographic one—that is, to stimulate rather than to inform the reader.

Do you think middle-class American women are becoming increasingly narcissistic, and if so, why? JUNE 1967

No, I do not. I think American women are increasingly overworked. The ideal of the all-purpose wife is perhaps the most difficult any society has set for its women.

Consider the exacting standards the modern married woman and mother must try to meet. In spite of her seven-day-a-week schedule of domestic chores, dishes and laundry, she is expected to look well groomed and well dressed on all occasions. No matter how burdened she is with the care of small children, she is expected to work at being attractive, even glamorous. Whatever her family responsibilities are, she is expected to be relaxed and companionable. In fact, it is taken for granted that she ought to be able to do everything, however hard and tedious, and still give the impression that she spends her days pleasantly and restfully, that she has the leisure to keep her hair shining and smoothly waved, her skin soft and glowing, her clothes fashion-model perfect and her smile warm and welcoming.

As long as her children are young she can concentrate on her home and family. But as soon as they all are safely in school she should be eager to add a job to her other activities. Working often is phrased as a form of self-fulfillment. But our high standards of expenditure may make it imperative for both adults in a family to earn money; and today, because of the shortage of educated labor, increasing pressure is put on women to go out of their homes to work.

Educated women have never before been asked to pay so high a price for the right to be wives and mothers. The demand that in spite of their hard work they should be *soignée,* perfectly turned out and always charming puts an almost intolerable burden on them. Calling them narcissistic simply adds insult to injury.

How do middle-class American men compare as fathers with men in other cultures you have studied? JUNE 1967

We are evolving a new style of fatherhood, in which young fathers share very fully with mothers in the care of babies and little children. In this respect American men differ very much from their own grandfathers and are coming to resemble much more closely men in the primitive societies I have studied. One question one can ask is what effect this is likely to have on the next generation and the life of the wider community.

Among the South Seas peoples I know, fathers carry and care for and play with their own small children. But when a baby becomes fretful and hungry, the father turns it over to the mother to care for. Usually a man's interest in small babies is confined to his own children. In contrast, a woman takes an interest in many babies, and women will suckle and care for one another's children. This differentiation begins in childhood, when boys may be pressed into service to look after their own younger brothers and sisters while girls without younger siblings may act as child nurses for younger cousins and neighbors. In these communities it is recognized that men enjoy children but that their care and rearing is primarily women's work. This is related to the fact that breast feeding is necessary for an infant's survival; there are no substitutes.

All this has changed in our society. The invention of bottle feeding and artificial foods especially adapted for infants has meant that men are no longer handicapped in caring for a little child. Whatever a mother can do for a child physically, a father can do also. And in American society, in which servants have disappeared and it is considered inappropriate for female relatives to live with a married couple, fathers are the only persons who can assume part of the burden of child care carried by young mothers.

Under these circumstances men have taken to the care of little babies with great zest and enthusiasm. They find watching the early development of their small children an engrossing occupation, one worth hurrying home from the office for every evening. These fathers are very close to their young children, and the kinds of formality and distance that used to characterize the relationship of middle-class father and son have disappeared.

There are several consequences of this new situation. Many fathers are less entranced as their babies grow beyond infancy and tend to press their wives to have another and still another new baby. What they fail to take into account is the extra strain on the mother who must look after three or four young children. And young fathers may become so delighted and preoccupied with their home and children that they are much less concerned with competitive advancement in their work than their fathers were. Furthermore, their very willingness to come home and help with their children at night and over weekends has the effect of isolating each small family in its own home. So there is little to counteract the isolation created by modern living conditions—small homes in suburbs, frequent moving and the increasing separation of work and residence.

The fact that both parents take care of babies may in part be responsible for the blurring of differences between boys and girls. Under older systems of child rearing characteristic of high civilizations, child care was wholly a woman's occupation. Taught by one sex, boys and girls went through a very different learning process. Girls were taught to relax while boys were taught to move away from their mothers, not to behave like girls and to enjoy activity, strength and masculine achievement.

Today, a boy or a girl can identify with either parent's tastes or type of mind or character and so may become like that parent without becoming like or different in terms of sex identification. A girls who feels free to follow her father's

29

love of hunting or flying may also adopt his kind of clothing. A boy who becomes a musician like his mother may also identify with her way of standing and moving.

Perhaps we are in the process of developing a style of parenthood that has never before been attempted by a civilized people, a style that will set children of both sexes free of some of the constraints that have forced on them narrow occupational and personality choices because of narrow sex identification. On the other hand, we may be destroying the set of motives that have made men the great achievers and innovators of civilization. At the same time we may not be developing enough ambitious and highly motivated women to take the place of the men whose chief delight is their children. It is still an open question how our children, as adults, will respond to the challenges of the wider society to become active in its concerns and interests.

How does suburban living complicate women's lives?
OCTOBER 1967

For many women with children, a move to the suburbs holds the promise of release from the restraints and monotony of living in a small city apartment. However, when the excitement of finding a new home and settling in it has simmered down, the newcomer finds that better living for her family means a highly segregated life for herself. Her neighbors are women who want the same things for their children, have the same hopes for their husbands, have the same anxieties about the future and face many of the same problems. All the picture windows seem to look out on the same vista.

Living in a one-class, one-age-group suburb (and most suburbs are communities of this kind) deprives women of the stimulus of complementary relationships. They are cut off from the enjoyment that comes from knowing people who are older or younger, differently educated and immersed in a variety of activities that can open up new ways of thinking. Living so close to others who are busy with exactly the same preoccupying details of homemaking, harried by exactly the same difficulties, often encourages a narrow and uncomfortable competitiveness rather than friendly co-operation. But the alternative—exclusion from one's neighbors' interests— would be an unbearable solitude.

Except in those small communities where the elderly congregate, there are very few older people. Parents, uncles, aunts and older family friends usually are far away. Especially in a new suburb, there may also be few adolescents. Recently a young mother told me that she had counted the children living on her street, and discovered that there were more than ninety, only two of them older than twelve. In such a suburb there is no one with leisure time, no one to take over responsibility for a few hours except another young mother as burdened as the one who needs to go to the dentist or who longs, just once, to go alone to the movies.

In a suburban area many services that are easily available in a city—an emergency clinic, specialists, places for getting repairs done—are far away. Shopping often is a major undertaking that involves the whole family. Necessarily, all of life depends on the automobile. Children must be taken everywhere and adolescents must be turned loose to drive on crowded highways long before they have acquired judgment based on experience. Women are constantly at the mercy of their family's diverse needs; they have little freedom to develop and follow up their own individual interests.

Families move to the suburbs to provide better living conditions for their children. Once they are there, however, women often discover that to maintain the new standard of living or to vary the deadly monotony of endless lonely housework, they need to find work outside the home. But that work is almost never conveniently close to home, and the household helpers who will replace such mothers in their homes do not live close by either. Then, soon enough, children grow up, take jobs, marry and make their homes elsewhere. And as a widow a woman may find herself living in a comfortable home filled with memories, but isolated, far from a meaningful life.

It is women, I think, who could do most to change the

contemporary form of suburban living, for they have experienced the full measure of its complications. If we could build communities in which there was room for many kinds of people, married and single, of different ages and with different backgrounds, skills and interests, it would be much easier for each woman to realize a life that is satisfying for her family and rewarding for herself.

ॄॖॖॖॖॖॖॖॖॖॖॖॖॖॖॖ

Many people think that women are basically unco-operative. They say that each woman wants to live in her own home, alone with her husband and children, as the mistress of her household; that women accept co-operative arrangements only when they appear to be unavoidable. Is this true?
JANUARY 1968

It is true, on the whole, in our own society. But this does not mean that women are incapable of co-operation.

Women's willingness to co-operate with one another is based primarily on the kind of experience they have growing up in the family. Among the Arapesh of New Guinea many men have two wives, but each wife acts as if she were the only one. The first wife will not welcome the second wife or co-operate with her to get work done. Elsewhere, in some African societies, for example, wives form a close-knit co-operative group; there, an only wife may shame her husband into marrying another woman to share the work load with her. These are extreme examples, perhaps, but girls growing up under such different circumstances will have very different conceptions of women's relations with one another.

Another type of household is that in which the husband goes to live with his wife and the household consists of two, sometimes three, generations of women, each with her husband and children. This was the accepted arrangement among the Zuñi Indians and in some African tribes. Characteristically here, the women form a solid mass of kin, quarreling as only relatives do, but essentially are accustomed to sharing every household task. In such a home there is always someone to hold a baby, to prepare the next meal and to carry out the ritual tasks that are part of women's responsibilities.

A somewhat similar situation is sometimes found in extended families in which fathers and sons live together and in which, as among the Tchambuli of New Guinea, a boy customarily marries his father's sister's daughter. The bride is no stranger. She comes into the household not only as a daughter-in-law but also as a niece, and aunt and niece can form as solid a front as mother and daughter. Tchambuli women, in fact, are conspicuously co-operative in social situations that go beyond the immediate family. When twenty women gather to cook for a feast, each brings her own clay stove.

There are also other ways of forming co-operative groups that may last through a whole lifetime. In some societies girls who are close in age form an age-grade group that cuts across family ties. Sometimes they are initiated together; sometimes they live for a period in a youth house where they share common tasks. Instead of looking to an older and a younger generation or to another woman who as co-wife shares a particular position, girls who grow up in an age-grade group form their closest ties and their most trusted associations with their own age mates.

Elsewhere girls may seldom see two women working together amicably. Among the Manus of New Guinea, men objected to their wives' making friends with other women; and the ghosts, the household guardians of good behavior, looked with special disapproval on women's gossip about men. A man's wife and his sister were always assumed to be jealous rivals. When a woman was angered by her husband's actions, she would accuse him of incestuous behavior, telling him: "Your sister is really my co-wife!" An insult of this kind was severely punished by the ever-listening ghost. Growing up in a Manus household, little girls had no adult models of feminine companionship, and even sisters broke away from one another. Nevertheless, in old age Manus women used to

33

speak nostagically of the only occasion when, as adolescents, a group of girls lived at the home of one of their number in a month-long house party.

There are a few societies in which the very idea of friendly association is lacking. Among the Dobuans, a Pacific island people in Melanesia, the whole house of a married couple is excessively private. On reaching puberty a boy no longer sleeps at home. Instead he wanders, looking for a girl who will receive him, and soon afterward a marriage is arranged. Each married couple live in alternate years in the home village of the wife and the home village of the husband. Wherever the couple are residing, one of them—husband or wife—is a stranger among strangers, distrustful and distrusted. And that stranger is safe only at home, where the wife watches over her cookpots lest the food be magically poisoned.

In general, women learn to be co-operative with one another by growing up in a household among co-operating women. It is through their experience as daughters that they learn whether or not women can trust one another and work together in amity. By contrast, men usually learn forms of co-operation outside the home in games with other boys and later by taking part in various kinds of masculine activity. In this matter they are less dependent than girls on what they learn at home. However, they do learn at home how women regard one another and whether, and in what ways, men and women can co-operate loyally with each other.

In an older American tradition the women for whom a man took responsibility in his household often formed a very solid feminine front. This broke down under the newer expectation that widows and single women should accept responsibility for themselves. In the future it may be that new forms of co-operation may develop out of the working relationships in which men and women together share common interests and responsibilities.

In a discussion of the draft, you were quoted as saying that you would not want to have women accepted as combat soldiers because "they are too fierce." Would you explain this?
JUNE 1968

I was speaking in favor of universal national service for girls as well as boys. The question then was raised about military service: If military service were part of national service, should girls be drafted into the armed forces? My answer was that women should be permitted to volunteer for non-combat service, as they were in World War II. But I also stated my belief that they should not be accepted, voluntarily or through the draft, as combat soldiers.

We are all familiar with myths about women warriors, and from time to time, though very rarely, women have taken part in combat, as, for example, the Soviet girl snipers in World War II, or the girls who fought in the Israeli war of liberation in 1948, or the women troops in Indonesia. However, throughout history most societies have consistently avoided arming women for battle, or even, among primitive hunting bands, teaching them the use of hunting weapons. The fact that something seldom has been done is not necessarily a good reason for avoiding it forever. However, it is a good reason for examining the possible consequences.

One way of thinking about the problem is to look at the behavior of other species. Among animals, as Konrad Lorenz pointed out in his book *On Aggression,* it is necessary to differentiate between hunting and defense against predators, on the one hand, and intraspecies fighting, on the other. In many species, combat between males, whether its purpose is to gain dominance or win control over territory or attract females, is highly ritualized and typically nonlethal. Females do not engage in these ritual trials of strength. Normally they fight only in defense of their nest and their young, and then they fight very fiercely and to the death.

Coming back to our own species, human beings unfortunately are able to define some of their fellows—strangers, members of another culture or another race, members of op-

position groups—as nonhuman and to picture them as predators or prey. At the same time, however, human beings are
able to make rules governing the conduct of fighting and
controlling the techniques of warfare. Throughout history,
among primitive peoples as among the members of high
civilizations, it has been boys and men who have been trained
and tested for their ability to keep within the bounds of these
learned (not inborn, as in the case of other species) rituals of
fighting. Whether it is through training for the hunt or by
playing games, competing in sports, taking part in mock battles or listening to the sagas of great heroes, boys learn to
accept the rewards of keeping the rules and the punishments
for breaking them. So also, in warfare they learn to restrict
killing, honor a truce and negotiate for peace, at least with
those they regard as human and like themselves.

We know of no comparable ways of training women and
girls, and we have no real way of knowing whether the kinds
of training that teach men both courage and restraint would
be adaptable to women or effective in a crisis. But the evidence of history and comparative studies of other species
suggest that women as a fighting body might be far less
amenable to the rules that prevent warfare from becoming a
massacre and, with the use of modern weapons, that protect
the survival of all humanity. This is what I meant by saying
that women in combat might be too fierce.

**People often criticize women drivers. Do you think there
really are differences in the way men and women drive cars?
If there are not, why are criticisms made so often?**
SEPTEMBER 1968

In the judgment of those who set automobile insurance
rates, girls are a better risk than boys among young drivers. In
some states, for example, men (but not women) under
twenty-five years of age pay especially high rates—as long as
they are single. Marriage evidently is considered to have a
steadying effect on the way young men handle their cars.

In the long run, however, wherever men and women drive the same kinds of cars, under the same conditions, with equal frequency and for the same general purposes, I think one is unlikely to find sex-determined differences in styles of driving. Some women are better drivers and others are less skilled than their husbands or other men and women.

Differences in expectation change the situation. When there is a belief that men can better stand long-distance driving, driving at night or driving in heavy traffic, it is likely to have some effect on how many women handle a car in such circumstances. It also adds to the visibility of the woman driver and to the likelihood that men will criticize her performance on superhighways, in night driving or in making her way through city traffic.

I am often amused when I hear an exasperated driver attempt to categorize the source of his annoyance—the idiot at the wheel of an offending car is a Sunday driver, an out-of-state driver, a foreigner, a teen-ager, a farmer and so on. Women drivers, as the most readily identifiable and frequently encountered opponents on the road, get a tremendous share of these explosive criticisms.

Special circumstances also may shift the balance. Where physical strength is a factor, as in driving a heavy truck or a tractor, men on the average have the advantage. Where endurance of routine is concerned, the advantage may be with women. Where knowledge of machinery is concerned, men have a great advantage in our culture; girls are not expected to learn about machines or to enjoy tinkering. But nowadays, when driving a car is more or less a matter of pushing the right button in total ignorance of the internal working of the engine, this is not an important consideration.

One thing worth emphasizing is the widespread tendency to treat access to new forms of high mobility as a male prerogative. In the early days of cars, horseback riding was relegated to girls. When men became pilots, women drivers of cars became commonplace. Later women pilots were permitted to ferry planes, though they still do not pilot commercial passenger planes. And at present, although there are women with the appropriate qualifications, no American woman has been chosen to be an astronaut. Perhaps when rockets carry men to the moon, women will be allowed to orbit the earth. [Editor's note: American astronauts made the first moon landing in July of 1969, ten months after this column was published. In 1978—nine years after the moon walk—women were admitted to the American space program as astronauts for the first time.]

Clearly, in these matters of skill it is much less a question of what women, as compared to men, are able to do well than of what, under given circumstances, women are permitted and are willing to do well.

ቈ

Does the ever-increasing use of prepared foods cut down on women's importance as culinary artists? JANUARY 1969

One generalization that can be made about cooking is that although wives and mothers usually are the most willing cooks, it is men who are the "culinary artists." This is not to deny that there are superb cooks who are women, but rather to emphasize that it is usually men, as chefs, who professionalize styles of cooking as an art outside the home.

But within the family, of course, food and its preparation play an extremely important part. Being fed has a tremendous significance in childhood, and as adults most men place a higher value on having a meal cooked especially for them than they do on eating very superior food. The story of the burned soup (or pudding, or stew, or bread) that Mother made is a joke that has crossed innumerable cultural boundaries. And the value of home cooking may well be accentuated today, when so many of the activities through which wives and mothers once could express their care for husbands and children—spinning cloth, making clothes, preserving food—have become impersonalized work carried out by strangers.

In this setting, in which men value the art far more than the results, it is a real question whether a wife's role is diminished and depreciated when she uses prepared foods in her cooking. Of course, a major selling point of partly prepared foods is that by using them the housewife can offer her family fresher, tastier and more eye-appealing dishes that become, through her final efforts, "homemade." This appeal is used today even to domesticate exotic and sometimes difficult dishes in whose basic preparation ingredients and implements are used to which home cooks may not have ready access.

If it is the sheer expenditure of effort that matters, using prepared foods can become a symbol of shirking by a wife or mother. But too often, I think, women spend long hours fussing over food and cooking elaborate dishes as a way of demonstrating to their families—and particularly to themselves—that their housewifely role is an important and a fulfilling one. There are other ways of spending time that are less associated with things and more gratifying to family relationships.

For a woman who is a talented cook, using prepared foods may give her greater freedom and more time to devote to the dishes she makes well and her family enjoys. And for the less-talented cook, prepared foods can help a woman introduce greater variety, with a greater chance of success, into her family's meals and give her time to develop other talents both she and her family can enjoy.

Is it a good idea to let fathers share the kitchen chores or even perform as master chefs? FEBRUARY 1972

There is very little to be said for letting fathers "share the kitchen chores" or, for that matter, do any work at home defined as chores. It is denigrating not only to the man who is asked to do them but also to the woman who defines homemaking tasks in this way.

I think we should treat homemaking tasks with greater respect and, where it is desirable to do so, divide the responsibility for making our homes pleasant and comfortable in ways that enhance each person's contribution.

The tasks a man can visualize as appropriate for himself

are, of course, culturally defined. But one also has to take into account generation differences and each man's sense of his areas of competence. Pushing the baby carriage, vacuuming the rugs, polishing the floors, mixing the drinks, stuffing the turkey, putting in new light bulbs, weeding the garden—any of these activities can be defined as male or female.

I know one elderly man who takes pride in making beds beautifully but who stays far from the kitchen. I know young husbands who are completely competent shoppers and others who extend their enjoyment of handling tools to using mechanized household equipment, large and small. Whatever the tasks are that a man takes over as his own, he has a right to regard his contribution with pride.

There is no reason why keeping a home going shouldn't be a matter of specialization. Certainly, in some families, enjoying the occasions when Father takes over as master chef, appropriately dressed and equipped to preside over the dishes he prepares, is one way of highlighting his partnership in the enterprise.

ह‍

In your anthropological studies have you found women to be stronger than men, physically or emotionally, as many of the Women's Liberationists claim they are? JULY 1973

No really satisfactory comparisons have ever been made. In general it can be said that the strongest men are physically stronger—in the ability to lift or carry or throw, for example—than the strongest women. But the overlap of physical strength is so great that different societies have put the burden of heavy work sometimes on men and sometimes on women or they have differentiated between the kinds of heavy work suitable for men and women. In actuality the difference in strength required may have been negligible; women carried all the heavy loads, for example, but men felled trees and dragged them through the bush. The difference lay in the social definition of the appropriate task.

There is some evidence that women have a greater capacity

to endure monotonous tasks and that men do better at work requiring periodic bursts of concentrated activity. There are societies that reverse this; we do not know at what cost. Tasks such as caring for small children, the sick or the old, or repetitive work, such as fine weaving or embroidery, women usually find less stressful than men. But there are a great many societies in which men have adapted themselves to monotonous hand work and repetitive machine work.

Cultural expectations are not always a sure guide when the problem is one of matching an old skill to a new task. During World War II, when a great many workers were quite suddenly needed in the United States for special tasks demanding very fine hand skills, the first to be recruited were male watchmakers. But it was soon found that manicurists and women who had done fine needlework were superior at these tasks. This did not mean, however, that women necessarily were superior at the new work but only that, contrary to expectation, the more useful training for it had been in tasks that customarily were assigned to women in our society.

The best we can say, I think, is that when men—or women—are required to perform any task that is assigned by their society to persons of the opposite sex, they will show some signs of emotional strain. There is encouraging evidence, however, that our own society is moving—gradually, at least—toward recognition of individual aptitudes and inclinations, away from the automatic assignment of tasks based on stereotyped expectations of the capabilities of either sex.

In other cultures to what degree are women valued for— and judged by—their appearance? JUNE 1974

Why just women?

Appearance matters everywhere for both men and women. But in other cultures what men and women value—and are valued and judged by—may not be the particular qualities we value.

In some parts of the world fat, jolly men and women—or

big, imposing men and women—are valued more than slight, skinny ones. Some peoples look first at the shape of the nose; a fine hooked nose may be an essential characteristic of a handsome man or woman. Others concentrate on the eyes— their color or shape, their piercing glance or their soulful inwardness. Or hair may be most important; for example, honey-colored hair among a predominantly dark-haired people, or abundant hair or long, straight hair. A great deal of body hair or a body free of hair may be the ideal. Turning women—or young boys—into pretty toys is something that often happens in affluent societies as one way of using leisure.

Can real sexual equality ever exist in a society such as ours, which apparently was founded on male chauvinist principles? OCTOBER 1974

"Male chauvinist" is a contemporary pejorative term for men who accept current practices in our society to which women—sometimes with equal chauvinism—are objecting.

In any case, I think it is nonsense to say that our society was founded on male chauvinist principles. Our society was founded in an attempt to attain certain kinds of freedom different from the kinds that existed in Europe—the freedom, for example, to oppose religious conviction to the will of the state; the freedom to change one's social status; the freedom to form communities of like-minded persons. In doing so our Founding Fathers—Women's Liberationists object to the phrase, but they were men—made an extraordinary leap forward in their statements of principle.

For these very principles, so imaginatively conceived, later made it possible to abolish slavery; to extend the franchise to the unpropertied, to the socially oppressed, to women and most recently to eighteen-year-olds; and to provide a basis for the kind of pluralistic society we have not yet attained. In fact, the principles on which our society was founded can provide for new freedoms that later generations may envision and demand.

True equality between groups that are different in any way can be attained only by providing for the differences. We cannot make children equal to adults in a contest of strength except by giving them a handicap; we can make them equal to adults before the law only by giving them certain kinds of protection. We can make working women who have—or wish to have—children equal to men only by providing for the time it takes a woman to carry an unborn child and to care for a newborn infant. We can make the currently uneducated equal to the educated only by giving them more and special education, even if we conceive of equality as equality of opportunity only. Those who deny or attempt to overlook such differences obfuscate the issue.

It has been pointed out that if we establish a meritocracy based on any single standard, only those who meet that standard have a chance to reach the top; all others inevitably will be limited in what they can accomplish. This would have the effect of disenfranchising all those who did not meet the standard as surely as would be the case if voting were limited to any particular group. It does not matter whether the single standard is male-oriented or female-oriented or is oriented to a group of a particular background or religious belief. In order to attain any kind of equality of opportunity and achievement, we must have a diversity of standards so that many different kinds of people may excel.

The basic inequality in the way Western society treats men and women is that no matter how much women are—or may be—welcomed in public roles that have been in the realm of male activity, they still are responsible for their older tasks of caring for their children and homes. This will not necessarily be changed as women gain new legal and economic rights or as day-care centers or precooked meals or housekeeping services lighten the actual double load carried by women. We will not achieve equality by making women into substitute men. What we need most to work out are new and diverse ways in which men and women can share equally in the responsibility for the children they want to have and the life they lead together.

ও

Why is marriage so different from other male-female relationships, especially that of boy friend and girl friend? MAY 1975

Marriage presumes a permanent relationship. For most Americans it still means total commitment to one's partner—to share a home and one's time and one's worldly goods, to bring up children together, to be faithful in sickness and in health—throughout life.

The most significant thing about a boy friend–girl friend relationship usually is its tentativeness, its lack of commitment beyond the present. Breaking up a marriage, even the most hastily and thoughtlessly contracted marriage, means going back on a deeply important pledge. According to one's temperament and culture, it may mean admitting a failure or the death of a relationship from which much was hoped. But boy friends and girl friends come and go with such ease that later their very names may be forgotten.

Marriage includes all that a child has learned about commitment, and every marriage re-enacts in a thousand ways the early-childhood scene, especially the division of sex roles between mother and father. Whether these parental roles are imitated or flouted, they are always a factor in a marriage. Everything the two partners ever felt through their long and happy, or unhappy, childhood is there to be revived and re-enacted by a carelessly left toothpaste cap or a struggle over vacation plans. Marriage is also, in itself, a reiteration of each individual's development in coming to terms with her or his own temperament, impulses, capacities and gifts.

In other sorts of relationships into which the question of marriage does not enter, some of the conflicts and contradictions are consciously or unconsciously ruled out. Whereas a wife has to worry about her husband's success as a provider, a mistress may be able to give her lover wholehearted, uncritical and flattering approval. Whereas it is possible for lovers to meet only on stated occasions during which each can concentrate on pleasing the other, wife and husband have to see each other at all hours—she in her oldest clothes, without make-up and her hair in curlers, he unshaven, tousled, sleepy and harassed.

The difference between the hours, or even months, spent together by two people not married to each other and a married couple also can be highlighted by the requirements of other kinds of permanent households—a household made up of mother and son, father and daughter, two sisters, brother and sister or two friends. Each of these includes many of the trying components of marriage: economic difficulties, differences over the way resources are to be used, conflicts over ideas, what flowers to plant on the terrace, whom to invite to dinner and whether to take a summer or a winter vacation. But there also are subtle differences. Each person realizes that the other must have areas of privacy into which one does not intrude, that each has interests that do not involve the other and that separation, sometimes for long periods, does not mean a severance of the relationship.

But frequent as divorce is today, marriage remains for us the model of complete commitment. Traditionally it was so strong a metaphor that it could be used by Christians to stand for the relationship between Christ and His church. In contrast to this insistence on irrevocability, medieval Judaism permitted divorce, but the person who maintained a difficult marriage was highly regarded; a good wife, according to Judaic belief, was permitted to listen in on the discussions in which her learned husband participated when they both reached heaven.

Marriage as we have defined it is a demanding and difficult institution. This is true whatever the circumstances may be—whether the couple live in isolation, as pioneers in a new world or alone in a modern suburb; or live surrounded by too many in-laws and relatives; or whether they must conduct their lives under the supervisory eyes of a church congregation, a school board, the husbands and wives of professional colleagues or simply the eyes of the neighbors.

It has become more difficult as people live longer; a couple whose children are grown face the prospect of thirty more years together. It is a question whether very many people will be able to achieve a lifelong union when women are no longer dependent, families are small and completed early in married life and men face discouragement and the need for new experience long before they are ready to retire.

At present it seems increasingly clear that we have reared a generation of women and men few of whom know how to make a success out of a first marriage. But as long as we hold on to our conception of marriage as a total commitment, it will be exceedingly difficult to bring into marriage the beliefs and practices we associate with basically different kinds of relationships.

ह्ल

Is it because of the male chauvinist and the female liberationist that young people today are avoiding marriage?
AUGUST 1975

Let's first clarify our terms!

The feminine form of a male chauvinist is not a female liberationist. It is a female chauvinist—a woman who, living in a changing world, still insists on her traditional rights to support and privilege, a woman who calls the money she earns "my money" and treats the money her husband earns as "our money," a woman who refuses her husband a divorce on any grounds or, if she finally consents to a divorce, insists on full alimony and sole custody of the children.

The male form of a female liberationist is a male liberationist—a man who realizes the unfairness of having to work all his life to support a wife and children so that someday his widow may live in comfort, a man who points out that commuting to a job he doesn't like is just as oppressive as his wife's imprisonment in a suburb, a man who rejects his exclusion, by society and most women, from participation in childbirth and the engrossing, delightful care of young children—a man, in fact, who wants to relate himself to people and the world around him as a person.

It is difficult enough in a period of transition to see where we are headed. Keeping ourselves clear about the terms we use is one step in the right direction.

I do not think young people today are "avoiding" marriage. What they are avoiding is an obsolete style—marriage for the sake of being married. They have seen that early marriage for everyone—a style set in the 1950s—ended in disaster for far too many families as essentially uncongenial wives and husbands discovered that they had altogether different and conflicting ideas of what marriage and parenthood were about.

Young people today have become far more serious about commitment. They have found it takes time—and effort—to find out who you are, what you care about and want out of life and with whom you can enter into the partnership of marriage with full commitment.

Even so, marriage is not easy for this generation. It will take genuine commitment, not to labels such as chauvinist or liberationist, but to the value of human relationships to work out new ways for men and women to live together.

ॐ

Do you think that most men today are willing to accept the fact that women should have wider choices? And if men feel threatened by women's growth and liberation, do you think they will ever get over it? AUGUST 1975

It isn't really a question of men's "getting over it," but of men's *and* women's finding a new balance in their relationships.

Whenever there are changes in the way tasks and roles, obligations and privileges, opportunities and responsibilities are apportioned between the sexes, among people of different ages or among people of different national backgrounds or races, some group is bound to feel threatened. But the curious thing is that those who are proposing—insisting

47

on—change tend to believe that those who feel threatened must be hostile, and often they themselves become hostile in response to what they believe they perceive.

I emphasize these feelings of threat and counterthreat because I think that today, in the face of the Women's Liberation Movement, we are making far too much of the point of necessary anger on the part of women and inevitable hostility on the part of men.

Roles are changing for both women and men. Women are being pressured on every side to insist on living in a different way and to believe that their past status was brought about by male oppression. At the same time men who thought that they were being good husbands and fathers and were working hard to care for and protect the mothers of their children are being accused of being oppressors—and angry oppressors at that. The whole process of change is taking place in an atmosphere of the greatest bad temper and a tremendous amount of secondary hostility is being generated that in itself poses a threat to a good outcome.

But let's go back just a little way in time—back to the mid-1950s. Then it was the young men who talked about the way they were being forced to marry and spend their lives accumulating money and possessions, only to die and leave everything to their widows to enjoy. Innumerable articles in the mass media advised women how to take better care of their husbands so that they would not be left alone in old age. There were even proposals that women should marry men ten years younger than themselves! But that was before early marriage for everyone went out of style.

There have been many periods in human history when for a time and in one society or another events have seemed to favor one sex more than the other. And there have been trends that have sometimes favored men and sometimes women. Long ago women's freedom was advanced by the invention of transportation, which meant that women did not have to walk, carrying their babies, wherever they went. Much more recently bottle feeding meant that even nursing mothers could sometimes leave their children in another person's care. Women have been further liberated by the development of various methods of birth control, and by the medical advances that have made it possible to keep alive almost all the children who are born. Now no woman need be worn out simply by childbearing.

But in our modern small homes, women have been imprisoned in lonely domesticity, and when in addition they have not had to work outside the home out of sheer necessity, they have been relegated to a consumer role. But this is no longer viable.

What we should begin to realize is that both men and women need liberation from a life-style that is stultifying and destructive to both sexes. I think it is likely that many marriages which were not good marriages will founder on the ideology of Women's Liberation. But where relationships are based on mutual love and trust, men and women together can work toward new styles of living. The present atmosphere of threat and counterthreat is making this more difficult than change need be. But I believe we are already beginning to create new manly and new womanly roles that will permit a great deal more individual choice as well as better health for men and a fuller, more gratifying sense of themselves for women.

Can women achieve "independence" without having economic independence? JUNE 1976

Today, no one, woman or man, can achieve independence without the ability—and the opportunity—to be self-supporting. Anyone who is forced to accept economic support is necessarily dependent.

In the past in most traditional societies, women were a very important economic asset. They worked in the fields. They spun and wove and made clothing. They cared for the children and the old, nursed the sick and comforted the sorrowing. Almost any household was better off for having another able woman living there.

This meant that an adult woman who was not living with a husband had some choice in deciding where to live. An unmarried woman had a useful role in her father's or her brother's home. A widow could contribute her work to the household of a relative. The frail old woman and the failing old man without any relatives or means of support have wrung the hearts of people at all levels of civilization. But the woman who had working skills to offer any one of several households was secure, and in some sense independent.

Today we associate independence for a woman not with the number of households in which she can have a place but with an income of her own. Only those who have some money—from salaried jobs, from legacies, trusts, savings, Social Security or a pension—feel independent. A woman without money of her own usually is financially dependent upon her husband and upon the compact of trust and love she shares with him. Should that compact fail, she may find herself in desperate circumstances, often with children to support.

Dependence represents a lack of alternatives. That is why the best gift American parents can give their daughters is training in some marketable skill. For a woman equipped to earn her own living need never feel trapped as a dependent—need never feel she has to keep up an unhappy marriage or live with inhospitable relatives just to keep a roof overhead. Independence begins with economic independence.

My father's mother lived with us. She earned her own living as a teacher for many years after my grandfather died. He was a Civil War veteran, and when finally Grandma retired, my father had her apply for a veteran's widow's pension. It was not that he could not support her, for of course he did. But the pension gave her money that was rightfully her own to spend as she saw fit. Social Security has given independence of this sort to many older women.

But we have not yet recognized how unjust it is for a full-time, competent wife and mother to have to live as a dependent, a situation we have ceased to respect for an adult. In a home in which a wife and husband see themselves as equal partners, surely the wife should have a share of her husband's income that is hers to spend or save as she wishes. In fact, she may choose to use most of it to help pay the house mortgage, the children's tuition or everyday running expenses. But the decisions about how to use this money should be hers.

Independence for women will be closer to achievement when women who devote themselves to the hard work of making a home are as fully recognized as economic contributors as are women who work outside the home.

ટેસ

Do you approve of the new "old-girl" networks—the contemporary variation on the "old-boy" networks that help business and professional men by passing along information and sharing contracts in the working world? OCTOBER 1978

Networks in themselves are neither good nor bad. They facilitate rapid and meaningful communication—for whatever purpose they may be used. And nowadays, in a world that is overloaded with information that an outsider or a newcomer finds inaccessible or very hard to interpret, networks have become an almost indispensable means of communication based on face-to-face meetings and shared experiences.

Of course old-boy networks of many kinds have existed in all larger societies for thousands of years. They have provided ways of introducing the newcomer—the novice, the promising peasant boy, the newly recruited cult member, the married-in member of another class or ethnic group, a man's own son or more distant, favored relative—into the existing working group of people who count, those in power and leadership positions at all levels. Old-boy networks based on schools, universities, fraternities and athletic-team membership are only modern versions of the many kinds of associations that have given men confidence in one another— sharing the experiences of a crusade or a pilgrimage, serving together in the same theater of war, taking part in the same voyages of discovery, belonging to the same religious group and, everywhere, backing the same candidates for public office.

In the past, women relied much more on the associations of kin and neighborhood. Today old-girl networks tend to be

51

made up of women who have worked together recently on the same causes. And, increasingly, because nowadays women and men have worked *together* for causes in which they passionately believe—for the Civil Rights movement, for the protection of our natural and manmade environment, for the election of political candidates, for women's rights in all their different aspects—membership in networks has brought men and women closer together through good communication.

As long as networks function to increase opportunities for action, I can see no objection to them. Such networks are necessarily open-ended as new individuals enter and become part of an expanding system of information and action. Where a network goes wrong is where it is closed—where pull, knowing the right person, is the only means of access to a job or a kind of information or club membership—or the only way of doing business. Such a closed network becomes rigid and destructive of enterprise and initiative.

What we have to keep in mind is that networks can be effective in increasing any kind of activity—evil activities, conservative activities, forward-looking activities. As women enter into a network system, whether it is an old-girl network or one that involves both women and men, they must be aware and proud not just of belonging but of belonging to something significant for the world we all have to live in together.

ह्ब

Do you have any suggestions for young couples as to how they can stay happily married today? OCTOBER 1978

Much of the damage to contemporary marriages comes about because young people, however sophisticated they may be, are not prepared for the fact that marriage at best is a difficult way of life. There are many rewards, especially for a couple who share children to love and care for, but there are also many necessary compromises and inevitably some very rough periods.

It will help a young couple to realize that they will often

disagree about what will work best for both of them and that they are embarking on a course for which they will get little guidance from what they know of their parents' solutions and from stories they have read about marriage in the past.

In the recent past there was a tendency for couples to devote the early years of their marriage almost exclusively to child rearing with the idea of thinking about themselves, and their relationship to each other, later "when the children are grown." So those early years became symbols of drudgery and sacrifice which had to be compensated for later.

Now, instead, there is a growing realization that neither a woman nor a man should try to stop the process of becoming a person. Women and men both must be individuals as well as parents and spouses, breadwinners and homemakers, sharers in joint expenses and in responsibilities. And if they realize as well that what they are trying to do is much more difficult than it was for their grandparents who lived in communities with many relatives and friends and that having children today is a matter of happy choice, no longer a burden forced on them, I believe they can face the future with some optimism.

It can also help to recognize that not every marriage is viable for a lifetime and that the decision to part need not mean that one's marriage was a total failure. But at the same time, the aim of keeping a marriage going until the youngest child leaves home can have a stabilizing effect. So also can the recognition that co-parents, even when they have not made it as husband and wife, can remain friends as they plan together for their children's present well-being and future happiness.

The first step toward staying happily married is the understanding of these changes in our society and in our own expectations.

ૈૐ

Why are sports on television (football, baseball, basketball, ice hockey) usually of interest to men but only rarely to women? JANUARY 1979

The simple answer is that sports are defined as activities that appeal to males from the time they are little boys and are given bats and balls and toy racing cars to play with, whereas their sisters are given dolls and dishes and toy household equipment. Newspapers and radio as well as television have "women's" programs devoted to food, child care, beauty and fashions and home furnishings, whereas "men's" programs are devoted to such things as racing and betting and so-called masculine sports.

But does anyone know how many young women watch tennis matches and know the relative standing in any recent season of the women tennis stars? If we took the trouble to find out, we might discover that women enjoy and may be knowledgeable about women in tennis or skiing or skating but that there are few events to watch. Or we might not.

Throughout history, women on the whole have been less interested in games than men, even when, as women of rank and wealth, they have been freed of household chores. Sometimes women are simply conforming to a particular style of femininity; sometimes they have been so weighted down by the clothes proper to a woman that any kind of active sport was impossible.

But it also may be true that women prefer to deal with the real world rather than with the tightly structured world of a game. All kinds of games—cards, baseball, chess and even gambling games—are constructs in which special rules take precedence. Women—most women—appear to have less patience than men with such constructs, even those women who are addicted to one or another card game or (in China in the past and in our own country more recently) a game like mah-jongg. They are likely to be more closely related to the everyday events of living, as well as with birth and nurture and death—more concerned with comforting the bereaved than with playing dice on the coffin.

But perhaps when girls and boys are treated more evenhandedly from their earliest infancy, such differences may disappear. We do not know because as yet we have not tried it.

◄ 2 ►
CHILDREN

M any psychologists believe that children are born knowing how to love but are taught to hate. Do you agree?
JANUARY 1969

No, I do not. I think love and hate are two aspects of the same human capacity to react to other human beings in terms of experience. The infant whose world is warm, giving and reliable responds with love that echoes the love he has received. But the infant who is continually hungry, cold and neglected will come to hate those who hurt him and do not attend to his needs. In a sense, both love and hate are learned: the infant is born with the capacity to respond, and experience guides his learning.

It does seem true that hatred of a given person or a category of persons or things must be learned. We have to be taught whom to hate, and if we are not taught to hate people in categories, we won't.

Most people discuss this problem today in the framework of aggression, war and race conflict. In fact, warfare has never had much to do with hatred, except as, for example, people in a conquered or an occupied country may come to hate those who oppress them. Wars are fought not out of hatred, but because they are an institutionalized method of settling disputes that arise between identified war-making groups. Especially in modern warfare, in which there is so little face-to-face confrontation, hate is usually irrelevant.

Learned hatred is much more relevant to race and ethnic conflict than to war. Children's initial response to the strange often is one of fear. A brown-skinned child, seeing a white person for the first time, may scream with fear. A white-skinned child, seeing a dark person for the first time, may also. If the screaming, fearful child is comforted, reassured and given a chance to learn to know and trust the stranger, he will have one kind of response—one of trust and expectation of friendship. But if his fear is unassuaged or is reinforced by the attitudes of the older children and adults around him, he may come to hate what he has feared.

This is why it is so important in a multiracial world and a multiracial society like ours that children have many experiences with individuals of races different from their own. Only in this way can we hope surely to dispel their early fear of the strange and enable them to distinguish among individuals, caring for some and disliking others, not because they belong to a category of loved or hated people, but because of their own personality, as individuals.

Do children have a shorter childhood today? JULY 1973

Both shorter and longer.

How one judges the relative duration of childhood depends on the period in history chosen for comparison and also, I think, on one's definition of childhood and adulthood as stages of living.

Among the first generations of settlers in America, children were hurried toward adulthood through early work experience and sometimes early marriage. In the Plymouth Colony, as John Demos has shown in his delightful book *A Little Commonwealth*, children began to work alongside their parents at the age of six or eight; this also was the age at which they were sent to live in other homes as apprentices. Where the need for work by able-bodied adults was so great, there was little time for childhood play. No special recognition was given to adolescence. There was only the "steady lengthening of a young person's shadow" as a boy or girl gradually achieved autonomy and took on full adult responsibilities.

All this began to change in the 19th century as styles of adult work were altered and the years of formal education were extended. This period continued well into the 20th century. Correspondingly, the years of childhood stretched out until people came to include the years of adolescence as part of childhood, in the sense that adolescents were not expected to be self-sustaining and responsible. Then, as in the past, we equated self-sustaining work with adulthood. What changed mainly was the age at which the individual was deemed to be ready to stand on his own feet and make his own decisions.

Today almost all children begin school earlier and remain in school longer than ever before. Even among the very poor, few children do any kind of regular work. At the same time, children of both sexes are hurried into adolescence. They are reaching puberty earlier and look more like young adults at an earlier age. In our time childhood has contracted; it is the years of adolescence that have stretched out.

Today neither children nor adolescents are subjected to the formal restraints of strict obedience and conformity with adult standards that once were the mark of dependence. Instead even quite young children are encouraged to display autonomy by exercising freedom of choice.

But I think the independence of the young is more apparent than real. From an early age children are at the mercy of time. The school bus, the television program, scheduled activities and the continuing necessity of moving from grade to grade of formal schooling set severe limits on children's freedom to grow at their own pace or to explore the world opening to them. Adolescents may roam the world, but few of them do so as fully self-sustaining persons. They may marry, but few of them think of marriage as a responsible, lifetime commitment.

What has happened, I think, is that we have split off autonomy from self-sustaining responsibility as a characteristic of adult life. Privilege without responsibility and dependence without the acceptance of authority characterize the life of young people today. The real question, it seems to me, is not whether childhood is longer or shorter than it was in the past. Instead it is what use we are making of the years between true childhood and adulthood in encouraging young people to become mature, responsible men and women.

Were your children brought up to believe in Santa Claus? If so, what did you tell them when they discovered he didn't exist? DECEMBER 1964

Belief in Santa Claus becomes a problem mainly when parents simultaneously feel they are telling their children a lie and insist on a literal belief in a jolly little man in a red suit who keeps tabs on them all year, reads their letters and comes down the chimney after landing his sleigh on the roof. Parents who enjoy Santa Claus—who feel that it is more fun to talk about what Santa Claus will bring than what Daddy will buy you for Christmas and who speak of Santa Claus in a voice that tells no lie but instead conveys to children something about Christmas itself—can give children a sense of continuity as they discover the sense in which Santa is and is not "real."

Disillusionment about the existence of a mythical and wholly implausible Santa Claus has come to be a synonym for many kinds of disillusionment with what parents have told children about birth and death and sex and the glory of their ancestors. Instead, learning about Santa Claus can help give children a sense of the difference between a "fact"— something you can take a picture of or make a tape recording of, something all those present can agree exists—and poetic truth, in which man's feeling about the universe or his fellow men is expressed in a symbol.

The multiple appearances of Santa Claus during the Christmas season—sitting in regal splendor in different settings in different department stores or stamping his feet on a cold street corner collecting money for charity—can be confusing for a child or can ease him into the experience of discovery ("Look! There's another Santa Claus!") that Santa Claus is not a person but an expression of gift-giving at Christmas. Seeing half a dozen Santa Clauses—tall and short, solemn and gay—need not lead to disillusionment; instead, it can lead to the realization that on Christmas Eve, when "not a creature is stirring, not even a mouse," one's own parents will be playing the part of Santa.

One thing my parents did—and I did for my own child—was to tell stories about the different kinds of Santa Claus figures known in different countries. The story I especially loved was the Russian legend of the little grandmother, the *babushka*, at whose home the Wise Men stopped on their journey. They invited her to come with them, but she had no gift fit for the Christ child and she stayed behind to prepare it. Later she set out after the Wise Men but she never caught up with them, and so even today she wanders around the world, and each Christmas she stops to leave gifts for sleeping children.

Children who have been told the truth about birth and death will know, when they hear about Kris Kringle and Santa Claus and Saint Nicholas and the little *babushka*, that this is a truth of a different kind.

ࡥ

Why are you advocating a world in which "we don't need children" as we did in the past? When you speak of the importance of contributing to society, are you willing to accept the possibility that raising a child can be one of the greatest contributions people can make? JANUARY 1976

Of course we need children!

What we no longer need is parenthood at any price. In a world in which population presses so close upon the food supply that one failed harvest endangers the lives of millions, we must find ways of removing the social pressures that force men and women into parenthood. In a world in which there are millions of children who are hungry and cold, neglected and unloved, undernourished and doomed to brief and anguished lives, we need a great many people who are willing to devote themselves to the care of children who are not their own.

In Sweden, where there is economic support for all

mothers, there are very few adoptable children. Adopting parents there reach out to countries in which the poverty and misery are so great that the society is willing to send children away so they may have a better chance to survive as whole persons. And there is a Swedish motto that reads: Parents need children need parents need children.

I would add to this that adults need children in their lives to listen to and care for, to keep their imagination fresh and their hearts young and to make the future a reality for which they are willing to work hard. And children, all children, need adults to care for them, to feed and comfort and trust them, to provide role models and role alternatives for them and to create a living link between past and future.

Not everyone need have children. Instead we need couples who *elect* parenthood as a conscious vocation, with some assurance that they will remain together and devote themselves to rearing their own children, who will grow up to make a contribution to society. But even the best parent-child relationship can no longer be exclusive. Children need adults other than their own parents to open their eyes to a wider world, and adults need children's companionship.

Some adults will choose to adopt children. But as long as millions of children are in need, adoption is not the only answer. We need to invent new ways for adults to devote themselves to the care of children who will remain in their own country, where the talents of every able person are desperately needed. To some degree this is possible today through our gifts of money to organizations that send workers to poor or developing countries to help care for and educate children. How to create programs of this kind on a much wider scale is a new challenge for those who feel that their best contribution to the world is caring for children.

Some children's books are now being written according to graded word lists so that words not within a child's vocabulary won't appear in the books. How do you feel about this?
FEBRUARY 1963

I feel it is disastrous. How are children to learn new words unless they encounter them in context where they are swept along by the story, and so are eager and willing to try to grasp new ideas or new descriptive phrases? Furthermore, simplified vocabularies are boring for the adult, who then tends to read to the child in a bored, unenthusiastic voice.

Rudyard Kipling was one writer for children who made a game out of the vocabulary differences between adults and children. First he would use a rare word, and then he would reassure the child reader that he need not try to understand it fully. Such words—sonorous, mysterious and tempting—stay in children's minds, and each such word opens a door into the unknown wider world.

In the United States we often try to find out what people are doing, and then tell them that they are doing it and also that they should keep on doing it because this is what everyone of the same age or sex or class is doing. This produces a vicious circle. As a result, children are permitted to learn only what other children know, and each generation, living in a world where the demands on vocabulary are greater than before, gets a little further behind.

Do you approve of letting children have toy soldiers and guns and play war games? JULY 1963

In a world in which real soldiers, real guns and real bombs are continually pictured, toy soldiers have less significance than they may have had in the past. Pacifists may well want to outlaw toy soldiers with all the other trappings of war. But today, games with toy soldiers may be a way of teaching children the difference between past wars and a nuclear catastrophe—which would not be a war at all because no one would win and all would lose. Just as Indian suits and playing Indian have become part of a daydream world in which children re-enact a past way of life, so toy soldiers dressed for bygone wars and war games based on outworn strategies can be used to teach children about the kinds of battles and the kinds of bravery the world has outgrown. And imaginative parents have more choice in selecting the soldiers and in constructing the plots of games than they have in selecting television programs.

The Soviet Union places a great deal of propaganda emphasis on the need to ban children's games with warlike toys. But at the same time it preserves vivid and graphic memorials to earlier wars. And those in this country who recognize both that past wars were sometimes necessary and just and that modern nuclear inventions mean holocaust, not war, may well use children's games as a way of impressing this recognition upon their children.

Do you think small children should go to funerals?
SEPTEMBER 1963

Two different questions are really being asked. One is the question of whether a child should attend the funeral of someone who has been very close to him. And then there is the larger question of how a child should generally experience death, the inevitable end of human life. The experience can be seen as one that gives meaning to life or as one that destroys all meaning.

We are in a transition period in which a serious effort is finally being made to halt the dishonesty with which Americans have dealt with death in the past half century. The early half of the 20th century saw the battle for a more realistic and honest attitude toward sex or the "facts of life." Today it is the facts of death that are hidden under a pall of evasion and need to be brought back into the open.

A funeral is the expression of a common attitude toward the whole complex of feeling that surrounds death—personal loss, resignation, revived memories of others who have died, preparation for the loss of people still living, rearrangement of ongoing life and preparation for each individual's later life and eventual death. It is extremely important for all human beings to learn about death as a universal part of our humanity, not simply as an unaccountable personal attack of fate on their happiness and security. If a child can share in a funeral before he has to face the loss of someone who is very close to him, he will become familiar with the idea of death. Then when he does encounter a close personal loss (even if he is still very young), the knowledge of shared grief and the very ritual of the funeral may sustain him and protect him in his personal grief.

If a child's first experience of death is the loss of someone who was very close to him—a parent or a brother or a sister— the decision as to whether or not he should attend the funeral must depend on the emotional state of the adult from whom the child will take his cues as to the meaning not only of death but also of this death.

Is there any equivalent to toilet training among primitive peoples? JANUARY 1965

I find myself very puzzled by this question. It is rather like asking whether an unwritten language has a grammar— which of course it has. Everywhere in the world children, born without ability to control their sphincters and without any knowledge of appropriateness, must gain control and must learn how and when and where urination and defecation are permissible.

Of course, styles of child training differ very widely. At one extreme there are societies in which a child is beaten for making mistakes; at the other extreme are societies in which the mother or nurse watches the infant's expression so as to anticipate its needs. Styles differ also in regard to such things as the age at which a child is expected to take responsibility and the kind and amount of responsibility expected of it. There are great differences also in the clothes children wear. In some parts of Asia small children wear pants without a seat; in some societies small children wear no clothes. In still others small children must be assisted to undress and dress in order to relieve themselves. In some societies the child is expected to learn habits of control before it can understand what is required—a kind of learning that is easily lost. In other societies children learn slowly, simply by accompanying their parents and doing as they do.

Comparative studies suggest that the way people teach children to control their sphincters is closely related to the way they teach them many other things—about cleanliness in general, about whether the human body should be accepted joyfully or should be treated as something shameful, about the importance of property, about punctuality and routine. Each of these lessons carries with it a great deal more information about what it means to be a responsible human being, and learning one lesson helps the child to master the others as well. But the relative importance of these several lessons varies in different societies. In all societies, children are trained in—are taught and learn—the accepted rules of their own society.

ॐ

Are you in favor of busing children to schools outside their home neighborhoods? MARCH 1965

Busing children to schools outside their home neighborhoods is a desperate measure carried out in an attempt to correct, mostly at the expense of the children, conditions that should have been corrected by other means.

When a white private school decides to integrate, perhaps as much or even more for the sake of the white children as for the Negro, the most generous scholarship program usually cannot prevent Negro children from having to travel farther than their white fellow pupils. Everywhere, the handful of Negro children who carry the burden of the integration are made to bear a terrible load. For these youngsters, who might have been among the best scholars, the chosen leaders and the athletic heroes in their segregated schools, must stand up to hostility, loneliness, condescension and ostracism in their new schools so that in the future all American children, whatever their background, may live in a free world.

No parents, white or Negro, want their own children to suffer by attending school under unfavorable conditions. And busing children from good neighborhood schools to more-distant schools that are run-down and neglected, poorly equipped and understaffed is something no parents could possibly want for their children.

The only possible answer is the rapid construction of good schools with good teachers and good equipment in locations that make integration feasible without causing hardship to any group of children. Instead of quarreling about our failures, we should put our energy where it is most needed for the protection of all our children.

How does your daughter feel about being an only child? Zero population growth encourages one-child families, but many psychologists say it is bad for the child. JUNE 1974

My daughter thinks it is so advantageous to be an only child that she would like someone to write a book about it. One of my goddaughters, also an only child, is thinking of writing it.

In the 1920s there was a great deal of discussion about the disadvantages of being an only child. However, more recent investigations of the lives of creative and eminent people have indicated that there are definite advantages, in terms of adult achievement, in being an eldest, a youngest or an only child. A middle child, who is in a much less exposed position within the family, is somewhat less likely to achieve eminence as an adult.

I think it is very bad to be a *lonely* child—a child who is wholly dependent on her parents for companionship. The situation is very different for the only child whose family lives in a community surrounded by friendly neighbors, who can go to a good nursery school and who has playmates of different ages. Under these circumstances it is gratifying for a child also to have the undivided attention and affection of her parents.

Actually, a strong case can be made against the two-child family. Almost inevitably the two children are drawn into an extremely competitive relationship. Now one and now the other has the advantage in being taller or brighter or hand-somer, a better student or a better athlete, more active or quieter, sunnier or more serious. Simply by being older and younger, a boy or a girl, the two are expected to compete.

We do not know as yet the kind of family style that will develop as Americans work toward a balanced population. But I believe we should look forward to a new kind of mix: more families with one child than there are today; some couples with no children, except the ones they borrow over weekends, perhaps; and a very few families with a lot of children.

A big family gives children some very special qualities that we would not like to lose. We can't afford to have many large families any more, but where there are good ones other people, especially childless adults, can help give each of the children some of the adult attentiveness an only child enjoys.

What do the games children play reveal about human nature? Do they reveal anything about the society in which children live? OCTOBER 1974

Delight in play, which human beings share with other living creatures, is universal. But there are no "natural" games. Children learn to play games as they learn other activities in the society in which they grow up.

However, some kinds of play seem to have a universal appeal. Children almost everywhere play some form of running and chasing game; often the pursued, when caught, becomes the pursuer. Hiding also has great appeal to young children, and games of hide-and-seek in many versions are found all around the world. There also are innumerable games based on the idea of simultaneity—all the participants move in rhythm, say or sing the same rhyme and make the same formal gestures. (An example is our own singing game, "Here We Go 'Round the Mulberry Bush.") Once invented, games based on activities like these spread far and wide. Although they are continually modified, they still are based on a very ancient model. Blindman's buff, prisoner's base and ring-a-levio, different as they are, all are versions of tag.

Whether games are highly organized and have elaborate rules or are merely simple, slightly patterned forms of play varies somewhat in relation to the society in which children grow up. In some societies, for example, children play only games that involve a single group. All the children form a line and hop along one after another in the same bent posture. Or each child may leapfrog over the backs of those in front in a never-ending succession. Or the group may play a kind of crack-the-whip until the line breaks at some point, and then the game begins again. Or the "head" may attempt to bite the "tail" of the line.

In other societies the games children play take the form of contests that test individual skill and self-discipline. Among the Blackfoot Indians of the Plains, boys belonging to the same age group competed against one another in the skills a warrior needed and replayed old battles. Long before they actually became warriors who took part in raids, each boy knew where he stood in relation to all the others.

Games in which the players take sides fit well into societies of organized opposing groups. But it does not follow that games of this kind are always found in a society organized around opposed and competing groups. And even when they are, it does not necessarily follow that the aim is for one side to win. Instead, the aim may be for each side to encourage—or force—the other to perform well. Among the Iatmul on the Sepik River in New Guinea, a very uneven contest is frowned on and may break up in a roughhouse that involves even the adult audience; the ideal is for teams to be so closely matched that in the end everyone will say, "Both sides are the same—both sides have won."

There are societies in which adults make all kinds of miniatures for children—dolls, household articles, weapons and tools—and children earnestly imitate in play the activities of the adult world—keeping house, rearing children, hunting or raiding or performing ceremonies. The curious thing is that these games occur only in some societies. Elsewhere children may have no dolls or toy weapons or tools; their play is unrelated to adult activities. Instead they are expected to perform real tasks that are within their growing strength and skill. Or, as in medieval Europe, where children were considered miniature adults, even the smallest children may be included in the games played by adults.

However, attitudes toward children and play can change quite radically even within a short time. In a recent study of the Bushmen of the Kalahari Desert it was found that as long as Bushmen continue to live their traditional roving life of hunting and gathering food far from their camps, children take no part in work. They are free to play all day; adolescent, unmarried boys and girls are described as "the owners of the shade," that is, a group that lives at leisure. But when Bushmen groups move closer to towns and begin to cultivate gardens and keep animals, the children are expected to perform a great many chores and have little free time for play.

One generalization can be made, I think. Whatever children in a society do will be defined as desirable by other children in that society. Where children are free to play, this is what children will want to do, and they will want to play the kinds of games they learn from other children. Where children are given pigs to raise or water buffalo to tend, small children will look forward to the day when they too can take on these tasks. As far as the children themselves are concerned, it is other children who set the style of what is desirable.

There are societies in which adults sigh and look back with deep nostalgia to what they remember as the carefree days of childhood. In other societies adults leave childhood firmly behind. There, games, rhymes and sayings may pass from one child generation to the next with little adult awareness. In Bali, when we began to collect the rather salacious songs the children sang, our Balinese secretaries laughed with delight. "We had forgotten," they said. "We had forgotten how naughty we were!"

◆§ 3 §◆
CONTEMPORARY
SOCIETY

Do you think our astronauts really deserve the adulation they are receiving? Are they any more courageous than millions of other American men who have risked their lives for their country? JULY 1963

I think the word "adulation" is ill-chosen. It places the astronauts in the same class as matinee idols, where they do not belong. Americans have had only a limited opportunity to know men who have consciously, voluntarily and within known conditions chosen to risk their lives for their country. And in most cases the risk has been taken in wartime, and those who have risked their lives were at the same time defending their own lives and the lives of others whom they valued.

The astronauts are not war heroes, and even though our space race with the Soviet Union places their activities within a framework of patriotism, they are not primarily risking their lives for the sake of their country. In their activities they represent a different—and a very new—combination. They are pioneers and explorers who bear a burden as great as the leader of a great country, feel an excitement equal to that of a great scientist and need the courage required only of those who must face the unknown.

The astronauts represent a new kind of hero patriot—one who serves his country and so the whole of humanity not by dying for it but by living for it, under conditions requiring extreme endurance and steadfastness.

69

Would you favor changing our abortion laws?
FEBRUARY 1963

The problem of abortion goes to the very heart of any ethical system. When is a human being a human being? At conception? When life quickens? At birth? An hour or a week after birth? If a choice must be made between the life of the mother and the life of the unborn child, how is the issue to be resolved? Is it ethical to endanger the life of the mother of several little children when a new pregnancy may end in the mother's death? Should children be brought into the world fatherless or, because of the state of the mother's emotional life, essentially motherless? Should parents do anything to prevent the birth of a child who is likely to be mentally or physically defective?

Who should decide these questions? Some of them, of course, can be resolved privately and be met by the use of contraception or the proper exercise of self-control. But some cannot.

Conflicts over abortion are generally based on either religious or political considerations. In countries like Japan and the Soviet Union, legislation has been controlled by national policies dictated by alternating desires either for more manpower or for a higher standard of living. In this country religious differences have been the most important. The various religious groups—and people who belong to no religious group—differ in their beliefs about abortion. In the eyes of some, our abortion laws are too stringent; in the eyes of others, too lax. A very wise psychiatrist, speaking about patterns of human behavior, used to insist, "You must not legislate in areas of heterogeneity." Yet this is what we do when we make the kind of laws about abortion that we have today—in 1963—laws which, in most states, permit abortion only when a woman's life is endangered by childbirth.

I believe that our abortion laws should be changed. In a country where there is a genuine and convinced divergence of ethical belief, I believe that we should not prescribe the conditions under which abortion is permissible. What is im-

70

portant is the provision of optimum medical protection for any woman who undergoes an abortion. Wherever abortion is illegal, unnumbered girls and women, married and unmarried, run frightful risks, and the danger of bearing damaged infants is greatly increased.

We will be a better country when each religious group can trust its members to obey the dictates of their own religious faith without assistance from the legal structure of the country.

ᔪ᠊

Do you believe that our laws on drug addiction should be revised? How? MARCH 1963

Yes, I do. Far from fulfilling their intended purposes, our present laws make it almost inevitable for the person who once begins to use drugs to become involved in other criminal activities and for the use of drugs to spread in ever-widening circles. Attempts to carry out our drug laws have a distorting effect on the lives of many people in our society.

With the high cost of illegal drugs, the addict—especially the young addict with limited earning powers—is rapidly driven to crime as a way of obtaining money to buy drugs. The waves of petty crime that sweep over a city when large drug supplies have been confiscated by the government are vivid testimony to the connection between theft and drug addiction. In addition, the new addict is readily induced to become a "pusher"—someone who seeks to involve others in the use of drugs so that, by selling the drug, he may get some for himself. In religious and political movements one of the most effective forms of recruitment is summed up in the rule "Bring the one next to you." In this, drug addicts are undoubtedly very much like others who are engaged in activities which their companions do not understand—they want to bring in their friends. But the main inducement is the economic one; they urge the use of drugs on others as a way of keeping up their own supply.

Our present laws on drugs and addiction are dangerous, illogical and inhumane. It would be no more intelligent for us to treat people with certain contagious diseases as criminals, to provide only the minimal hospital care for them and to make it illegal for them to buy medicine. In these circumstances we would not be surprised at the development of a bootleg market in medicine, or at a tremendous upsurge of crime among those who could not pay the exorbitant prices.

The sale of drugs to addicts should be legalized, put under strict medical control, as has been done in England, and the drugs should be sold as inexpensively as their real cost permits. If this were done, those who became addicts would lose most of their reasons for seducing their companions. Under such a plan there would be more opportunities and incentive for addicts to accept help in freeing themselves from their addiction, and they would be under far less pressure from their former companions to begin using drugs again. The illegal sale of drugs should continue to carry heavy penalties. What is imperative is that the drug addict should be regarded as a patient and adequate care should be provided for him, just as we provide medical and hospital care for other ill persons. As in the case of other illnesses, not every stricken person will recover. But the illness can be reduced to a state in which it is virtually noncommunicable—and so the danger of infection to others can be minimized.

Has homosexuality in America increased in recent years, or does it only seem so because it is more publicized and more accepted than previously? JULY 1963

It is always hard to answer a question of this kind about behavior that is socially disapproved and legally punishable. There has been much more open discussion of homosexuality in contemporary literature, on the stage, in films and over television and the radio. This tends to give people the impression of a great increase. The McCarthy period also brought homosexuality into unexpected prominence by linking it with subversion and thereby making it a more acceptable, if highly criticized, subject of discussion.

It cannot really be said, however, that we are becoming more tolerant of variations in sexual behavior. I think that for the most part we are simply more willing to permit discussion—sometimes with pornographic intent, as a way of feeding a commercially developed appetite for the titillating and the unusual; sometimes on the pseudoscientific level of homosexuality as a "curable" or "incurable" malady.

Such discussions almost always confuse three kinds of person: the individual who prefers a member of his own sex within the same limits of monogamy and fidelity as those set for current heterosexual preference; the individual who is compulsively driven to an endless and almost inevitably exploitive and antisocial search for new physical satisfaction; and the individual whose involvement in homosexuality is also an involvement in crime—because our laws make homosexual practice a crime, and so some individuals become involved in a variety of criminal activities such as drug addiction (another example of a criminal activity by ill-advised laws), prostitution, procurement, and so on. The failure to distinguish among these very different types results in the furtherance of a large number of socially undesirable activities—the harassment of socially harmless individuals, blackmail and police corruption and an actual increase in crime.

One partial explanation of the seeming growth of homosexuality might be an increasing sophistication among Americans as we have shifted from a frontier society, with very primitive codes of human relationships, to a cosmopolitan society, which like all cosmopolitan societies has more room for the nuances of human behavior and a greater toleration of individual choice.

Another partial explanation might be an increasing scientific sophistication based on knowledge of other cultures, other periods in our own culture and the behavior of other living creatures. Out of this knowledge comes a recognition that bisexual potentialities are normal and that their specialization is the result of experience and training.

Many liberal statesmen and scientists have criticized the enormous effort and sums of money we are spending on our

**race to the moon when these resources are desperately
needed to fight problems—such as disease and poverty—
right here on earth. Would you comment on this?**
SEPTEMBER 1963

This would be valid criticism if our country were suffering
from a shortage of resources and if, by diverting capital
equipment to the moon race, we were interfering with the
construction of schools and hospitals or, by diverting manpower from agriculture, we were letting people go hungry.
This was the case in the United States during World War II,
when many essential services were neglected to speed up
war production. And the criticism can be applied with some
justice to the Soviet Union today. But for the United States,
the argument is a specious one. And it is a pity when those
who are deeply concerned about the human race join
others—and there are too many—who oppose our space activities simply out of a lack of military or general imagination.

We are not a poor nation. We are not a recently industrialized nation like the Soviet Union. We are not a nation,
like China, with both a new political system and all the new
problems of industrialization, as a result of which tens of
millions may face famine. We are not a new nation, like
Nigeria, with scanty resources to meet skyrocketing aspirations. Nor are we an old nation, like Egypt, with few resources and a desperately poor majority. The United States
has resources, space, know-how, plant, materials and people.
What is lacking is only the will and imagination to put as
much energy into the fight against disease, poverty and illit-
eracy and into meeting our obligations to the underprivileged
of this nation and the world as we are putting into a quasi-
military, international sports event. We can well afford to
carry on the moon race *and* to work on other pressing
problems—both.

Our race to the moon may be questioned on two other
counts. It can be asked: Is it wasteful to have the United
States and the Soviet Union duplicating each other's activities instead of co-operating with each other? This charge is
questionable. Co-operation in as many fields as possible is
important. But competition leads to the development of dif-

74

ferent and novel solutions, and a race for prestige is far safer than an armaments race in which dangerously explosive nuclear weapons are stockpiled. It can also be asked: Does the moon race absorb too much of our scientific manpower and is it directing research into too-narrow channels? The answer to this double question seems to be yes.

ट≫

Your columns generally take an optimistic tone about such forms of "progress" as automation. Isn't it equally possible that instead of freeing man's spirit, all these engineering triumphs are simply dulling it? DECEMBER 1963

There seems to be some confusion here between "automation" and "mechanization." When the mechanized factory system developed in the 19th century, man became part of that system as hour after hour he tended a machine, performing some monotonous, routine task. This did dull the human spirit, and critics of the social order rightly protested and called for a return to the spirit of individual workmanship and for the development of ways in which men could do more diversified and meaningful work. In contrast, automation is a method that removes the need for human beings to act like cogs in a machine. The subhuman, routine tasks once performed by factory workers can now be performed automatically by machines.

It is certainly not conducive to human dignity to have men perform any kind of repetitive, meaningless labor that can be done by some other method—for women to carry loads of bricks on their heads, for men to stoke furnaces, for girls to work hour after hour pouring chocolate into molds. The whole history of civilization has been the history of how first some and then many individuals have been freed from drudgery so that they might have time to think, to paint, to pray, to philosophize, to observe, to study the universe. Leisure and the cultivation of human capacities are inextricably interdependent.

But even though automation makes possible high productivity and great leisure, there is no guarantee that we shall

75

make good use of this new freedom. Indeed, if we think of automation chiefly as something that deprives whole armies of men and women of their livelihood and the means of acquiring necessary goods, then we are certainly making poor use of it. The effect that automation has on us depends on our own attitudes and reactions to it. It is not "engineering triumphs" but men themselves that create the conditions that dull—or free—the human spirit.

Are funeral practices in the United States really more garish and outrageous than those in other cultures, as charged by Jessica Mitford in her best-selling book *The American Way of Death*? MARCH 1964

Cultures vary in the importance given to death and burial. People in many lands have expended more than they could afford on funeral rites, sometimes destroying the house and all the possessions of the dead. What is shocking about American funeral practices is the combined denial and commercialization of death.

Our usual method of changing our value system is to turn those who participate for profit into whipping boys. So the mortician is now accused of having caused the denial of death, when actually he has only responded to what mid-century Americans wanted. When commercial interests pick up a theme in our culture, they simplify it in such a way that it comes back to us bizarrely overemphasized. So the embalming of a corpse may be seen as a method that makes it possible for a funeral to be postponed until relatives arrive from the four corners of the nation to share a common grief. But if it is represented as making the corpse "lifelike," a different note is struck. The serene appearance of a relative who has died may be a tremendous comfort to the survivors who knew his last painful months or years; as an advertisement for a flourishing business, it grates on our sensibilities.

Yet I think it is a mistake to forget that we are not a society in which the dead can be washed and laid out by the women of the household, while the coffin is shaped and the grave dug by the men. We depend upon an industrialized and technical group for these last rites; as we wish them celebrated, so they will be celebrated. It would be a pity if, in our present national turning toward a greater realism about death, we should also reject and punish those who have only ministered both to real need and to our fears and prejudices.

It is always a temptation in the United States to make a needed reform by going to extremes. So, accompanying the present furor about expensive funerals, there is a tendency in some quarters to reject all ceremony. Yet burial without ceremony is so empty, and often so damaging to at least some of those who would have wished to mourn, that almost inevitably the pendulum will swing back again. An era of flowerless funerals and gifts to CARE or the Home for Crippled Children will only usher in a return to more extravagant mourning behavior a couple of decades from now.

A religious funeral with flowers and music, and afterward food and drink at the home of the mourners, need not be treated as an alternative to a set of idealistic good works. Instead of "please omit flowers," we could have "no set pieces," or some equivalent that would suggest moderation. In the case of those who have bequeathed their eyes or their kidney for others, or their brains or bodies for research, the notice of death could include a statement of what they had done, perhaps with the phrase "closed casket" as a positive rather than a negative statement.

Right around the world it is the people who take death simply, who openly sorrow for someone who has gone from their midst and can speak easily of both the virtues and the vices of the recently dead, who are able to have the simplest funerals.

How do you explain the fact that the Chinese, who live as unassimilated a life in America as Negroes do and who have suffered similarly from the effects of poverty and prejudice, have been so remarkably free of a criminal record? MAY 1964

In spite of superficial resemblances, the experiences of

Chinese in America and of American Negroes have been very different. For the most part, Chinese migrants to the United States came of their own accord, and while they lived and worked here most of them remained closely related to their own society, to which, in theory if not always in practice, they expected to return. The Chinese have an ancient tradition of living in extraterritorial communities, and those who settled here organized a way of living which in some respects paralleled the way of living organized for Europeans and Americans who went to Chinese cities. Except for the scholars who came as students, most of those who left China were very poor, and they bettered their lot—and sometimes the lot of their families in China—by coming. Until recently the overwhelming majority were men, and the few women and children were protected within the Chinese community.

The Chinese living in American cities had their own system of community administration; this meant that they could preserve order, exact conforming behavior and punish infractions of accepted rules without, in general, appealing to American law-enforcing agencies. Abandonment of his fellow Chinese was something an individual was seldom prepared to risk, and intervention in Chinese affairs by the larger American community was something most Chinese hoped to avoid. Poor communication and the sense of dealing with an alien people, a feeling shared by Chinese and Americans alike, helped keep the Chinese communities in America apart and intact. The Chinese were, in effect, members of a self-selected colony who were temporarily exploiting the economic possibilities of an alien land.

When Americans exploited the Chinese through their unfamiliarity with our style of life or treated them to the kind of racism we have meted out to the other non-Caucasians (or sometimes to non-Northern Europeans or non-English-speaking peoples), the Chinese colonists were angry and resentful, but the individual was not effectively damaged as a person. The greatest damage was to American clarity—to our own ability to see and understand a people different from ourselves. For this lack of clarity we paid heavily in our unpreparedness for dealing in wartime with the members of another Oriental civilization, the Japanese. And today, on a world-wide scale, a heavy price is being exacted for the fact that Chinese and Americans have traditionally regarded each other as alien peoples to be excluded from each other's way of life.

The condition of the American Negro was and is strikingly different. The ancestors of these Americans were brought from Africa by force, torn from a score of very different societies, speaking many different languages, without any traditional way of bridging the gaps between them and without a means of communicating with their own people still in Africa. Under slavery the family system, which was as strong in Africa as it was in China, was destroyed, and men were denied the right to have responsibility for their women and children. From the beginning, white men ruthlessly abused African women, and a new population grew up that was both bound in speech and custom to its white ancestry and punished by social ostracism and poverty for every trace of its African ancestry.

Throughout most of their history Negro Americans, defined by visible color or simply by some remembered American Negro ancestry, presented no picture of social solidarity. The differences among them were in themselves a cause of disunity. Unlike the Chinese, Negro Americans have had no ongoing style of social regulation to fall back on; what they have shared is the knowledge that the law is administered in one way for white men and in other ways for themselves. Whereas the Chinese community has been able to protect its members, control its children, mete out informal punishment and reward, and cover for its members who break American laws, Negro Americans have had until very recently few means of protecting themselves to give them a sense of security and pride as a group.

The U.S. Court of Appeals has ruled that a pacifist should be permitted exemption from military service even if his pacifism is not based on a belief in a Supreme Being. What do

you think are the implications of this ruling? JULY 1964

I agree with the recent statement by the World Council of Churches that freedom of religion includes the freedom to question all religion. I also think that on an ethical issue for which the community is willing to make sacrifices, the individual who takes a contrary position should also be willing to make sacrifices. The treatment of a conscientious objector should not be conceived of in a punitive or self-righteous spirit, as has so often happened in the past. Instead, the tasks he is asked to do should be in keeping with the ethic he has advanced. If this is a lively concern for the well-being of his fellow men, for whose sake he is trying to speed up the elimination of war, he can be given a task concerned with his fellow men—working in a hospital, for example. If his concern is only for his own soul, he should at least give up, temporarily, involvement with this world's goods and spend the same number of months spent by his fellows in the armed services in some overtly self-sacrificial manner.

However, our present methods of selecting men for the armed services are themselves manifestly unfair and discriminatory, working to the advantage of some and to the disadvantage of other young people. We should have national service for every able-bodied young person. In such a setting there would be room for everyone to serve the community for a period of time.

ॐ

Aren't today's chores of washing, ironing, cleaning and meal preparation infinitely easier than they were fifty years ago? NOVEMBER 1964

Taken individually, yes. Each of these activities has been mechanized and streamlined over the last fifty years. An electric steam iron is easier to handle and more efficient than the first clumsy electric irons, and much easier than the old irons with detachable handles that used to be heated on the stove, or the still older box iron (known as a "goose") into which one put burning charcoal.

But in making this kind of comparison we forget the change

80

in our whole style of living. All the washing and ironing equipment is there to make work easier. But whereas in the past the family laundry was done as routine once a week, today women may load the washer every day, sometimes more than once a day. The vacuum cleaner is a wonderful invention, but today few people are as careful about tracking in mud or spilling ashes as they were when a thorough housecleaning was a major, semiannual event. Nowadays men wear clean shirts (instead of clean, starched, detachable collars and cuffs) and children wear clean clothes from top to toe every day, and the housewife almost literally follows in her family's footsteps, vacuuming, waxing and polishing away the unwanted residue of their activities.

There is only one way in which household work can be said to be easier than it was—it takes less muscle and so it is less backbreaking and easier on the elbows and the shoulders and the knees. But in fact, the largest part of homemaking is a continuous response to the recurring needs of others— another meal to be prepared, a message to be taken and delivered, a child to be chauffeured somewhere away from home and back again. Only by keeping a careful count of the hours a homemaker spends looking after the house and responding to the needs of her family could we find out whether her life actually is easier than her mother's or her grandmother's was.

Are there really so many more youth crimes today than in previous eras, or are we simply more aware of them?
NOVEMBER 1964

This is not a question that can be answered simply by quoting statistics. There are many factors that must be taken into consideration.

First, there is our constantly growing population. At the time of the Revolution, in 1775, it was estimated that there were 3 million people in the thirteen colonies; in 1850 our population was just over 23 million; in 1910, approximately 92 million. And since the turn of the century our population has more than doubled. Even if the crime *rate* had not changed over the last fifty or one hundred or one hundred and fifty years, we would have a constantly increasing *number* of crimes.

Second, our cities are enormously larger than they were and the proportion of people living in cities has increased tremendously; between 1900 and 1950 our *urban* population alone increased by 66 million. The mass movement to cities had begun by the time of the Civil War, but today's urbanization is a phenomenon of this century. And crime flourishes in the big cities.

Third, the practice of treating delinquent youngsters differently from adult criminals, of sending young offenders to reformatories rather than to adult prisons, is a process that started only in the 19th century. And the first children's court in the United States (in Cook County, Chicago) was not established until 1899. So it is very difficult to assess accurately changes in the actual number of juvenile offenders.

Fourth, we have a national communications system hungry for news, and much of it hungry for news of a morbid character. The sensational press gives preference to crime news that occurs far beyond any one locality; so the reader, the television viewer or the radio listener is continually given the impression that the nation is crimeridden. This is particularly the case where juvenile deliquency is concerned, for both those who batten on crime news and those who, for the best reasons, want to goad the authorities into action—to clear the slums or improve the schools or deal with the problems involved in school dropouts and unemployed youth—keep the picture of juvenile crime, especially violent crime, before everyone's eyes.

Fifth, the age at which juveniles become involved in lawbreaking activities is becoming lower. This is to be expected in our society, of course, as we permit ever-younger children more freedom of movement outside the home and the school without in any way providing new kinds of protection for these young people who, with adult encouragement, are set loose on the streets.

But there is also an important factor of confusion. People tend unthinkingly to lump together school and college pranks (which have, it is true, become more and more expensive and destructive), the teen-age crimes of undereducated and un-employed young people, the casual crimes committed by juveniles who have fallen prey to drug addiction, the crimes in which young offenders are associated with adult criminals. Taken together, the various ways in which young people clash with the law can be the source of very formidable statistics.

Yet we must seriously consider whether, in a rapidly chang-ing social world, the statistics gathered today are fully com-parable in kind and in meaning to those gathered twenty-five or fifty years ago. The fact that there are more people who care—more people who do not take it as a matter of course that we must expect to waste a large proportion of our young people who grow up in difficult and deprived environ-ments—in itself affects what we look at and try to quan-tify. When people become conscious of some social evil, the evil is made more visible and seems much "worse." And if we are to come to grips with the problems we are beginning to identify, it will not do to concentrate on comparisons with the past. Instead we must sort out and think about the sources of maladjustment and lawbreaking and violence in the ex-pression of disturbance in our contemporary life.

Do you think membership in the John Birch Society should disqualify a man from being a policeman? JUNE 1965

The status of the John Birch Society is ambiguous. If the Department of Justice were to pursue the identification of possibly subversive organizations with the same zeal it dis-played during World War II, very probably the John Birch Society would be included on a list of those so defined. In that case police departments, federal, state and local, would have acknowledged grounds for excluding from the force a known member of a local chapter. But in the absence of con-sensus, it can be claimed that exclusion by reason of mem-bership alone constitutes capricious persecution on the grounds of guilt by association, and that this is no more desirable when it is directed to the extreme right than when individuals belonging to liberal organizations are indiscriminately branded as Communists by members of the John Birch Society and its sympathizers.

However, an important distinction must be made between the extreme left and the extreme right in their advocacy of change in governmental form. Extremists on the left give great importance to the ideological positions of other countries—both those with which they do and those with which they do not sympathize. In contrast, extremists on the right are preoccupied with local, domestic battles. They pursue a course that endangers the country from within through their accusations against responsible elected and appointed leaders of the people. This preoccupation with dangerous neighbors, rather than with foreign ideas, is a particularly precarious ideological position for a policeman, particularly a policeman who carries arms.

There is also another important consideration. Both groups, the adherents of the radical left (particularly in earlier years, in the 1930s and 1940s) and the adherents of the radical right (in the present as well as in the past), include many deeply *sincere* people. But in neither case is sincerity alone a guarantee of good sense or effective patriotism. Sincere, unsuspecting fellow travelers could be—and have been—manipulated by ruthless, purposeful Communist leaders; and sincere, unsuspecting sympathizers with the extreme right by their very sincerity and naïveté may enable fanatical leaders to attain the ends toward which they are working. Then, when one realizes that the immediate consequence of the rightist position is a deep suspicion of elected and appointed officials and of a military leadership that has been exemplary in its devotion to the causes espoused by the American people, one may well ask whether sincerity that is linked to distrust and suspicion is not in itself a potential danger.

Why do you think our public schools get involved with such trivia as how their students wear their hair—as in the case of

the boy in Connecticut who was expelled because he refused to cut his hair to the proper length? JUNE 1965

Your question raises another question: What *is* the "proper" way for a boy to wear his hair? Clothing, ornaments and hair styles are extremely important in every society, for they provide a series of necessary clues as to the sex, age, caste, status, occupation and sometimes even the religious, artistic and political position of the individual. Every change in these very significant markers reflects a change in public attitudes. I remember very well the evening when a famous sociologist, a friend of my father's, pointed to my bobbed hair and said, "That girl's short hair is more significant than all your theories!" It *was* significant—in 1920.

While people are adjusting to a change of this kind— women in slacks, men in colored vests, women with short hair, men with long hair, men with beards, students with bare feet, old ladies in Bermuda shorts, tourists without ties— many people feel embarrassed. Embarrassment tends to make people angry at whatever has caused it, and they are likely to demand special rules aimed at banning or at least limiting the questionable behavior. So a rule is made that bathers must take a special stairway to the beach, that girls must wear skirts to school, that all males must shave or that only males wearing coats and ties will be served.

Demands of this kind and the responses made to them test the strength of feeling for and against some new practice. If the protests fail, eventually there is a new "proper" way of wearing one's hair or dressing for some occasion. But until a change has withstood such tests, it will be opposed as "improper" for certain places, occasions or persons.

In other societies, do the adults attempt to control adolescents in the consumption of alcohol? OCTOBER 1965

The handling of adolescent drinking depends both on the way a people thinks about alcohol in its various forms and the way it thinks about childhood and adolescence. In most of Western Europe the use of alcohol is highly ritualized, and different kinds of alcoholic beverages are defined as appropriate for different kinds of people at different times. There "drinking" in the negative sense of the term means inappropriate drinking. Men drink "spirits" or "hard liquor," but women and children do not. Traditionally, students drink beer but no spirits. Family groups drink in public what family groups also drink in private. The Italians, who think of wine as part of man's normal nourishment, give children a little wine as they also give them bread. The French, who regard drinking with moderation and discrimination as something that must be learned, give children wine as a matter of course. For just as children must learn to read and write correctly, so also they must learn what and how much to drink.

In every European country there are also class and regional differences in custom. For the peasant or the workingman, beer or a simple wine is part of everyday life. For members of the upper class, connoisseurship adds to the complication of the ritual. In England, children and young adolescents who are sent away to school have for the most part a stern and rigorous diet. For them a glass of sherry is a holiday symbol, just as beer is a holiday symbol for the working class and the country child, and once a wealthy English father laid down wine for his son's coming of age. In countries where different patterns of drinking alcohol are highly elaborated, the question is not, "Do adolescents drink?" but, instead, "What do adolescents drink?"

In the United States we run into two major kinds of difficulty when we try to regulate drinking among young people. The first is that we tend to include every form of alcoholic beverage, from beer to brandy, under the single rubric of "drink." The second arises from the distinction we make between children, adolescents and sometimes women, on the one hand, and adults, sometimes excluding women, on the other, in our thinking about things that are "bad" and "bad for you." Whatever is bad for adults—and here "drinking" is classified with a whole set of activities that may also include smoking, gambling, card playing and dancing—is worse for children, adolescents and women than it is for grown men. Adults (or at least men) may be able to set limits for themselves or may be able to recover from a lapse, but others should as far as possible be protected from temptation. So even though the prohibition laws failed dismally when they were applied to adults, those who wish to regulate others' lives still insist on what amounts to a prohibition law for youth.

Our feeling about this is strengthened by our traditional linking together of moral and physical well-being, particularly where anything that is taken into the body is concerned. This in itself makes a disapproved substance "worse" for women and children—the two groups whose health we care for most vigilantly—than it is for men. Perhaps this is why cigarettes—"coffin nails"—were especially strongly disapproved of when they were taken up by young boys and women. Cigar smoking was, strictly speaking, an adult male habit. Cigars made boys go pale and the very smell of stale cigar smoke nauseated many women. But cigarettes made tobacco available to those who needed most to be protected from its dangers, moral and physical, as we saw the problem.

Much of this feeling is breaking down today as Americans have brought drinking into the home and many other formerly forbidden activities have become everyday, harmless pleasures. Many parents feel that it is all right for adolescents to have a drink at home "with us." But we are still struggling with confusion about what is "a drink"—beer? wine? spirits?—and with the problem of how to become more discriminating in our patterns of serving and drinking. Meanwhile, as we continue to combine vague moral disapproval and general toleration of law-breaking, young people "drink" as a way of testing out the pleasure of doing things that are "bad for you" and that adults somewhat uneasily reserve for themselves.

Will you comment on the changing role of grandparents in American society today? JUNE 1966

In relatively unchanging, traditional societies, closeness to grandparents means closeness to old, accepted modes of life.

Intimacy with their grandparents gives children a sense of how a whole life is lived into old age, and unconsciously they set their sights to follow in the same path. Among American Indians, the most conservative peoples have been those among whom grandparents have played a decisive part in rearing children.

In our American past, many grandparents were immigrants who, though they lived in new homes in a new country, kept up customs that related them to the life they had left behind. Their American grandchildren, to whom these ways seemed increasingly old-fashioned and strange, felt separated from them by an almost unbridgeable gulf. Later, when the grandparents died, parents and children adopted fully American ways, and nothing remained of old customs but the memory that they were unyielding and different. This picture, true of the past, still shapes our American image of grandparents. Even when grandparents have been American-born and speak English as their native tongue, there is a tendency to equate them with whatever appears to be out-of-date in contemporary life. Pediatricians, public-health nurses and schoolteachers are likely to depreciate grandparental advice, and housing authorities plan for modern homes in which grandparents have no place. As we still visualize them, grandparents are old people—old physically and old in the sense of being set in their ways and probably better off and happier living in Florida and California with others like themselves.

This picture of what grandparents are supposed to be like masks a very different reality. In a changing society, grandparents themselves change. Far from representing what is stubbornly old-fashioned, they are the men and women who in the contemporary world have the greatest experience in incorporating new ways and ideas. Very often their daughters are mired down in a thousand details of baby care and housekeeping, and their sons are struggling to establish themselves in the world. But grandparents have the leisure to follow up what is most modern and new. And unlike their own parents, who grew old early under physical stress, today's grandparents generally have years of vigorous living ahead.

More often than we realize, grandparents who move away from the homes where they brought up their children are not settling into "retirement," but instead are launching into new activities. Some of them have—and many more could have—a very important role in their grandchildren's lives. Because as adults they have lived through so much change—the first "talkies" and television, the first computers and satellites— they may well be the best people to teach children about change. With a lifetime of experience of how far we have come and how fast, grandparents can give children a special sense of sureness about facing the unknown in the future. Having experienced so much that is new, they can keep a sense of wonder in their voices as they tell their grandchildren how something happened, what it was like the first time, and open their grandchildren's eyes to the wonder of what is happening now and may happen soon. And as men and women who are making new beginnings, developing new interests, they can demonstrate to children that growing up is only one stage in a lifetime of growth. As in the past, they represent continuity. But now, in a changing society, this continuity includes the future and acceptance of the unknown.

Would you impose any limitations on scientific research into the creation of life and the alteration of genetic patterns?
JANUARY 1967

I do not think we can impose limits on research. Through hundreds of thousands of years, man's intellectual curiosity has been essential to all the gains we have made. Although in recent times we have progressed from chance and hit-or-miss methods to consciously directed research, we still cannot know in advance what the results may be. It would be regressive and dangerous to trammel the free search for new forms of truth.

It is true that research findings are almost daily becoming more significant for our understanding of human life. But it is in the *application* of these findings that new controls and new canons of responsibility must be developed. This necessarily involves not only research scientists and professional practitioners but also the citizenry of every country.

The recognition that this is so is the basis of the Information Movement, organized in different parts of the United States by scientists who have banded together to inform the general public about problems of great consequence, such as the use of nuclear power, including nuclear tests; problems of water and air pollution; the need for population control; and problems of race relations.

Two things are necessary for the success of the Information Movement. There must be groups of dedicated scientists who can organize information about the applications of science in such a way that it is meaningful to laymen. But also there must be groups of responsible citizens who want this information and who are willing to grapple with the problems that are posed by the new possibilities of its application. Those of us who are involved in this venture believe that scientists should take the responsibility for informing the public; we do not believe that scientists can take the sole responsibility for decisions on the applications of science. Without technical information, discussions are likely to produce more heat than light. But decision making is a process in which scientists and citizens, working together, must take part actively, continuously and responsively.

The question of positive, purposeful intervention in human genetic processes is certain to arise very soon. It is important that we be prepared to think about it. Of course, certain types of intervention already exist. Examples are found in sterilization laws, in voluntary abstention from parenthood by individuals bearing a known heritable defect and in changes in endemic disease patterns. Negative intervention also occurs wherever there are so-called apartheid laws that prevent free interbreeding between different races. Many older social customs and legal measures must now be called into question in terms of the doubtful genetic theories underlying them and in terms of human rights as well. As our knowledge grows, new ethical issues will always arise, and we must be prepared to reconsider practice in the light of human values.

The answer is not to limit research. What is needed instead is careful and profound discussion based on the best knowledge we have—knowledge that is shared and understood by all responsible citizens, not only those who are scientists. This is the step we must take, and soon.

Professor Hans Morgenthau has indicted the academic community for having abdicated its social responsibilities in failing to speak out on crucial issues. What is your view of the matter? JUNE 1967

Society accords the academic community, as a whole, special rights and privileges, and its members carry special responsibilities. Universities and colleges are tax-exempt, endowed and supported in the public interest. Young men and women wishing to work toward an academic career receive fellowships and grants. Older members of the academic community, who are trusted with the induction of the young into the intellectual traditions of their culture, are treated with respect. And today, in a changing world, they have the responsibility of developing new knowledge and applying it to the basic problems of our lives.

I consider teaching and developing new knowledge to be the primary responsibility of the academic community. Taking a stand or speaking out *without* the appropriate knowledge is a betrayal of trust. I would indeed criticize many parts of the academic community today for failing to do research on critical problems, as well as for failing to alert the public to issues on which members of certain disciplines have special competence, such as the hazards of radiation; the dangers of air, water and land pollution; and the vital necessity of controlling urban growth and overpopulation. But I would also indict those members of the academic community who speak out without special competence or who substitute political passion or individual conscience for the competence they are believed to have.

The problem of acquiring and interpreting data on human races illustrates what I mean. In the 1920s and 1930s anthropologists devoted very considerable research time and effort to certain problems that puzzled the general public, such as the apparent association between skin color and various forms of education and economic "inferiority" or "superiority." One outcome was the demonstration that members of a racial group might make significant contributions to civilization in one period, but in another period, when they were cut off from the main stream of development, might sink into insignificance. Similarly it was possible to demonstrate the critical importance of social expectation on children's achievement in situations in which invidious comparisons were made in terms of racial heritage. This research and its application to everyday life contributed materially to the creation of a new social climate of opinion within which Americans could reformulate the goals of democracy.

More recently, however, younger anthropologists have concentrated far more effort on "speaking out" than on careful research and critical analysis of problems related to race. A few of them have even denounced research that undertook to explicate the relationship between long-continued malnutrition or endemic disease and poor performance in groups defined as racially distinct or—as in the case of American Negroes—racially mixed. These anthropologists have been particularly vehement in their denunciations of research which has demonstrated that the effects of deprivation are real and lasting, though they are the result of conditions that could be eradicated for a new generation of children. In doing this, they have hindered the public understanding of the incapacitating effects of social conditions that can be changed. This is a situation in which members of the academic community *have* spoken out, but in doing so have failed in their primary responsibilities.

It appears to me that wherever demonstrations, manifestoes, sit-ins, teach-ins and other similar activities are treated as substitutes for the search for new knowledge and ways of applying it to the living world, the academic community is failing to take responsibility for its position of trust. In contrast, when scientists have taken the initiative in organizing their knowledge so as to make it really available and have worked on the problem of how best to inform the public on areas of urgency and danger, I believe they are meeting their responsibilities. The rapid dissemination of knowledge about the dangers of atomic fallout and its effectiveness in leading to social action locally, nationally and even internationally is an outstanding illustration of wholly responsible standing up and speaking out.

§æ

With American crime rates on the rise, do you think it possible that our police and courts are taking the wrong approach? Are there any lessons we can learn from primitive cultures and other societies? MARCH 1968

Our police system and our courts, like our school system, are essentially localized and diverse. This makes it difficult to generalize about "the" approach to crime. Two things can be said, however. One is that almost every kind of reform that has been suggested is being actively advocated or tried out somewhere in the United States. The other is that while most such reforms aim at altering particular procedures or methods of organization, or attempt to eliminate injustice rooted in prejudice, they also tend to be regarded as keys to change on a larger scale.

A few examples are enough to show the range of thinking about new approaches to crime and law. Legal experts working on a project initiated by the Vera Institute of Justice are trying to eliminate bail requirements in New York City's Borough of Manhattan for persons accused of crimes other than homicide, narcotics violations or some sex offenses, holding that detention before trial of those unable to put up bail works against justice for the poor. Police forces are steadily upgrading their educational requirements. There also are advocates of differential requirements for police-recruitment at various levels of education for varying jobs connected with public safety. Especially in large cities there is interest in automating settlement of minor traffic cases that clog court calendars.

Another wide variety of reforms aims at the redefinition of

criminals. In a growing number of prisons and reform institutions, experiments are being carried out to replace punishment with remedial care and rehabilitation. A parallel development is the "halfway house," where those re-entering the community can live during the difficult period of job hunting and social readjustment.

A related way of thinking underlies the various efforts that are being made to redefine drug addiction not as a criminal offense (as one result of which an ever-increasing number of addicts are becoming involved in crime), but as a medical problem that can be handled through research and, in practice, by treatment. At further remove, but still part of the effort to try new approaches, are the attempts that are being made to alter conditions in slum schools and to devise new ways of training and finding work for young people who otherwise may be alienated from society.

Taken alone, none of these reforms can eliminate crime. But each can contribute to its reduction.

Comparing the kind of society in which we live with small primitive societies, we cannot avoid realizing that crime as we know it is a by-product of complex civilizations and written codes of law. For diversity and crime appear to be related to the extent that codes of law representing the beliefs and moral standards of only part of the community are imposed on the community as a whole. In a small primitive society there is much greater homogeneity, and although occasional deviant individuals may become disturbed enough to break known and accepted rules, there is little crime. Crime as we know it develops in urban settings.

In such a society a major problem arises when one group in the population is in a position to incorporate its special values and code of morals into the law and tries to regulate the behavior of all members of the society. Some of the quainter efforts of our ancestors, such as a law forbidding a man to kiss his wife on Sundays, seem ludicrous. What we do not see is that many contemporary laws, such as those that forbid drinking or the use of marijuana or that prescribe the private sex life of adults, are similar.

The difficulty is that laws that attempt to enforce special

forms of moral behavior breed disrespect for the law and for law-enforcing agencies among those who do not share the beliefs on which these regulations are based. And where disrespect and lawbreaking by the respectable are combined, one also finds connivance with crime in other areas of living.

The more complex a society becomes, the more fully the law must take into account the diversity of the people who live in it. The approach to crime is not a matter for the police and the courts—or even the lawmakers—alone. It is a matter in which the whole society is involved.

ৡৡ

Why shouldn't we have schools of homemaking whose graduates would receive diplomas? Wouldn't this give greater dignity to the work that most women spend most of their adult lives doing? MARCH 1968

The first question is: For whom would the training course and the diploma be intended? For the future homemaker who expects to manage her own home and care for her family? Or for the domestic worker who will earn her living by taking over the tasks in a home not her own? Or for a member of a profession in a career that is not as yet defined?

In the applied arts and sciences a diploma carries with it the assurance that the recipient is qualified to begin practicing a set of skills as a professional person. The student who has majored in home economics at the college level has various occupations open to her. She can teach homemaking to others, for example, or she can become a dietitian. Going a step further in her training, she can enter the applied scientific field of nutrition studies.

A few attempts have been made to provide domestic workers with very elementary training in household work. Usually such courses have been arranged for new immigrants, young women who have never worked in a city household, who are unfamiliar with our standard equipment and the routines of American family living. Such a course does no more than prepare a woman for the labor market—but now even newcomers prefer almost any employment to that in homes.

So far, American women have not been willing to accept real professionalization of domestic workers in their homes. Perhaps hotels and inns might be willing to try the experiment as one way of cutting down the tremendous turnover of their employees. But would a professionally trained domestic worker be willing to do the kinds of chores that are part of room service? Paradoxically, women in their own homes take on the most exacting tasks of housekeeping—tasks they would regard as beneath their dignity if done for pay.

At the same time, over the years the skills practiced by the homemaker have been separated one by one from homemaking into specialized occupations. Cookery, performed by a man, may be treated as a fine art. Performed by a woman, even when she is paid for her work, cooking is regarded as drudgery. The exception is when it is treated as the avocation of a professional woman, such as an opera singer, or a professional hostess, such as the wife of an ambassador.

In the past, women who looked after small children in a crèche had little standing. It was only when girls of good families, backed by college courses in child development, entered the new field of nursery-school education that work with little children acquired the dignity of a profession. Much earlier, nursing also acquired high status when gently bred women, moved by compassion and religious dedication, undertook to care for the sick and the wounded. And today nursing and specialized teaching of children are among the few sex-typed professions for which women themselves have a high regard. Social work, in contrast, has risen in esteem to the extent that it attracts both men and women.

Even today, when the battle to open the doors of "masculine" occupations is all but won (except, perhaps, in some women's minds), women accord higher prestige to those professions formerly confined to men, and relatively few men would be willing to choose an occupation traditionally defined as "feminine." Up to the present, caring for small children, for example, is only occasionally a masculine vocation.

In spite of the proliferation of specialties that have separated off from homemaking, the skills of the homemaker as a *whole* have remained remarkably intact and unchanged. And

96

the tendency is still very great to regard homemaking as a tradition-bound occupation and the homemaker as someone trained at home who passes on to her daughter the lore she acquired from her mother. In fact, of course, this is not so; what does remain unchanged is our attitude, sometimes expressed with enthusiasm and sometimes with chagrin.

It is our attitude that must change if we want to give those who work in homes, as homemakers or as paid professionals, special training and a new kind of dignity. This, of course, leads to a second question: Would such training be limited to women or would it be open to men as well?

Today young fathers—as the only collaborators available to their wives—have taken over many aspects of homemaking. How many have acquired special skills that could be part of a new but growing tradition? Including men in the planning for courses in homemaking might well initiate changes that would lead in the direction of greater dignity and a new view of homemaking as a real profession.

§∾

In California and several other states, single women are being permitted to adopt children. Do you think this is a good idea? JUNE 1968

Basically we have developed three forms of adoption in the United States. The first is modeled on the ideal of the American family. The adopting couple want an infant who will resemble as closely as possible the child they long to have. Adoption agencies, in turn, set very high standards for the prospective parents, specifying good health, financial solvency, a desirable age combination, demonstrated compatibility and suitable social circumstances.

The second form of adoption is contrapuntal to the first. Although there are long historical precedents, this form of adoption really became popular in the years after World War II, when returning servicemen and their wives began to bring small children from distant lands to live in towns all over the United States. The prospective parents look for a child who not only needs a home but who also is different from themselves; sometimes such adopting parents seek two or more children who are different from each other. Here it is quite clear to the children and to the world at large that these are adopted children—Japanese or Chinese or Vietnamese or Cook Islander children, even children from newly contacted tribes of the New Guinea highlands—who are being proudly brought up by adoptive parents in an American home. Adoption agencies were slow in approving adoptions of this kind, in which the older rules were reversed. Yet this form of adoption also is related to the ideal of the American family, which accords each child recognition as an individual.

Both these forms of adoption emphasize parental choice of a child. The third form emphasizes instead the child's need. In adoptions of this kind the central consideration is the provision of a home for a child who would otherwise have none. The child may be a member of a minority group, deprived of his parents by illness or accident; or he may have a serious physical handicap; or there may be serious doubt about his health or intellectual abililities or emotional stability. Many such children have lived in institutions or have been moved in and out of unsatisfactory foster homes. For these children good homes are hard to find. Any home where they are really welcome and can hope for understanding of their troubled lives—with a single woman, with aging and less-ideal parents, with an adult brother and sister who live together in the family home—offers a kind of security they may never otherwise be fortunate enough to receive.

So I would say yes—where the need of the child is great and is matched by the willingness of a single woman to create a warm human relationship, this form of adoption is a very good thing. Mutual love and acceptance are fundamentally important to the development of a good human being.

What changes do you foresee as a result of the liberalization of abortion laws? JULY 1971

I foresee a great deal of trouble.

Initially the passage of legislation liberalizing practice in a matter such as abortion may seem to have a good effect. It encourages those who have been fighting the old restrictions and it has a mildly modifying effect on negative opinion. Surveys have shown that more doctors now are accepting the idea of legal abortion and that more laymen think abortion may be justified under a wider set of circumstances.

But the liberalization of laws about which there is deeply felt conflict of opinion is asking for trouble. Those who disagree with the new restrictions still will try to evade the law or, alternatively, will continue the fight for greater liberalization. Others, consciously or unconsciously believing that abortion is wrong, will attempt to hedge the law with new kinds of restrictions in the name of good medical or social practice. So the question of how liberal or how restrictive laws about abortion should be will be opened again and again, always in an atmosphere of tension and conflict.

Where abortion laws have been modified, new arguments already have been raised.

Some groups in the Women's Liberation Movement are protesting the fact that the whole burden falls on women in a situation for which both sexes are equally responsible. It is likely that increasingly noisy demands will be made for male sterilization as the better method of dealing with the problem of couples who seem to be unable or unwilling to take contraceptive measures.

Psychiatrists are expressing concern about the effects of abortion on the women who feel bereaved but cannot mourn as they can when they have lost a child as the result of a miscarriage or of a stillbirth. Of course, women vary in their response to abortion, depending on how they envisage a conceived child.

The woman who thinks of her unborn child, no matter how young, as an individual, the potential bearer of a name, with a soul and an innate personality, cannot lose that child without a sense of deep loss. The woman who reacts to an abortion as she might to the loss of part of her own body—her tonsils or appendix—in an operation has somehow to come to terms with an altered self-image. Still other women seem to treat an abortion simply as the process of removing an unwanted intrusion into the body.

All these attitudes exist, and we are only beginning to understand what the different consequences are. Researchers in Catholic countries are discovering the effects on women who are unable to live out the experience of mourning. From Eastern Europe, among groups that have rejected religious belief, we are obtaining accounts from women who have had many abortions, apparently without significant disturbance.

These are long-term problems. There are others as well. Almost no one has asked about the effects of abortion on men's attitudes toward and feelings about the unborn child, toward the woman who has the abortion or toward themselves. Continuing conflict about liberalization and law enforcement simply deflects our attention from these very serious issues.

In the long run, the only viable solution is the repeal of *all* restrictive laws controlling abortion. Only then will we be able to face the basic issues.

For the truth is, reliance on abortion is at best a poor solution. It is humane to interrupt a pregnancy in certain circumstances—when a woman has suffered rape or when disease threatens the normality of the fetus or the life of the mother. But abortion, no matter how phrased, is too close to the edge of taking life to fit into a world view in which all life is regarded as valuable.

Once abortion as such has ceased to be the issue, we can concentrate on establishing widespread knowledge of contraception and on the development of life-styles and personal relationships that are consistent with the idea of conceiving, bringing into life and caring for children, all of whom are desired and loved.

Do you believe that young people today are more realistic about love than their parents? Or are they more idealistic?
JULY 1971

I think that young people today are typically the children of their parents. Their feelings about love and marriage are a response to their parents' attitudes as they have understood them.

The generation that came of age in the late 1940s and early 1950s—the parents of most of today's young people—was singularly unromantic. What most young people of that generation wanted above all else was to *be* married. They wanted to marry early and they settled for marriage at almost any price. The idea of waiting for someone for three or four years was inconceivable. Few couples thought of each other romantically, as lovers. They were too intent on matrimony. They made love in order to get married, rather than marrying because they were in love.

A great many young people today distrust the institution of marriage, into which their parents rushed so precipitately and single-mindedly. They want to be much more sure of each other before they marry. They want to see themselves and each other as individuals. When they make love it is as persons, not as a way of acquiring a mate. They are not more or less idealistic than their parents. They have a different ideal of personal relationships.

However, their relationships are more fragile than their parents' marriages were. They meet and part even more readily. In this they are the children of their parents—who wanted marriage but not the responsibilities of a loving relationship. Far too few people in these two generations have thought very intensely about the seriousness of taking the responsibility for another person's happiness or of the mutual responsibility of parents for the happiness of children.

§∂

With increasing international communication through radio, television and films, do you believe that social values and ways of thought and behavior are becoming more standardized—and Westernized—around the world? Or do you believe there is a reaction occurring as evidenced by the interest in the United States today in the philosophies of the Far East? FEBRUARY 1972

All the various forms of popular culture are becoming more alike around the world. At any one time the same hit records, television shows and newest dance steps can be heard and seen from New York to Indonesia. There are, as well, highly standardized reactions against what is popular. Some take the form of nativistic cults, in which people wish to throw out everything that is Western (or modern) and return to the ways of their forefathers. Others take the form of anti-nativistic cults, in which people turn, for example, against the Western culture into which they were born and decide to study Zen or attach themselves to a guru.

Fascination with Eastern religions and philosophies is by no means new in the Western world. My own great-granduncle became a Muslim during his travels in the East. Periodically, critical young Americans, and some not-so-young Americans, become enthusiasts of the art, the ethical system or the religion of some other area of the world. Fifteen years ago it was Zen. Later, India was considered more interesting. Since the choices are limited, one must expect repetitions over time.

What is new and an intrinsic part of our present flat, over-simplified, world-wide mass-media culture is our handling of fads. Each new one, as it sweeps the cities of the world, expands into a major portent of disaster or an indicator of some significant change of heart. At the time, as we look at ourselves and one another continually and anxiously, without critical cross-cultural or temporal perspective, we see only our own reflections magnified and infinitely multiplied, like people gathered in a room of grotesque mirrors. Then we move on. For a fad is still what it always has been—a fad.

In time, as the world becomes in a real sense an intercommunicating network, we may hope for change in two directions.

On the one hand, we may achieve world-wide standardization in those activities on which safety, health and some kinds of convenience depend—as we have already done to some degree in international controls connected with air and sea travel, currency exchange and protection against epidemics. On the other hand, with better communication people may be led once more to care about and develop their own half-abandoned traditions and also with respect and a deeper awareness to draw on the highly developed traditions of other cultures, as in recent years architecture in the United States has drawn on Japanese models in creating new forms.

ॐ

Is the world really coming together into a "global village," as Marshall McLuhan claims? FEBRUARY 1972

I do not think that the figure of speech "global village" is well chosen.

It is true, as McLuhan has so aptly put it, that we live in a simultaneous world. That is, we are constantly exposed to news about events taking place even in the most distant parts of the world. Wherever we are, information about what is happening reaches us by television and radio more quickly—and often more accurately—than the news that was passed by word of mouth from one village to another even in the recent past. In this sense we are living in a shared—a simultaneous—world.

But in a village everyone knows everyone else. People know the family history of almost every individual and children who have grown up together know just what to expect of one another. True villagers speak the same language, laugh at the same jokes, share the same expectations and remember the same past. Their lives are inextricably interwoven.

In this sense I think McLuhan's "global village" is inappropriate and a deceptive metaphor. The world's population exceeds 3.5 billion people and is increasing at the rate of some 200,000 persons every day. We may know something *about* many of the world's people, but we have face-to-face contact with only a few. Wherever a person travels, most people are strangers with whom there is little or no possibility of real communication.

The news media bring the peoples of the earth within view of one another. But the sheer numbers of people of whom we are made aware diminish the possibility of any feeling of closeness and community.

Seen from space, our planet may look like a little, blue, spinning top. But the world is not, nor is it likely to become, a global village.

ॐ

Do you agree that American television is a cultural waste-land? SEPTEMBER 1972

American television is what Americans make it.

Our national news programs are among the best in the world because there is a vast, diverse audience for them. And if the majority of those in search of entertainment on television tune in on sports and talk shows, Westerns and soap operas, the networks, responsive to the techniques for measuring audience appeal, will provide more programs of the same kind.

Others—the people with different preferences—seldom take the trouble to praise the kinds of programs they like and approve of. Instead they simply grumble and tune out the programs they dislike. And so far, in spite of all their complaints about the fare offered them by the networks, they have signally failed to support the heroic efforts made by public and educational television to provide more varied and intelligent programs.

Television is what we—the viewers and the nonviewers, the producers and the reviewers—make it. We cannot blame "television" for something in which we all have a share—those who turn it on, those who turn it off and those who are turned off by it.

ॐ

What has happened to the generation gap? SEPTEMBER 1972

The "generation gap" is the phrase we have been using to describe the deep break between the generation of those all around the world who grew up before World War II and the generation that has grown up in the changed world of the past twenty-five years.

Most people first became aware of the generation break in

communications in the 1960s, when members of the new generation began to arrive in college and to express their dissatisfaction with attitudes, beliefs and ways of looking at the world and organizing society that appeared to them outworn and unbearable. Some of them dropped out and went their own way. Others rebelled and gathered around them very large numbers of other dissatisfied and alienated students.

These students were rebellious, not because they were the young rebelling against the old, but because the world as it was presented to them and the world as they perceived it were quite different—and they wanted to initiate changes that would be in keeping with what they saw as the new realities.

These realities included the life they were expected to live in college. They wanted student voices to be heard in policy making. They wanted places on the boards of trustees; they wanted more student choice in the organization of teaching and the curriculum; they wanted greater freedom to decide how they, as young men and women, would live. They wanted their colleges—as the one place where students could form organized groups and bring pressures to bear on the faculty and administration and, through them, on the community—to take a stand on matters of great importance to them: the draft, the war in Southeast Asia, civil rights, the conditions of urban living, the right to education.

In response to student dissatisfaction, expressed sometimes in mass demonstrations, sometimes in threats of destructive action and often in long, long meetings, most college administrations and faculties have moved in the directions advocated by the student rebels. And in the country at large students won—in record time—the right to vote at the age of eighteen.

The students who started the movement are no longer students. The older members of the new generation are now out in the world as young lawyers, teachers, doctors, architects, engineers and politicians. Their successors in school know where many of them are and what they are doing. The struggles that began on the college campuses have been carried off-campus to outside spheres of action.

And in many cases, today's students who have inherited from their activist predecessors a part in college policy making have found that it is a rather unexciting, time-consuming activity. It is exciting to take part in mass demonstrations against a particular company known to make the deadly chemicals used in the Vietnam war. But trying to change the real-estate policy or the investment policy of a university board of trustees is a far slower and more tedious business, and at any particular time this kind of effort seems to be less rewarding.

As only a few students can actually participate in policy-making discussions, the excitement of being temporarily unified in a common cause dies down. What does go on is less enjoyable and far less publicized. The mass media look for trouble, and sober, quiet committee work seldom makes news.

But I do not think the students of the 1970s are less opposed to the war, less worried about the danger of nuclear explosions, less concerned about the environment or less committed to a democratization of life through change in the future of minority groups or in the rights of women. Rather, they no longer feel that they, while they are undergraduates, are the ones whose actions will be decisive. Many of them are working very hard, and they object to being politically manipulated by fellow students or by others, even in the best of causes.

These young people in college know something about what the students of five or ten years ago are doing now as working citizens to change political alignments, to alter institutional arrangements in the courts and in the practice of law, in the care of young children and the elderly, in the fields of education, equal rights and consumer and environmental protection. Many of today's students are dismayed by a national administration that takes away with one hand what it seems to be giving with the other. And many are biding their time. They are politically aware and waiting to see what they can do with the vote.

The generation gap is not something that will go away. It was brought about by changes that altered the life view and

106

the life expectations of a particular generation. But the older members of that generation, many of them now young parents, have moved out into a wider world. They are moving toward responsibility.

ॐ

Have we the right to demand that parents limit their families to two children? SEPTEMBER 1972

I would not restrict the matter to "parents." Have we the right to demand that people who are married and those who intend to marry limit their families to two children?

If "we" in this question means the human community, I do believe that the human community must now take responsibility not only for the present generation but also for the next and the next. We must establish a climate of opinion in which people will wish to work toward a balanced population for the whole world, so that our children's children will have a chance to have a good life, preferably a better life than ours.

I do not think that any government should—or can—legislate the number of children people may have. But we can demand that all governments take responsibility for extablishing a climate of opinion and for making it easy and desirable for people to limit the number of children that are born.

This means that contraceptives, with abortion as a back-up measure, must be freely available to everyone, adolescent or adult, single or married. It means that we must make it possible for large families to share their children with those who have none and much easier for people who wish to bring up children to adopt those who are in need of care. It means that we must cease to penalize the childless with especially heavy taxes. We must rearrange our mode of living so that children become true and considered members of the community.

In the past, when many children were needed because so many of them died, this need was incorporated in the ethical, social and economic framework of almost every society.

107

Today we must recognize a new need—to keep the conditions of human life humanly livable. And I believe we can develop a new ethic of responsibility for every human life only if we can accept responsibility for limiting the number of human lives to be cared for—in some countries because adults cannot care for an exploding population of children, in others because each child born lays such a heavy burden of energy consumption on our endangered planet.

This new social ethic will involve everyone very personally. Those who are thinking of having children—not two, but any—will first ask themselves why, indeed, they should have children. Will they—as a couple, not as individuals—make good parents? Will they be able to stay together long enough to rear those children?

If not, perhaps they should wait until each finds a more suitable partner. Or if they stay together, loving each other, perhaps they should adopt children or in other ways devote themselves to the care of other people's children, helping the overburdened instead of insisting on possessing children of their own. Or perhaps they should ask themselves what other contribution they can better make to strengthen their relationship and to further the well-being of the human community

But there also are those who joyfully hope for children, those who will welcome them with love and be able to raise them with thoughtful care. And these people, as responsive and responsible parents, will make their own vital contribution to the world.

Why do we have such a high homicide rate in the United States? And what can we do to curb violence? MAY 1975

Americans have a long history of violence. But one reason violence so often leads to bloodshed and homicide is the extraordinarily easy availability of guns, particularly handguns that have no other purpose than to kill human beings. Almost anyone who is enraged or frightened, who wants to threaten another person or who feels threatened, can acquire a gun.

The facts speak for themselves. In the 1960s, when the rate of violent crime was beginning to escalate, historian Richard Hofstadter pointed out that the gun-homicide rate in the United States was forty times as great as in England, Scotland and Wales, Japan or the Netherlands and that in the 20th century alone we had suffered over 265,000 homicides, over 330,000 suicides and over 139,000 accidental deaths from guns—a total greater than that of Americans killed in battle in all our wars up to then.

In other urban, industrialized countries of the world, governments very strictly control access to firearms—who can sell, buy or possess anything but a sporting gun. In large measure this is done to protect those governments against armed uprisings and rebellions. But it also protects the private citizen, the criminal and the peaceful man alike.

In the United States we have not feared armed uprisings. Americans habitually turn their aggressions against one another, not against the government. From the beginning of our history as a nation we have interpreted the right of citizens to bear arms—a right incorporated into the Constitution—as the right of every peaceful, responsible man to carry a gun to protect his own life and the lives of those dependent upon him. In our idealized picture, having a gun makes the good man equal in strength to the bad man—the robber, the cattle rustler, the burglar, the mugger. And the oftener crimes of violence are committed, the more necessary it seems for nonviolent people to be armed.

So we have a runaway system. The more guns are readily at hand, the more they are used by people with evil intentions. And as more people with good intentions feel they must be armed in self-denfense, the more the criminal will use his gun because he believes his victim must be armed—and the oftener the police will shoot first and ask questions afterward.

There is only one way we can break this vicious circle—by very strict gun control. And as the first step in this direction we must stop thinking of guns as a means of defense against dangerous individuals. That is, we must shift our emphasis away from people to guns as a prime source of violent danger.

It will not be easy. Again and again we will want to make exceptions. Today, every time a doctor is robbed or burglarized—and this is a very common occurrence because doctors' offices are a source of drugs—ten other doctors feel they must have guns to protect themselves. And it will take time, probably quite a long time, to gain control. Police everywhere admit that we have no knowledge of the number of unregistered guns Americans—peaceful citizens and criminals alike—possess.

We also shall have to convince the so-called gun lobby that there is an intrinsic difference between the licensed sporting gun in the hands of a skilled and presumably disciplined user and a handgun that, obliterating caution, can translate a moment of suspicion or fear or passion into death for a human being.

The more clearly we can differentiate between the idea of the rifle used for sport and the idea of the hidden handgun designed only to kill human beings, the more hope we shall have of winning consent to gun control, not only through legislation, but also in people's minds.

Gun control alone will not solve our problems of violence. But as we know from the experience of other countries, it will reduce enormously the number of homicides—accidental, self-inflicted or intentional—and this in itself will make a great difference.

Can we reconcile the democratic right to know with the glorification of individuals like Lynette Fromme and Sara Jane Moore and Patty Hearst, who have been charged with very serious crimes? JANUARY 1976

I see no good reason for doing so. In a democracy we have responsibilities as well as rights.

Certainly everyone wants to know something about a person, woman or man, who is accused of attempting to assassinate a public figure or who is charged with any other major crime. But this need not mean they should be given magazine-cover and day-after-day front-page publicity.

We have arrived at a dangerous state of mind when we cease to discriminate between the women and men whose actions we most admire and those whose actions are abhorrent to every sane adult. We bracket fame and notoriety, service to our country and crime, when we accord the heroine and the criminal essentially the same treatment—front-page headlines, cover stories in the national news magazines, repeated exposure on television and heavily publicized opportunities to talk or write about themselves.

Yet we know from long experience that this kind of false adulation of the criminal invariably leads to repetitions of the same kinds of crime, both by criminals and by disturbed people who are excited by the chance to become "famous." Robert Kennedy was killed only two months after the assassination of Martin Luther King, Jr. And it was estimated that overt threats against the life of President Ford tripled—from about one hundred to over three hundred—in the brief period between the failed assassination attempts with which Lynette Fromme and Sara Jane Moore are charged.

But we also know from experience that when the excitement dies down—when a kidnapper or highjacker, for instance, receives the most minimal notice—fewer people try to kidnap or highjack, for a time, at least.

Cooling it helps. And we have a responsibility, I believe, both to those whose life and well-being may be endangered and to those who may be led to commit some terrible crime against a fellow human being. Our responsibility is to keep our curiosity in check; the responsibility of newspapers, magazines, television and radio is to avoid the exploitation of crime and violence. New Zealand has recently passed legislation forbidding public mention of the very name of a person accused of a crime. We would never go that far, but we can, I believe, learn restraint.

ॐ

I must comment on your characterization of suburbs as non-supportive. I have just lost my husband and have had wonderful support from my neighbors. JANUARY 1976

Many people living in suburbs do have good neighbors. This is especially true in older suburbs where families have lived for two generations or more and have relatives and old friends living nearby. In other suburbs there are pockets of warmth for the newcomer and friendly help in the crises of birth, illness and death. But this is not usual.

Suburbs for the most part are places to which families move as their economic status improves or where they live for just as long as their company job keeps them in that area. Families like these have broken their deeper ties to the past and they are not looking for the kind of close ties they have recently given up. People who are bent on improving their status are concerned mainly with the chances for their own children, for whom they are seeking safety from the terrors of city streets, health away from dirt and pollution, better education and association with the children of parents who have achieved security. Families who are living in a suburb because of a job are always poised to take off again; the center of their lives is elsewhere.

All this means that neighborly relationships in suburbs usually are quite superficial. The play groups of small children provide temporary co-operation among mothers, but this is reduced as children grow older and make their own friends. Commuting husbands, and to an increasing extent commuting wives, often are too tired at night to enjoy the kinds of social contacts that are suburban substitutes for long-standing, affectionate relationships—clubs, associations, politics, causes.

Undoubtedly many women have found close and supportive friends in the suburb in which they live. But the support given a woman—or a family—in a time of crisis is likely to be more transitory than in a community in which neighbors have lived through many crises together.

With so many young couples living together without marriage, what do we call the pair who have this arrangement and how do we introduce them to other people?

JANUARY 1976

Institutions need names so that we can think about them, and having an accepted way of referring to a relationship between two people helps us to respond more easily and spontaneously when we meet them.

In the past there have been definite phrases: She's pinned, she's engaged, she's married. She's his wife, he's her husband. In different social settings such words as "steady," "intended," "betrothed" and "fiancée" have come and gone as appropriate descriptions of a girl preparing for marriage.

Today's young people are uncertain about what they prefer. "This is John Jones and Mary Smith; they are living together" is a frequent way of introducing two people living in such an arrangement. But some young women active in the Liberation Movement prefer simply—if the couple are at home—"This is Mary Smith. She lives here." They feel that "here" denotes sharing, but nothing connubial. Away from home, introducing to others a couple who live together is more difficult. There is no accepted style, no phrasing that young people agree is comfortable for everyone.

Many people are groping for words to describe the partners in this kind of relationship: girl friend and boy friend, companions, housemates? Others feel that any attempt to define may be an invasion of personal privacy.

I would, myself, appreciate knowing from young people who are living together as well as from older people who approve of this new form of relationship what they think is a suitable and unambiguous phrasing.

Since we seem to be approaching a time when we shall be able to select the sex of our unborn children and since many

**psychologists tell us that most people prefer to have boys, do
you think the world will ever face a woman shortage?**
MAY 1977

I doubt it. When psychologists refer to "most people," they
usually mean Americans or Europeans. They seldom are talking about the human race based on a good knowledge of
people all over the world.

Societies differ enormously in their sex preferences for
children. Sometimes girls are more highly valued, for example, because they bring a big bride price or constitute a valuable family working force. In societies in which male activities, such as hunting or herding, are very important, parents
want to have sons. And there are contradictory situations, as
among some Eskimo groups, in which polygamy exists
alongside female infanticide—that is, societies in which a
man may want to have two wives and yet girl babies are often
rejected.

There is also the well-known fact that the chance of having
a boy decreases with each successive birth to the same
mother. Almost everyone knows of a family in which the parents have gone on having girls in the ever-fainter hope of
producing one boy. Sometimes, of course, they succeed.

The discovery of a certain, ethical and humane method of
choosing the sex of each child would have enormously bene-
ficial effects. The birth rate would decrease immediately, as
couples could plan with certainty for the sex as well as the
number of children they wanted to bring up. Equally important, every living woman would know that her parents did not
merely accept or tolerate her out of necessity, but chose her to
be a girl.

It is possible that here and there around the world there
might be a temporary woman shortage. But as women come
to play their full part in the modern world, I believe, this
will change. For wherever women are accorded dignity
and importance, families welcome daughters. What is likelier
is that societies will differ in their sex preferences for elder
and younger children. Some American couples want a boy
first and then a girl; very probably many families will make
this choice.

The United States Supreme Court recently ruled that employers have the right to exclude pregnant women from sick-leave benefits. What are your views on this? FEBRUARY 1978

I think that a mother, before and after the birth of a child, and a father, before and after the birth of a child, are entitled to a childbearing leave of absence that should not prejudice their seniority or other job-connected benefits. The right to a childbearing leave should be accepted in the same way as is the leave to vote, to do jury duty, to continue one's education or to perform religious duties. The length of childbearing leave and whether it should be with pay are matters for negotiation.

I do not think that childbearing leave should be treated as sick leave. It is important, however, that a medical-benefits scheme include a physician's care both before and after birth, as well as hospitalization for health disturbances during pregnancy and medical care at birth.

There was a time when pregnancy was regarded as an act of God for which no one—neither the pregnant woman nor the man involved nor anyone else—was responsible. Today pregnancy is a matter of choice.

By treating pregnancy as an illness we obscure the fact that it is a normal, healthy process. And by combining demands for a childbearing leave with demands for affirmative action, we obscure the very real difference between women and men, as far as pregnancy itself is concerned.

We are right to make provision for working parents to spend some time with their newborn infants, rather than placing them directly in nursery care. Childbearing leave should not be coupled with sick leave, but should be regarded as a right that grows out of one's responsibility for another human being.

How do we reconcile population control with charges of genocide by minority groups and loss of personal freedom by all groups? FEBRUARY 1978

Personal freedom is a matter of cultural definition. Americans are likely to treat any new social restriction, even one that is essentially protective, as a blow to personal freedom. Currently a great many Americans are refusing to accept a lower speed limit on highways and are unwilling to invest adequate funds for the improvement of mass transportation. They act as if such measures constituted an invasion of personal freedom instead of somewhat isolated efforts to make better national use of limited resources.

Actually, the idea that individuals have ever been entirely free to decide about such a matter as how many children to have is an illusion. All kinds of social and cultural pressures always affect people's beliefs about having—or not having—children, when and under what circumstances.

And fashions change. In the 1950s in the United States, every young person, woman or man, was pressured into marrying and every married couple was pressured into having or adopting several children. Today the current is running the other way. No laws were passed. But as fashions change, most people float with the stream.

Others, usually only a handful, rebel. They have to be willing to pay the price: virtual ostracism in the 1950s for couples who insisted on remaining childless, heavy disapproval in the 1970s for couples with large families. But today it is not a matter of fashion that may change in a decade or two. It is a question of balancing the world's resources and the world's population. It is a question of acting responsibly in the light of our best knowledge.

As long as each country accepts the responsibility for balancing its population in accordance with both its own resources and the resources of the world, there can be no charge of genocide. But a claim by any group that it has a greater right than others to have children—because its members are richer or brighter or belong to a superior race—opens the door to charges of genocide. And keeping any group in circumstances of ignorance and poverty, as a result of which more of its children die, is a form of genocide.

I do not feel we are losing personal freedom by choosing to have fewer children. Instead we are ensuring, as best we can, that our children will be free to make choices of their own.

ટ≽

Have cities outlived their usefulness? AUGUST 1978

Cities have outlived many of the special uses that have been made of them since the Industrial Revolution that began in the mid-18th century. Cities near seaports, on rivers and later at important railway junctions and terminals became centers for gathering masses of cheap labor—recruits from the countryside and immigrants from overseas. These people were needed to work in the new factories and foundries and to amass the raw materials and distribute the products into which they were transformed.

As time passed, great urban populations grew up whose members had no ties outside the cities and knew only the life of city streets and tenements and sordid places of work. Some city people prospered but many remained very poor and dependent. Nowadays, those who work in industrial cities have to carry the great weight of those who are too old to work, the handicapped and the unfit, and especially all the children who must be cared for and educated.

Meanwhile, as new sources of power have been developed to turn the wheels of factories and to provide for transportation, cities have become less necessary for industry. Electric power can be transmitted over great distances and cars and giant trucks have replaced streetcars and trains as a means of transporting working people and the products of their work. So while the big city is no longer crucial for industry, industry—in the sense of providing jobs—is essential to the city.

In spite of this, planners all over the industrialized world are relocating industries and the effective workers for these industries. This, of course, leaves the cities with great numbers of dependent people, many of them too old or too young to work and others quite unfit for the labor market, and without clearly established ways of caring for all the unemployed—and unemployable—men, women and children.

Modern cities in the United States still carry all the financial responsibilities that were appropriate to smaller towns and that could more or less be met as long as industries paid their way in cities. At the same time, as industries have

117

moved out of cities a passionate struggle has developed over where the workers who have followed industry should live. Is low-cost housing to be built in the older suburbs that have widely spaced houses and pleasant green lawns and taxes already high for schools for privileged children? And if not there, then where?

In Europe many of these problems are being met by new cities, which are carefully planned to receive industries that have agreed—or have been ordered—to go there and to house both the needed workers and the technical staff. But the few new towns that have been built in our country are still primarily suburbs, better planned and with greater diversity in housing and among the residents, but places where people in general do not work.

We have not solved the problems of our outmoded cities or worked out adequate alternatives for all the people who work in industry.

Other uses of a city—as a center of culture, of government and of contact with the rest of the world—have not been outlived. The mass media can bring much of what is developed in cities to people who do not live in them. But wherever the distant audience may be, the symphony is in New York or Boston or San Francisco. Young musicians go to the city to study and stay there to play their music. And in the city authors seek publishers and publishers seek authors, art galleries show the work of artists and theaters struggle to survive and show plays and ballets and other works of the human mind and imagination.

The city as a center where, any day in any year, there may be a fresh encounter with a new talent, a keen mind or a gifted specialist—this is essential to the life of a country. To play this role in our lives a city must have a soul—a university, a great art or music school, a cathedral or a great mosque or temple, a great laboratory or scientific center, as well as the libraries and museums and galleries that bring past and present together. A city must be a place where groups of women and men are seeking and developing the highest things they know. This can never be outlived.

Do you believe that the violence shown on television has increased the violence in our daily lives? Or is it the other way around? And is there anything we can do about it?
OCTOBER 1978

It is a circular process, I think, in which violence in the world and violence portrayed feed each other.

National television draws on acts of violence of many kinds in the whole nation and elsewhere in the whole world. So there is always, somewhere, some act of violence—the more gruesome and bizarre the better—to feed a public that is believed to be voracious for sensations of horror and frightened thrill. The wider the base, in terms of the world's population, on which the media—television, radio, magazines and newspapers—draw, the more numerous the violent acts that can be, and are, vividly reported. In the past, before radio and television, murders, unless they involved people of great importance or notoriety, were matters for the local press. Now any murder—any violent act—anywhere is likely to be reported; any victim may be shown; any person who has committed a crime of violence may look out at us from our own television screen.

It is well known that violence breeds violence. A well-publicized crime increases the frequency of other similar crimes, whether it be a bank robbery, a kidnapping, a rape, a hijack or a spectacular multi-murder. This is true also of violence shown on the cops-and-robbers "series" programs and other weekly fictional shows that feature crime. The disturbed and suggestible individual has a recipe spelled out on television and may well act out an event that has become dangerously real and available.

Of course there is something we can do about this situation. Sponsors of commercial television are among the most sensitive and responsive people in the world. Well-organized, insistent and widespread pressure, such as that already initiated by Action for Children's Television and the Parents and Teachers Association, have brought and will continue to

119

bring effective change. But merely to complain is to accept what we deplore.

What are your hopes for humankind as of the year 2000?
JANUARY 1979

It is my profound hope that a sufficient number of people with a high tradition of literacy, learning and concern for other human beings may survive to keep alive the human experiment. Our chances of such a survival are becoming fewer every day that we allow nuclear weaponry and an economy based on the use of plutonium as a fuel to proliferate around the world.

But if we do succeed in overcoming these extreme dangers and other dangers related to the use of imperfectly understood and poorly controlled scientifically based technologies, I have no doubt that mankind will continue to develop in ways as yet undreamed of.

◄ 4 ►
PRIMITIVE PEOPLES

Do very primitive societies have humor? What forms does it take? MARCH 1963

Laughter is man's most distinctive emotional expression. Man shares the capacity for love and hate, anger and fear, loyalty and grief, with other living creatures. But humor, which has an intellectual as well as an emotional element, belongs to man. Primitive peoples laugh at surprise, incongruity, shifts in timing, wisecracks and reversals, just as civilized peoples do. They differ, as do individuals and civilized nations, in the kinds of humor they enjoy.

In many of the cultures of Africa, laughter seems to have been specially cultivated. The Pygmies of the Ituri Forest have songs as filled with joy as a six-month-old baby's crowing; when they laugh, they fall to the ground and roll in delight. While an outsider is often puzzled by the different ways some Africans express their humor, he almost always finds it contagious.

The amount of humor in a society—which invariably includes the ability to laugh at oneself and to feel that those who laugh at one are not hostile—can be used as a measure of the sense of freedom and security individuals feel in that society. The Manus people of the South Seas, for example, used to make up songs with disguised names in them; when they came into conflict with government, they took great pleasure in singing these songs in the presence of officials, trusting each other and laughing together against the foreigner. For genuine humor, there must be trust.

Laughter at the ways of the foreigner—at foreign words and foreign customs—is also common among primitive peoples. And sometimes they laugh at quite different kinds of things from what we do. We laugh at a failure—at a slip of the tongue, at someone who stumbles clumsily where grace is required; the Iatmul people of New Guinea, on the other hand, laugh uproariously when a child or a foreigner gets something *right*.

Do people in most primitive societies spank their children when they misbehave? FEBRUARY 1964

Many explorers have commented on the gentleness of various primitive peoples with their children. It is unusual to find a primitive society in which an adult, after the deed has been done and tempers have cooled down, will deliberately get out a whip or a switch and actually beat a child. Punishment of this kind is one of the unfortunate concomitants of great civilizations, as are the rack and the screw, the dungeon, the gallows and the electric chair. But in occasional outbursts of anger, all the primitive peoples with whom I have ever worked will express their annoyance physically by slapping a child, dragging it suddenly by one arm, even occasionally picking up a stick to reinforce the lesson. Shaking, cuffing, dragging—even, on occasion, throwing a bit of stinging pepper into the child's eyes—all these are expressions of momentary irritation and anger. What one seldom finds in a primitive society is the systematic, moralistic philosophy of "spare the rod and spoil the child" or "never strike a child in anger."

The difference between the blow given in anger and the blow given out of a desire to punish, whether to deter or to revenge wrongdoing, is highlighted by conditions among the headhunting Iatmul people of New Guinea. Iatmul tempers flare easily, and Iatmul children learn early to leap out of arm's reach at the slightest hint of trouble. The children occasionally avenge themselves on adults by destroying property, throwing away adult valuables, eating food that has been saved for some special purpose, or even burning down a patch of sago palms. Then they will run away until the mosquitoes drive them home again. There is a saying that though an angry father *can* wait by his son's mosquito bag and beat him when he returns at night, the high pitch of anger seldom lasts so long.

It is necessary to distinguish between deliberate beating—a moralistic, cold-blooded and usually cruel and sadistic proceeding—and a good hearty shake, slap or cuff that is not heavy enough to damage the child and yet is convincing enough to be remembered. Failure to make this distinction is responsible for much of the confusion about discipline in the United States. Deliberate corporal punishment, administered self-righteously, tends to beget not a healthy avoidance of the next smack but a deep and often murderous hatred of all authority—and often produces a child who in later life must be "disciplined" by that odious invention, legal corporal punishment.

Not all but most primitive peoples are free of this terrible self-righteousness that makes the person who is "free of sin"—either in appearance or by dint of an extraordinary denial of his impulses—feel that he has the right, sometimes even the duty, to inflict cruelty on a hapless victim, too often a small and helpless child.

ह&

I was very much interested by your column about the Manus people of New Guinea. I gather that you do not feel any regret at the passing of their primitive ways. Would you comment? JUNE 1965

I feel an aesthetic regret whenever a people give up an old, internally consistent way of life to take on the ways of the larger society. At present this means that they will be caught in a kind of living in which fashion and unregulated machine manufacture lead to the production of objects that are incongruent with each other and less aesthetically satisfying than the traditional handmade objects of a primitive or a peasant people. In the past the houses built by the Manus had more

123

attractive architecture, their dress was more picturesque and their tools and utensils were ornamented in a style that was special to the Admiralty Islands. Every time an old, consistent tradition disappears, we are the losers. That is why it is so important to make adequate sound and film records as a way of providing a treasury on which arts and crafts can draw in the future.

Today, however, when a people's way of life is out of step with the larger world, they cannot occupy a dignified place in that world. Once a people are in contact with a more complex civilization, see how its members live, and acquire or covet any of its goods, spiritual or technical, the unity of their old way of life is broken. They can no longer take pride in their own traditions, and shame—a sense of the inadequacy of one's own life—is a corroding state of mind. If a people are to have full access to the benefits of the modern world—medicine, education, technology, government and (in the case of a primitive people) one of the great religions—they must be prepared to make many new adaptations so that they may attain and enjoy their new desires.

Do people in primitive societies make pets of animals as people in other societies do? If so, what is it that makes people all over the world want to keep pets? MARCH 1966

Relationships between man and the animals he has domesticated are ancient and diverse. People keep animals for many different reasons. The dog, which is the most common domestic animal throughout the world, may be used in hunting, to pull loads, to keep watch and (when still a puppy) as a toy for small children. A few peoples, among them the ancient Aztecs, have bred dogs for food. In a great many societies, both primitive and civilized, dogs are treated almost like members of the family. In other societies they are treated as pariahs—unnamed and without individual identity—a pack of gaunt, hungry, detested and feared but necessary scavengers. In parts of New Guinea pigs are better treated than dogs. Each pig is named and piglets are reared with tender care. Thus trained, they develop a "conscience" and they cower with guilt when rebuked for misbehavior, as when they walk across a sacred place where women, children, dogs and pigs are not allowed to go.

Some peoples bring home wild creatures—young deer, pumas, monkeys or parrots—sometimes to gentle and play with them, sometimes to bait them for the entertainment of watching their savage response. In China, little boys used to keep crickets and match them in fights, as elsewhere in the world men rear fighting cocks. In many village communities, flocks of birds or bands of monkeys lead a privileged existence, half tame, half wild—much like the squirrels in our parks.

Where people live in crowded communities and food is scarce, there may be very little feeling for pets and only the strictly utilitarian domestic animals may be tolerated—chickens and goats, donkeys to bear burdens, oxen to plow the fields. But many herding peoples regard their animals as individuals, naming each one and remembering the individual traits of each cow or horse or goat.

A people's attitudes toward animals, both wild and domesticated, are intimately bound up with their attitudes toward life and with their concepts of acceptable and unacceptable behavior. In civilized societies especially, a child's first lessons in kindness and sympathy, in the control of impulses to tease, bait or torture, often are learned through handling animals. The child may be taught how to kill noxious or dangerous insects or reptiles quickly and without needless pain, how to be gentle with a long-suffering animal that tolerates heedless play, how to care for the physical needs of a pet and under what circumstances an animal may or must be killed. All these lessons are aspects of learning how to respect life itself. Long before children are permitted to handle human babies they may be given young animals to play with and care for, and lonely children may be led to trust in life through a relationship with a devoted and dependent animal. And sometimes feelings about pets mirror very accurately a people's ideas about proper conduct in human relations—as when a Haitian woman, with a high sense of dignity, rejected the advances of a pet cat because, as she said, "he was disrespectful."

୧❦

What roles do dreams play among primitive peoples? Do dreams take similar forms in different cultures or are they specific to a particular culture? MARCH 1966

Where dreams are concerned, no real distinction can be made between civilized and primitive—that is, preliterate—peoples. In some cultures a great deal is made of dreams, in others very little.

In some cultures dreams are believed to have a predictive value. Where dreams are regarded as forewarnings, people remember their dreams, discuss their interpretation and treat them as keys to action. Elsewhere dreams are recounted only after some event which they are said to have foretold. Dreams may also be treated as a source of inspiration, as a way of creating new songs or new charms. Sometimes dreams give the individual a way of gaining magical or curative powers, or they are the means of coming in touch with the supernatural world.

Every culture has its own style of dreaming, and dreams reported from one culture will show this style so clearly that they cannot be mistaken for those of another culture. However, a careful analysis of dreams that includes associations an individual draws from his own dreams shows that the same general laws of dreaming apply everywhere. That is, there is a kind of universal grammar in dream thinking in which one finds reversals, regressions, condensed images, the part standing for the whole or the whole for some part; there is the complex process of substitutions in which, for example, one thing that is loved or hated, feared or desired, may stand for other things of the same kind. Many attempts have been made to apply theories of universal symbols to dreams and myths without reference to cultural style or the meanings that particular dreams have had for specific individuals, but these necessarily fail in their purpose.

One primitive people in Malaysia actually taught promising dreamers how to dream more creatively. Those who were chosen presented their dreams at a kind of seminar, where they were discussed and criticized by the older men. In our own society we use dreaming as one means of communication between a psychoanalyst and his patient. The patient learns to treat his dreams as a language, which he and the analyst decode in their joint effort to gain deeper insight into the unconscious sources of his behavior.

Do women in primitive societies follow any special routine—or are they subject to any taboos—during their menstrual periods? Do they commonly feel discomfort?
MARCH 1966

In many primitive societies women are subject to a variety of taboos during menstrual periods. Sometimes the menstruating woman is prohibited from taking part in ceremonies, or she may have to stay away from roads on which men walk. Sometimes she is not permitted to cook or to touch food; often she must spend several days shut up in a special hut, lonely and cut off from everyday affairs. During this period of isolation she may worry about how her children are faring and whether her husband or co-wife is taking good care of them.

Men, of course, also are affected by the restrictions imposed upon women, and so they also have cause for worry. Will his wife's condition compel a man to miss some important tribal event? Have his possessions been contaminated? Has his wife followed all the prescribed routines? These concerns are easily conveyed to the wife, whose state of mind may already be affected by her fear or hope of pregnancy.

This combination of social and practical anxiety, nervousness about the possibility of breaking an important taboo and concern about pregnancy can produce in the woman considerable physical discomfort, although the woman may fail to recognize the causes. Under these circumstances it is impossible for an outsider to distinguish between subjective and physiological discomfort and discomfort that is essentially sociological.

We read a great deal these days about caring for and educating retarded children, and about special opportunities for the highly gifted child. How are exceptional children—both under- and over-average—treated in primitive societies?
JUNE 1966

In no primitive society I have studied have I ever seen a child below the level of intelligence we would define as characteristic of a moron. Severely retarded children rarely survive in primitive societies, for the majority of such children are also physically defective and cannot live without a great deal of special care. Lacking medical remedies of any kind, a mother needs tremendous energy just to keep alive a seriously ailing or incapacitated child. When an infant cannot respond to normal care, the energy to rear it is likely to be withdrawn. I have never seen a child who was totally blind from birth in a primitive community, and I think such a child would be unlikely to survive. One exception, however, is the deaf child. It is not easy to diagnose deafness in very young infants, and as the child grows he may compensate with extra activity and unusual responsiveness. Such a child may have a chance for survival, since by the time the deafness is recognized he is already less dependent on his mother's milk and is integrated within the family. Later the deaf child's fate may depend on his ability to make his wants known and on the willingness of those around him to interpret pantomime.

Sometimes the exceptionally gifted child can find a niche where he is protected. Born into a society whose craftsmen have developed art forms, the artistically gifted child may grow up to make the single set of carvings that stands out among all others as a masterpiece. Or in a society in which trance and possession are recognized as special states, some very gifted children may be given scope for their talents as dancers, as curers or as interpreters of the will of the gods.

But in general the gifted child cannot go beyond the limits of his culture. The mathematically gifted can do little among a people who count only to four or five. The political genius can accomplish little in a community of three hundred people without the kind of political forms on which more complex organizations can be built. As a rule, such gifted persons are subdued to the norm of their culture. Occasionally they may be feared and hated as witches.

In a primitive society an exceptional occasion may give a chance to the exceptional individual. In the face of some great disaster, or in a period of rapid change following the arrival of members of a more complex culture, greatly gifted individuals may break through the confining restrictions of their own culture and display their talents.

When you are in the field, living among a primitive people, what kinds of food are available? OCTOBER 1966

Housekeeping in the field, especially keeping the larder stocked, depends on a large number of considerations. Some are familiar to anyone who runs a household. Others are peculiar to the field situation itself.

Cost, of course, is an important consideration, one that in the field is often determined by transportation facilities. If you depend even partly on imported foods, how will they reach you? Do they come by ship? Can supplies be delivered upriver by canoe? Then you may be able to afford some canned and dried foods and staples that come from a distance. But if they must be flown in by plane, every box and tin, whether it contains oatmeal or *pâté*, is a luxury. So you ask yourself, "Do we need this food? Or is it more important to use the money to buy film?" And when everything must be carried over mountains by human carriers, it is necessary to balance your needs very precisely against the ability and willingness of the carriers you depend on.

Food storage and preservation is another consideration. In the tropical areas where I have done most of my work, ice is almost unknown, and fish and game must be eaten at once or smoked. On my 1965 field trip to Manus, in the Admiralty Islands, I had a kerosene refrigerator for the first time. The chance to have a cold drink, to stow away half a dozen fish on a day when the fishermen had a good run, to keep an opened can for the next meal, to have some fresh sliced pineapple ready late at night when I had been working—all these were marvelous new luxuries. Nothing like it had been possible under earlier conditions. But the cost in effort was high. It took hours of precious time for a man who was patient and skilled to keep the refrigerator working, especially when winds of hurricane strength swept the village and, over and over, blew out the kerosene flame.

Depending on native foods has many complications. Will buying food for your household—consisting of two Europeans and three natives who have been withdrawn from the community's continuous search for food—overstrain the tiny hamlet so that some people will go hungry? Is buying food a matter of endless bargaining that may result, besides, in bad feeling? How much time will it take? Each individual vender comes whenever he or she is ready. One brings a few limes. Another has a small bunch of bananas. The third offers some taro. Each one wants to be paid at once. So each time, you get up from your work, discuss the worth of each item and measure out the salt or get out the razor blades, the tobacco or the beads that represent payment. Then, a little later, another vender arrives and you have to start all over again.

Native foods also may represent health hazards. It is safe enough to buy uncooked pork or accept it as a gift, providing you supervise its cooking very carefully. But what will happen when you are invited to eat half-cooked pork at a feast? Isn't it safer to explain, at the beginning of your stay, that eating pork (or other foods that may be tainted) is tabooed in your family?

Then there is the question of food preparation. Time spent on housekeeping is time lost from work. The natives who come to work in your household are chosen for many reasons; their ability as cooks may be of minor importance. How well can you teach adolescent boys and girls to cook local foods so that they are edible and not too monotonous? Many anthropologists grudge the time and effort spent trading for food and supervising its preparation, and men living alone have often paid heavy penalties for not bothering with fresh fruit and greens. Today, of course, vitamin capsules make some difference.

Each field situation is unique. In Manus in 1928 we lived almost entirely on fish. Fresh fish was very good, but since fishing success came in spurts, we usually depended on fish smoked hard as a board. Once, late at night, someone brought us a chicken. I prepared this delicacy myself—seasoned it carefully, roasted it in an iron pot and stowed it away in the hanging food safe for the next day. Before morning a savage robber dog broke into the safe and ate the chicken. Another time, when a little schooner came by, to entertain the captain I opened the one box of biscuits and the three little jars of hors d'oeuvres we had been cherishing. But before we sat down to eat, a storm blew up and he had to sail away without his dinner.

When we worked among the Arapesh in New Guinea in 1931, all our stores had to be carried inland and up steep mountain trails. Since there was no guarantee that carriers would ever make another trip, we never opened a can except in an emergency. Instead we lived on wild pigeon (very tough and barely edible even when the meat was ground up), papayas, taro and various kinds of greens. Rice and prunes were luxuries saved for times of illness. I had brought in a few scallions, which I have planted at the foot of a coconut palm. After three months we could cut up a quarter of one scallion as a condiment for one meal. The constant laborious battle to get enough food for ourselves and our native boys and the effort to keep the stores intact made a tremendous impression on me. Later, when we came down to the coast, and arrived at a plantation where milk came not from an irreplaceable can but from goats that were milked every day, I almost wept with delight.

Sometimes the best plan is to standardize a meal and eat the same food every day. In the late 1930s, up the Sepik River in New Guinea, pigeon was the most readily available meat. I taught my cook how to roast pigeon and also how to prepare a kind of small, bony, tasteless fish that several small girls working together could debone in a morning. These were the staples. Once in a while we were lucky—someone would kill a hornbill. The breast of this bird tastes remarkably like beefsteak.

Native New Guinea food offers no temptation to the gourmet. Most foods are boiled and there are no interesting seasonings. The problem for the field worker comes down to getting enough local food, having it cooked in a way that is safe and bearable and not losing time over housekeeping. Employing local small boys and adolescents nominally to do the housework is one sure way of keeping them at one's house to answer questions, to make running comments on the things that are happening and to hurry across the village to find out who is screaming or crying or shouting and why. Too much attention to housework interferes with these more important activities. No anthropologist, as far as I know, looks forward to eating "exotic" foods in the field, but we all have long, lingering memories of the food that kept us going while we got on with our work.

Do members of primitive societies ever commit suicide? And do you believe that suicide bears any relationship to homicide? JUNE 1967

Yes. Suicide is a socially recognized practice among many primitive peoples. Elsewhere the threat of suicide, rather than its actual performance, is an acknowledged and dramatic way of dealing with an impasse. Of course, the socially recognized motives for suicide vary exceedingly from one society to another. In a tribe in which premarital pregnancy is deeply disapproved of, a pregnant girl may kill herself in desperation. Among other peoples a young girl thwarted in love may threaten or actually commit suicide. Among the Plains Indians of North America, a young warrior who was crippled through some injury preferred to ride out bravely to his death on a last war party to the prospect of living on, helpless and unhappy. Among some peoples it is not the idea of death but the fear of shame that is intolerable.

But there are also primitive societies in which the idea of suicide is unknown. I studied one group in New Guinea among whom there had been a single case of suicide. This occurred not long after the government had introduced the idea of hanging as a punishment for the newly forbidden act of headhunting. No other suicide was known. It has also been reported that suicide as such was unknown among the Zuñi Indians of New Mexico. However, a Zuñi who was filled with anger at his fellow tribesmen might secretly invite their traditional enemies, the Navahos, to attack his village. He then readied himself, went out to meet the enemy and was the first to be killed.

In some situations it is not easy to define a death. Many American Indian tribes attempted to control extreme forms of antisocial behavior by expelling the guilty individual from the group, thus in effect cutting him off from human society. In this situation it is possible to regard the man who walked away to almost certain death either as a suicide who had taken his guilt on himself or as someone who had been condemned by the judicial verdict of his fellows.

The line between suicide and homicide is a very narrow one. Some forms of homicide are essentially ways of forcing others to carry out an execution. Among the Malays there is a traditional form of insanity known as *amok*. Characteristically, a man goes into a deep depression. Then, suddenly and without warning, he starts to kill people, until he himself is killed. During the Western colonial period among Malay peoples it proved possible to control the syndrome of running amok by insisting that the man should not be killed, but should be brought in alive. In China, a man who felt he had been treated unjustly might commit suicide by hanging himself at the gate of his oppressor, who by implication became responsible for the death.

In compiling national statistics it is customary to use both suicide and homicide rates as indices of social malfunctioning in different countries. From a psychological point of view this is justified, as the motives are often compatible. But the social consequences are very different. Where suicide is recognized as a response to two equally valid but totally conflicting demands on an individual, as it is in Japan, it can be regarded as an ethical and a responsible act. In contrast, homicide violates one of the two essential taboos on which the existence of human society depends; that is, the taboos against incest and against the murder of a member of one's own group.

Of all the societies of which you have firsthand knowledge, which has the most effective means of disciplining its children and which has the least? What are those methods?
AUGUST 1967

In the matter of childhood disciplines there is no absolute standard. The question is one of appropriateness to a style of living. What is the intended outcome? Are the methods of discipline effective in preparing the child to live in the adult world into which he is growing? The means of discipline that are very effective in rearing children to become headhunters and cannibals would be most ineffective in preparing them to become peaceful shepherds.

The Mundugumor, a New Guinea people, trained their children to be tough and self-reliant. Among these headhunters, when one village was preparing to attack another and wanted to guard itself against attack by a third village, the first village sent its children to the third to be held as hostages. The children knew that they faced death if their own people broke this temporary truce. Mundugumor methods of child rearing were harsh but efficient. An infant sleeping in a basket hung on the wall was not taken out and held when it wakened and cried. Instead, someone scratched on the outside of the basket, making a screeching sound like the squeak of chalk on a blackboard. And a child that cried with fright was not given the mother's breast. It was simply lifted and held off the ground. Mundugumor children learned to live in a tough world, unfearful of hostility. When they lived among strangers as hostages, they watched and listened, gathering the information they would need someday for a successful raid on this village.

The Arapesh, another New Guinea people, had a very different view of life and human personality. They expected their children to grow up in a fairly peaceful world, and their methods of caring for children reflected their belief that both men and women were gentle and nurturing in their intimate personal relations. Parents responded to an infant's least cry, held him and comforted him. And far from using punishment as a discipline, adults sometimes stood helplessly by while a child pitched precious firewood over a cliff.

Even very inconsistent discipline may fit a child to live in an inconsistent world. A Balinese mother would play on her child's fright by shouting warnings against nonexistent dangers: "Look out! Fire ... Snake! ... Tiger!" The Balinese system required people to avoid strange places without inquiring why. And the Balinese child learned simply to be afraid of strangeness. He never learned that there are no bears under the stairs, as American children do. We want our children to test reality. We teach our children to believe in Santa Claus and later, without bitter disappointment, to give up that belief. We want them to be open to change, and as they grow older, to put childhood fears and rewards aside and be ready for new kinds of reality.

There are also forms of discipline that may be self-defeating. Training for bravery, for example, may be so rigorous that some children give up in despair. Some Plains Indians put boys through such severe and frightening experiences in preparing them for their young manhood as warriors that some boys gave up entirely and dressed instead as women.

In a society in which many people are socially mobile and may live as adults in a social or cultural environment very different from the one in which they grew up, old forms of discipline may be wholly unsuited to new situations. A father whose family lived according to a rigid, severe set of standards, and who was beaten in his boyhood for lying or stealing, may still think of beating as an appropriate method of disciplining his son. Though he now lives as a middle-class professional man in a suburb, he may punish his son roughly for not doing well in school. It is not the harshness as such that then may discourage the boy even more, but his bewilderment. Living in a milieu in which parents and teachers reward children by praise and presents for doing well in school—a milieu in which beating is not connected with competence in schoolwork—the boy may not be able to make much sense of the treatment he receives.

There is still another consideration in this question about discipline. Through studies of children as they grow up in different cultures we are coming to understand more about the supportive and the maiming effects of various forms of discipline. Extreme harshness or insensitivity to the child may prepare it to survive in a harsh environment. But it also may cripple the child's ability to meet changing situations. And today we cannot know the kind of world the children we are rearing will live in as adults. For us, therefore, the most important question to ask about any method of discipline is: How will it affect the child's capacity to face change? Will it give the child the kind of strength necessary to live under new and unpredictable conditions?

An unyielding conscience may be a good guide to successful living in a narrow and predictable environment. But it may become a heavy burden and a cruel scourge in a world in which strength depends on flexibility. Similarly, the kind of discipline that makes a child tractable, easy to bring up and easy to teach in a highly structured milieu, may fail to give the child the independence, courage and curiosity he will need to meet the challenges in a continually changing situation. At the same time, the absence of forms of discipline that give a child a sense of living in an ordered world in which it is rewarding to learn the rules, whatever they may be, also may be maiming. A belief in one's own accuracy and a dependable sense of how to find the patterning in one's environment are necessary parts of mature adaptation to new styles of living.

There is, in fact, no single answer to the problem of childhood discipline. But there is always the central question: For what future?

136

What means of population control have been utilized by primitive societies? JUNE 1968

In most primitive societies, as in most modern societies until recently, people have been concerned not with reducing the population but with increasing or at least maintaining its size. Recurrent famines and epidemics, the dangers and hardships of men's occupations, the hazards of childbirth for women and the fragility of young children have meant that any small group, almost up to the present, has had to face the threat of extinction.

Primitive peoples usually have used every means at their command to produce children and rear them safely. In most primitive societies, grossly incapacitated children were allowed to die, and infants who did not prosper on their mother's milk also died because their discouraged mothers lost their milk. Abortion and infanticide at birth were used by some peoples to reduce the number of small children for whom a mother had to care at any one time. Some protection against a too-rapid succession of births was assured by taboos forbidding intercourse for long periods after childbirth and also by long periods of breast feeding. But these were methods of control that gave a better chance of survival to the mother and to each child she had in her care.

In spite of all that could be done, a very large proportion of infants died. Without improved, scientific knowledge of medicine, pediatrics and infant feeding, there were few ways of protecting mothers during·and after childbirth or of safeguarding the lives of the newborn. As long as this was so, safety for the group depended on keeping the birth rate high.

Today the situation is reversed. We can save almost every mother and keep alive almost every infant that is born. The safety of civilization now depends on our foresighted willingness to control conception in order to protect the ratio of children to adults and the ratio of people to food and living space.

Is it possible to keep primitive peoples from becoming civilized? Should we try to preserve primitive cultures?
AUGUST 1977

It is quite impossible to protect primitive cultures from the impact of modern civilization. Primitive peoples who come in contact with the modern world recognize the usefulness of at least some of its technology. As soon as they begin to use steel axes and knives, cloth, tobacco, alcohol, firearms and transistor radios—all the different kinds of things we make available—their economy and way of life are rapidly altered. They also learn very quickly that modern medicine can protect their babies and cure many of the ailments of the mature. This benefit they also want.

To deny a primitive people what they have newly learned to want, in order to keep them primitive—even if this is conceived of as a protection—is wholly out of key with the modern world.

But we need not treat primitive peoples as incapable—as most of them were treated in the past. We can see to it that they are given a chance to be consulted and that they learn how to weigh alternatives and make their own choices. We can prevent their lands from being invaded, stolen and devastated, as is still happening in many parts of the world. We can prevent the destruction that is brought about by pipelines, atomic reactors, experimental undersea nuclear reactions and the use of pesticides that alter the landscape. We can protect them from forced labor and from the traumatic effects of harshly imposed, alien laws. But we cannot prevent them from becoming civilized.

There are primitive peoples who have fled from civilization. They are peoples whose experiences with outsiders more technically advanced than themselves have been so terrible and devastating that their only chance for survival has been to refuse all further contact. Ishi, the lone survivor of such a remnant Indian group in California, threw himself on the mercy of white men in the early years of this century only when he was totally alone.

To the extent that we make contact more humane and civilized—offer primitive peoples medicine and real education instead of poor-quality tools and goods, alcohol and firearms, and give them a chance to reach for what is best in our world instead of restricting them to positions of illiterate, low-grade labor—just to this extent will they desire to accept in their own lives what is valuable in modern civilization. The more civilized we are, the more civilized primitive peoples will wish to become. I see no escape from this paradox.

☙ 5 ❧
GOVERNMENT
AND POLITICS

How do you feel about Senator Margaret Chase Smith's possible Republican candidacy for the Presidency or Vice-Presidency? MARCH 1964

It is very interesting that her candidacy is being seriously discussed. Senator Smith has many of the attributes that a woman candidate for either the Presidency or Vice-Presidency would, I believe, need. She is a mature woman, a widow, with political experience. But I think it unlikely that she will be nominated. I doubt if this generation of American men has the kind of experience that would lead it to accept a chief executive who is a woman. Cabinet posts are more acceptable, and we should have more of them filled by women.

There has been a great deal of controversy as to whether divorce or divorce and remarriage is a serious handicap for a candidate for high office in the United States. Would you comment? SEPTEMBER 1963

As a rule, Americans are concerned that public figures should present an image that is congruent with their particular notions of respectability, especially in those areas in which they are trying to control others—their children, their spouses, their neighbors, their employees. Among handicaps for a political candidate are divorce, marriage to a divorced person, membership in a religious minority group, conversion from one religious faith to another, association with

141

crime and so on. But American attitudes toward irregularities in the personal lives of candidates have some curious aspects. A middle-aged woman who is afraid that her husband might leave her for a younger woman will be very critical of a candidate who is known to have divorced a wife of long standing. She may actually take pleasure, however, in hearing whispered accounts of a candidates' infidelity. In fact, in our political history *whispering* has attributed illegitimate children, extramarital affairs, atheism, violations of trust, and so on, even to men who were candidates for the Presidency. But whenever such scandalous accusations cannot be printed for fear of libel, they play a relatively unimportant role in a political campaign, and often the two parties may tacitly agree to keep their respective candidate's weaknesses out of public notice. In such cases there is little harm done if the weaknesses are identified as rumors. People everywhere discuss the rumors in hushed tones to show that they are in the know, and sometimes this kind of talk is so gratifying that the slight, secret aura of disrepute may even enhance the candidate's appeal.

But a scandal that breaks into print during an election campaign can be fatally damaging to a candidate, and sometimes a politician will decide that presenting the public beforehand with a *fait accompli,* however much it may displease some segment of the population, is preferable to any possible future scandal. When a man or a woman has been divorced and has already remarried before a campaign opens, the possibility of scandal is removed. The event is no longer news; in fact, if it is repeatedly mentioned during the campaign, it is quite likely to arouse partisan feelings of protectiveness in undecided voters who react against "unfair" political tactics. In the United States it is still regarded as unfair to harp on a man's past. The one major exception is alleged sympathy with communism, for here we paradoxically have adopted the viewpoint of Soviet Communism that past events that are politically unpopular are irreversibly damaging. Otherwise, to mention a candidate's past personal history with the intent of reducing his chances for election may very well have the effect of increasing those chances.

ટ~

How do you feel about legalizing off-track betting and other forms of gambling and using the money in the public interest? DECEMBER 1963

The question of whether we should legalize off-track betting or any other form of gambling should be strictly separated from the question of whether the money gained is to be used in the public interest.

Many advocates of legalized gambling seem to hold that gambling, although wicked, would be less wicked if the proceeds or taxes on the proceeds went to a good cause. This particular formula usually draws the counterargument that virtue should not be supported by vice. These arguments only cloud the issue. The point is that gambling does go on, and by taking no action to regulate the conditions under which it takes place, by treating as illegal something everyone knows is practiced on a very large scale, we have been producing organized crime and supporting wide political and police corruption.

By legalizing off-track betting and other forms of gambling, we would open the way to taxing these activities and regulating them. A tax on the proceeds of gambling would be a particularly non-onerous form of taxation—for after all, no one is obliged to gamble. And gambling in a good private cause, of course, would be one permitted form of gambling, available to those who could soothe their consciences only in this way and available to the cause as a painless way of raising money.

ટ~

Is there any sense to disarmament talks that exclude Communist China, now reportedly developing an atomic bomb of its own? FEBRUARY 1964

To be really effective, disarmament must, of course, include all the countries of the world. But every step toward disarmament is a step forward. Every increase in understanding of the problems involved, every new device—like the

143

atomatic "box" for monitoring nuclear tests—gives hope and a sense of direction. We need to work toward a climate of opinion in which China will be included and in which China herself will want to be included. But it would be dangerous to use our failure to achieve this aim as a criticism of disarmament talks.

Are you in favor of government fluoridation of our water?
MARCH 1964

I certainly would not be in favor of Federal fluoridation of our water. Properly handled by each local community, the question of fluoridation is one in which a community can be educated in the whole field of preventive public health. In the first place, however, it shouldn't be treated as a single issue but should be discussed with the other preventive and protective measures—use of pesticides, smog prevention, noise control and so on. So often when an issue like fluoridation comes up, the real issues are obscured by scientific dogmatism on one side and irrational fear of too much governmental meddling with life on the other, and this does a great deal of harm, whether or not fluoridation wins or loses in the local vote. Single measures, out of context and not understood, re-establish magical thinking and undo all our efforts to spread a rational understanding of what science does and does not know, and where expertise begins and ends.

We keep hearing that undergraduates today are far more politically conservative than in previous generations. From your visits to college campuses would you say this is true?
MARCH 1964

No. But young people with conservative tendencies are more articulate today than they were in earlier generations. In the 1920s, 1930s and 1940s it was the liberal young people who were actively promoting causes and crusades—there

144

were far fewer organized groups interested in conservatism. The conservative young people went swimming or skiing or—in some colleges—spent their time cultivating the right people. Then there came the long dead period of the 1950s when young people seemed to be uninterested in anything beyond their immediate personal lives.

When the integration issue woke the country up, old-style liberals hailed the birth of new political interest on the part of college students—as long as it was on the liberal side. But they have been very much surprised to find that now young conservatives too want to take a hand in the affairs of the nation and of the world. Actually this is simply a reflection of what is happening in every field of American life—earlier participation of young people, whether in politics or marriage and parenthood.

As a larger portion of our young people go to college, it may be expected that campus life will become more representative of the whole population. And with a two-party system of government, it is healthy to have students interested in and articulate on both sides of every issue.

Senator Barry Goldwater [Republican Presidential candidate in 1964] seems to think that the poor are poor because they want to be poor, do not have jobs because they do not want jobs and collect welfare because they find this easier than working. What, if anything, is wrong with this point of view as it applies to the American poor in general? JULY 1964

The viewpoint you attribute to Senator Goldwater is based on a two-pronged argument: The poor will get richer (if not rich) if they work, and the poor deserve to starve if they do not work.

In most Western societies, which have built an ethic on work, the traditional attitude has been that those who worked and gave to the poor were virtuous; but those who could not work and were in need—the sick, the lame, the blind, the dispossessed—were somehow evil. In the Irish famine the soup kitchens that stood between the thousands and starvation were located far outside of towns, so that weak and famished people had to earn their dole of soup by walking long distances to get it.

At the time of the Great Depression the American attitude toward the poor began to change. When millions were dropped from payrolls and businesses were failing, the insistence that men should work for their living—no matter how strong an incentive—did not produce jobs. In this situation our moral sense was sharpened by the awareness that the millions without work—relatives, friends and neighbors, as well as distant strangers—could not have become lazy and vicious overnight. It became clear that in a system like ours there are inevitably fluctuations in employment for which no individual banker or worker or farmer can be held responsible, and that a complex and wealthy society like ours must begin to take minimal responsibility for everyone. Out of this recognition came national programs for welfare, home relief, assistance to dependent children, unemployment compensation, old-age insurance and other measures taken to protect our people and our economy against another great depression.

But now we face new problems. In today's society, in which the rate of unemployment is rising because the need for many skills is declining, the poor who work will not necessarily get richer. Instead they will continue to live in slum housing, send their children to overcrowded, dilapidated schools and try to keep well on inadequate, grudgingly given medical care. And the number of low-skilled city poor is growing as underemployed and undernourished people from deteriorating countrysides pour into the cities. Cities no longer can use their simple skills, and they go on welfare. Living on welfare for a long time may sap their will to work, especially when they realize that today, no matter how hard they work, they—unskilled, often illiterate, malnourished, suffering the effects of lack of medical care from childhood—will always be poor. No matter what they do, they will still be where they are. Today we have indeed removed the threat of absolute starvation. What we have substituted for its desperate urgency is the promise of a low level of living for

146

the unneeded and the helpless, whether they work or do not work.

But in the history of mankind no sort of compensation has been an adequate substitute for a place in society—for the opportunity to work as a man among other men, hunting or planting, herding or building, not to avoid starvation or to gain riches but as part of human life. In the past 5,000 years millions of men have been deprived of this dignity. But in recent centuries the groundwork has been laid for today's affluence. And now, perhaps for the first time, we in the United States are in a position to grant all men dignity. For we are in a position to abolish poverty and misery and hunger and ignorance in our land of plenty, where many millions more could be adequately clothed and fed and housed and educated—to the ultimate benefit of the whole economy as well.

Don't you think that the political system in America, whereby a man's election to the Presidency depends so much on his personal appeal to the voters, is less desirable than the English system, whereby the party winning the election chooses the Prime Minister and the voters' choice centers more clearly on the issues? SEPTEMBER 1964

I think it is necessary first to consider the two systems in the context of English and American history. The English system is an appropriate one for a constitutional monarchy, wherein the Crown provides a continuing personal stability and the Government represents a quite temporary alignment of men and ideas. The English system also fits a society in which people react with sufficient deliberation so that it is safe to risk the overthrow of a given government at almost any time. In the American system, stability depends on the election of a particular man for a particular term of office and, in the case of the Presidency, on the election of an alternate—as the tragic death of President Kennedy last November so abundantly demonstrated. The popularity of any president rises and falls in response to his actions. But a secure term in office enables a president to take an initially unpopular or controversial stand that can be fully discussed without risking a breakdown of government at the height of the debate.

Americans are especially aware of personal appeal today because of the new prominence of television. But so are the English, and many English people felt that the last Prime Minister, Mr. Macmillan, was being tailored into a film-star personality because of television. In both countries, current arguments about "personal appeal" reflect the confusion of educated people on the whole subject of television and for the most part ignore the central point—the opportunity that radio and television give a whole people to judge the *character* of a man.

Actually, there is little danger either in the United States (where we distrust newscasters who are too handsome) or in the United Kingdom (where newscasters are selected for their appealing voice and appearance) that the people will select statesmen on a wholly superficial basis. The opportunity to experience candidates for office directly gives the people a much greater chance to weigh their characters and, it is to be hoped, to reject those who are found wanting.

Do you think that the State Department is right or wrong in trying to prevent Americans from traveling to Cuba or mainland China? SEPTEMBER 1964

In forbidding travel to these countries, the Division of Passports and Visas is carrying out national executive policy. Accusing "the State Department" or "the White House" or "Congress" of being arbitrary only obscures the real issue.

We have a national policy that is based on the obligation of the United States to protect its citizens abroad and on the inability of the government to carry out this obligation when Americans travel beyond the limits of the ambassadorial or the consular arm. The only way the government can protect the interests of its citizens in countries with which we do not have diplomatic relations is by the threat or the actual use of force. And in a world in which it is crucial to avoid incidents that heighten the risk of war, a strong argument can be made against allowing United States nationals to travel where their activities—even their mere presence—may involve the government in an international incident.

An alternative solution would be to invent a kind of passport that is as far below an ordinary passport in its standard of protection as a diplomatic passport—which confers diplomatic immunity—is above an ordinary passport. In effect, such a passport could state: John Smith is an American citizen. When he uses this passport in a country with which the United States has no diplomatic relations, he travels at his own risk and with the express understanding that if his rights are infringed upon while he is in that country, the United States will not come to his aid. The government, in issuing this passport, guarantees only its willingness to have him return to the United States when he desires to do so.

The traveler who decided to use such a passport would know where he stood. And having accepted the personal risk, he could not expect his mother or his wife or his business firm to petition his congressman to get him out of trouble.

Why do we not follow such a course? One reason is that some Americans, having too little faith in our system, are fearful of letting impressionable young people taste the atmosphere of a country like Cuba or the People's Republic of China. They fear that they might be corrupted by Communist rigor—as the Communists, especially during World War II, feared that their young people might be corrupted by a desire for worldly goods through their contact with the West. Another reason is that journalists who traveled in such a country would write and publish. But would that really do any harm? Do we gain or lose by finding out what is going on in a country with a rival political system?

I do not think a free society can maintain its freedom by using any of the methods used by totalitarian regimes to maintain their power. Our strength lies in the fullest possible exercise of those values that we hold highest: protection of the freedom of the individual and protection of the world so that free men may live many generations hence. We are weakened by curbing the freedom of actively curious,

149

genuinely worried and professionally committed Americans, whether students, journalists or tourists.

Perhaps we should go to work and devise a "travel-at-your-own-risk" passport. In a short time insurance companies would be ready to estimate and cover the risks.

[Editor's note: Although the specific situation has changed considerably since this question was asked, the issue itself remains open, and Dr. Mead's imaginative and sensible solution will interest today's reader—and maybe even the State Department.]

ह

Isn't it true that nations should no more be financially irresponsible than individuals are, and isn't national indebtedness as bad as individual indebtedness? NOVEMBER 1964

It depends on the kind of indebtedness you are discussing. For one nation to be deeply indebted to other nations— because its imports far exceed its capacity to pay for them— may be as crippling to the nation as it is for a family to buy goods and services beyond their eventual ability to meet their cost. But when we speak of national indebtedness we usually mean *internal* indebtedness, that is, the money that citizens of a country owe to themselves. A family may lose their car or their house because they cannot pay their debts, or a business may go into bankruptcy. But it is a different thing for a nation to borrow money from its citizens in the form of bonds on which interest is paid.

People with money buy the bonds, on which they receive interest; and the government uses the borrowed money to improve on our national plant and to employ people who, in turn, have money to spend and invest as they need and like. This helps to increase the gross national income and the gross national product on which we measure our prosperity. Economy measures, so-called, on the part of the government do not, therefore, necessarily increase the country's prosperity. What is prudent for an individual or a family whose income, once spent, brings in no further return is not comparably prudent for a government or, for that matter, for a business.

But it is true that we need to develop new international devices for solving the problems that arise when too much money—too many dollars or pounds or pesos—flows out of a country without return.

Why do you disapprove of laws against homosexuality?
DECEMBER 1964

I disapprove of laws that are directed toward the control of private behavior, whatever aspect of life may be concerned. Essentially, laws are designed to govern people's public behavior. In the case of sex practices it is necessary to provide for decency of public behavior and to protect children and other helpless persons. But to decree how individual adults should—or should not—conduct their lives in private with adult partners of either sex seems to me to confuse the issue. For in doing so we are confusing the police power of the state, which has responsibility for the protection of all citizens, with the moral power of religious authorities, who should not need to call upon the state to support their position or enforce their moral tenets.

Are you in favor of our law that a man cannot be elected to the Presidency more than twice? DECEMBER 1964

Yes, I am. An essential component of our way of life is the recognition that no single man is indispensable to the nation's well-being. It is important to organize our government and our political parties in such ways that we will always have available for office a group of capable and experienced candidates. Failure to do this signals the failure of a political party.

151

When a leader in the Soviet Union loses his position, why is it necessary that he be vilified in the eyes of the people?
MARCH 1965

It isn't. When, for example, Nikita Khrushchev was consolidating his power and developing a new policy antithetical to Stalin's earlier one, repudiation of Stalinism served two purposes; it heavily emphasized policy change and it provided a way for people to declare personal allegiance to the new leadership.

Mr. Khrushchev's removal from office has been quite different. He was removed from office, after he had displayed signs of aging, in a legal manner according to the Soviet constitution, to make way for successors who would pursue the same policies without some of the personal preferences and antipathies displayed by Mr. Khrushchev.

The point is that in Western democracies the decision to retain or change leadership is reached openly, as well as legally, and *all* candidates may be "vilified" during the election campaign. The accusations made during this period are often a permanent handicap to the successful candidate.

As the Soviet system precludes active vocal opposition during the incumbency of a leader, critical discussion of alternative candidates would be out of accord with their insistence on unanimous adherence to the man selected for public office. Criticism (vilification seems a rather strong word, in the light of political campaigns in the United States) can be openly voiced only later, when a man no longer carries the weight of supreme leadership in party or state.

Do you believe we can ever achieve world peace through world law? JANUARY 1967

Most people, I think, picture world peace as an absolute state in which wars would cease forever all around the world. This picture of peace as freedom from war tempts us, for today we see each small war as likely to trigger a larger war that may be fatal to the human race and all life on this planet. But when we set peace as our goal, our aim is essentially a negative one of prevention.

What we need to think about, instead, is a higher level of organization on a world-wide scale and a higher sense of respect among the world's peoples. Both are necessary for the free exchange of persons, goods and ideas; I think this freedom of movement is more productive as a goal than the negative one of "preventing" war.

Through the ages men have developed rules about travel, rules of the road, rules of trade, rules of hospitality, rules for settling disputes and for protecting the safety of persons. Observance of such rules depends on the agreement of all those who live by them that they are right and just. This, essentially, is what we mean by the rule of law.

World law requires world-wide agreement on what is fair and just. A first step in this direction is agreement on what is "equality before the law" for small countries as well as large and for people of all races, all religions, living in all societies and in all walks of life. Today we have very wide agreement on some rules—the delivery of mail, rescues at sea, the protection of aircraft on landing strips. We are developing systems of gathering and disseminating health information that serve as virtually world-wide safety measures in controlling epidemics. Rules for the respect of persons have reduced the hazards of travel. But we cannot yet be said to have a real beginning of world law, for any powerful country can, and sometimes does, flout international rules.

There is a group of imaginative political scientists and jurists who are working hard to understand the general basis of law as it exists in different societies. Through such organizations as the World Law Fund and books like *World Peace Through World Law*, by Grenville Clark and Louis Sohn, their aim is to establish a minimum body of law which all men will find just. World law, and so world peace, does not depend on persuading the world's peoples to accept our own ideas or the ideas of any one nation. World law, like local law, must be rooted in the ethical agreement of all people who live within its tenets.

153

Can a democratic society continue to exist if such men as the Reverend William Sloane Coffin, Jr., feel that their conscience is above the law? JANUARY 1969

I think that our kind of democratic society can continue to exist only as long as there are men who responsibly consult their conscience in obeying or challenging the law, as the Reverend William Sloane Coffin has done.

The law is a human institution and laws change through time, but slowly, as the people who live by them change and grow. Change often comes about as the result of active protest. But when it is too long delayed, there is likely to be widespread—and dangerous—disregard of the law. For law enforcement of the kind we believe in rests on the consent of the governed. The orderly-minded may consent to wait. They may be willing to put up with an outmoded law while struggling within the legal structure to change it. But whenever the difference between what people believe is right and what the law decrees becomes too glaringly great, a challenge like that made by Dr. Coffin is essential. Otherwise our confidence in law itself may break down.

Civil disobedience based on ethical considerations is one of the strongest weapons in the arsenal of justice. Traditionally, the civilly disobedient have accepted as part of their protest the legal penalty for the illegal act they have carried out in good conscience. Today, however, the traditional ethic is clouded. In the trial in which Dr. Coffin was involved, the charge—conspiracy—was one to which the defendants could not in good conscience plead guilty.

A different problem is raised by the fact that many young demonstrators now demand amnesty as an acknowledgment that their protest, however illegal in form, is right. I believe their stand is a dubious one. There is greater strength in the position taken by the citizen who says, "I must challenge this particular law and I shall show my respect for law by accepting the penalty for my act." But a change in the ethic of civil disobedience may be coming about nonetheless.

At the present time the political process has got out of hand in that a very great number of people feel excluded from active politics and lawmaking. When this happens, those who are making social protest go outside ordinary channels to get a hearing. The issue of conscientious objection to war is an outstanding example. Many serious persons believe that the individual has the right to declare his conscientious objection not only to war itself but also to a particular war.

When the conflict in Vietnam is settled, we may hope that we shall modify our laws so that conscientious objectors to particular wars will have the legal right to declare themselves. For in situations in which the safety of the nation as a whole is not in danger, I believe it is no longer ethically feasible to exempt from military service only those who have conscientious objections to all wars on religious grounds. In the meantime, civil disobedience as a form of ethical protest is one way of establishing the strength of the demand for change.

Is international spying necessary? JUNE 1976

Spying is a predictable response of human beings who feel that their well-being is endangered by the existence of some alien group. Knowing something you believe those other people do not know that you know can give you an illusory sense of security.

But spying is neither efficient nor necessary for the orderly, intelligent conduct of human affairs. What can be learned by spying is inevitably piecemeal and subject to misinterpretation because it is torn from its context. In order to be effective, what we need to know about the political, economic and social life of any country depends in the first instance on a sound knowledge of the language and culture of that country. And what we need essentially is a well-trained and trusted career foreign service, whose members build up a sound working knowledge of particular areas of the world at first hand, and who are in good communication with similarly well-trained analysts and policy makers at home. Knowledge that is openly arrived at and openly discussed can always be tested against the realities of the current situation and can be corrected as situations change.

What human beings in difficult political and military situations have done for as long as we have any records has been to substitute intermittent and particularized spying for long-term, systematic knowledge of another people or country. In the past generation our means of collecting and transmitting "secret" information have vastly increased, and the armies of spies also have proliferated. But in the most crucial situations—for example, at Pearl Harbor, at the time of the German attack on the Soviet Union and, more recently, at the outbreak of the Yom Kippur war—intelligence systems failed utterly.

What is currently agitating Americans of every political persuasion is, not intelligence gathering, but enterprises that started out as by-products of traditional intelligence gathering and now seem to have become the principal activities of those agencies concerned with intelligence operations—that is, the Central Intelligence Agency abroad and the Federal Bureau of Investigation at home. Abroad, such activities have involved stirring up dissidence, bribing political leaders, distorting the flow of public information, arming guerrillas and, in effect, financing civil disturbance and open warfare of various kinds. This we can, if we will, check through the control by Congress of the intelligence budget.

More immediately destructive to ourselves are counter-intelligence (spying) operations within our own country against our fellow countrymen. The difficulty here is that as long as there is spying abroad there must also be a continual search not only for foreign spies but also for defectors and traitors at home. And for this there is, I believe, only one long-term, workable solution: the decision to build up a sophisticated, widely shared and mutually accepted fund of knowledge of other countries and our own. This also, of course, will move everyone in the direction of a more intelligible, orderly world.

Please describe what you consider the advantages of the two-party system as generally practiced in the United States.
SEPTEMBER 1976

A two-party system of government expresses in action the belief that there are at the very least two sides to every question and the supporters of both sides have the right—indeed, the responsibility—to make themselves heard. The give-and-take that necessarily follows makes it likelier that people will respect their political adversaries instead of wanting to annihilate them in order to establish the rule of one point of view.

It is also somewhat easier in the long run to arrive at workable decisions. In countries with multiparty systems, where each party works within a narrow framework of political ideas, necessary decisions may be long delayed while each party maneuvers for a leading position. Under these conditions a stable government may become impossible and the electorate divided into irreconcilable factions. Under the two-party system as it has usually operated in our country, each party includes people of very different viewpoints on particular issues. Co-operation—as well as opposition—across party lines shifts from issue to issue without destroying the integrity of either party. And the decisions, which may affect the welfare of millions of people irrespective of their politics, must be acceptable to a majority that almost inevitably includes legislators of both parties.

A two-party system provides a kind of balancing mechanism in which parties exchange roles, now one party and now the other taking responsibility for necessary actions. For example, it was easier for the Republican administration of President Nixon to carry through *rapprochement* with mainland China and the Soviet Union, with conservative Republican support, than it would ever have been for a Democratic administration opposed by conservatives in both parties.

There are hazards, of course, in a two-party system as in any other. The most extreme of these is civil war, as we are now witnessing in Northern Ireland, where each party has

157

become so totally committed to its own purposes that little useful communication across party lines is taking place. Less obvious but perhaps only a little less insidious are the hazards of keeping one party in power too long. When the Republicans returned to power after almost a generation under New Deal Democratic Presidents, they were faced with working out programs they had long opposed and had little experience in administering, and with a vast bureaucracy that had flourished under one party's patronage. The problem then was—as it always is—how to restore some kind of balance without destroying the system itself.

Children learn a great deal about politics while they are very young. The authoritarian family in which the wife, or occasionally the husband, is totally subordinate to the dominant spouse is a logical preparation for living in a totalitarian state or participating in other autocratic, hierarchically organized institutions, including the armed forces, many American industries and some American unions.

But in families in which there is a great deal of give-and-take, the child learns that two parents, both of whom she loves and both of whom love her, may differ—that sometimes one and sometimes the other, for example, seems to be on her side. And so the belief is born that there are two sides to every question and that both party loyalty and loyal opposition are necessary and desirable forms of behavior.

Do you believe we should adopt the principle of "triage" to solve the problem of famine in many parts of the world, as advocated by some authorities? JUNE 1976

No, I do not. The philosophy underlying the concept of triage is totally repugnant to me and to most Americans. Under this concept, food aid would not be sent to the neediest countries, but only to those that seemed to show the best prospects for survival. Deliberately and as a matter of policy to deny any people the basic necessities of life in a time of crisis would be contrary to the ethical system on which our society is based.

Our country has long stood for generous help to any people, wherever they may be, who are suffering from famine or earthquake, drought or flood, hurricane or tidal wave, war or war's aftermath. It is quite true that much of the aid given through our government has been ill-advised and self-serving. But the impulse on the part of the individual American to give help in a time of trouble is pragmatic only in the sense that we believe hungry people need to eat *now* before they can do something about the future.

Any nation that adopted a policy of triage—of deciding which peoples of the world had no right to a future and deserved no help in the present—would be paving the way for the deliberate sacrifice of the weaker members of its own society. In due course it would be "clear" that the country could get along better without the burden of the crippled, the blind, the aged, the orphaned and any others defined as helpless.

What we need to learn how to do better and more consistently is to translate our concern for pressing, immediate needs into a concern for longer-term problems and their solution. Of course we must be willing to help feed the hungry this year. But we also must be willing to help other peoples become more safely self-sufficient, sharing our technology to enable them to provide themselves with food in good times and bad.

~ 6 ~
PARENTHOOD:
PLEASURES AND
PROBLEMS

What steps can parents take to prepare their children for the future? FEBRUARY 1972

It is generally agreed today that the time in which parents have the greatest influence on their children is while they are under two years of age. During this short time parents can, if they wish, turn off the television, keep the radio out of reach and decide what mass media come into the house. From two on, children begin to receive the impact of the entire world, so the first two years have become crucial. In these years children acquire (or fail to acquire) the basic trust in others and in themselves that only parents and those very close to a child can give. This is what parents and children have to build on in later years.

For the rest, we can recognize the fact that the future is unknown. We can prepare children to take responsibility, to accept limitations and to obey unquestioningly a very limited number of necessary instructions. We can teach children how to form viable habits and how to break them as circumstances change. We can help them to feel at home wherever they go, to meet and come to know members of all races and cultures as human beings like themselves.

We can encourage children to listen to us as we listen to them. In doing this we can help them to form the expectation that within a few years they will have to be our guides in many things that are their birthright but that we came to too late. Teaching with this expectation, parents also keep open their own ability to live on within their children's world.

Recently Vice-Admiral Hyman George Rickover was quoted as saying that members of the Parents and Teachers Association are "an infernal nuisance and ought to stay home and take care of their husbands." Would you comment on this? MAY 1963

Vice-Admiral Rickover has been using his prestige in the defense field to make pronouncements on educational issues. His well-intentioned attempt to reform the schools has been accompanied by attacks on many of the carefully cherished innovations in American schools through which children are taught to be sensitive and responsible human beings as well as scholars. The PTA organizations have been essential in the struggle for more human schools as well as for better schools. Since the PTAs are made up largely of mothers, Admiral Rickover's remarks may be interpreted, among other things, as a desire to keep out of the schools the humanizing tendencies that women—as teachers and as mothers—have brought into them.

Probably nothing has done the PTAs so much good in the last decade as the Admiral's ill-considered attack on one of the most valuable and fundamental institutions of our school system.

PTAs have just one weakness—they are too exclusive. We need a further invention—a GTA, a Grandparents-Teachers Association.

Do you think there are any strong arguments against naming a boy after his father? DECEMBER 1963

Naming a son after his father is, of course, a very old custom in our historic tradition. Many common surnames—Johnson, Anderson, Williamson—are related to an earlier system by which a boy was designated as the son of his father. John Johnson was John, the son of John. Naming a son after his father is associated with pride of lineage and with the expectation that the new child will be an ornament—as his father has been—to the family name. This is even more pronounced in the use of "II" and "III" where there has been a break in the line but the name of an illustrious ancestor is claimed for the child.

For Americans there are objections. We have a society in which one of the most important freedoms is the child's freedom to follow his own bent. Naming a child after his father suggests, however gently and tacitly, however proudly and lovingly, that the child is a junior version of his father. It suggests that when he grows up he will somehow be like his father—a doctor like his father, or a champion tennis player or a good hand at poker. Being named after his father means that his name is not entirely his own; and if Old John and Young John or Big John and Little John are used, "John" is just a category of male in the house. The father seems to be the real John and the younger John a copy.

It is an open question whether children should not be given a choice of names. At birth they might be given several, from which they could later make a choice. If children felt that the names given them by their parents were not fixed for life, they would perhaps be happier with those very names. And as soon as one thinks about giving the *child* a choice, it is clear that it is unfair for the parents to give the father's name to one child, usually the oldest boy, rather than to another. Who knows which child would value it most or want least to be identified with his father? At birth so little is known about a child—not even the color of his hair or eyes is always certain—that names which please the parents' fancy or pride should not be binding on the child forever.

My mother gave none of her daughters a middle name. She objected to the tendency of girls to lose their identities by keeping their given names and dropping their surnames when they married. As a result, my sisters and I had a beautiful time trying on various middle names that fitted our changing sense of ourselves as we grew up.

If you had a son or a daughter who wished to join a group that would be exposed to the kind of dangers that confronted the students going to Mississippi to join the civil rights struggle, what would be your advice? DECEMBER 1964

I would give my daughter or a young male relative the same advice I would give to anyone who planned to volunteer for a dangerous task. There are several questions I would ask. Were they certain why they were making this choice? Were they certain they understood and accepted the responsibilities involved? Were they certain they were not endangering other lives or a cause they believed in just to satisfy a personal desire to undertake a risk or to gain notoriety—or even to seek martyrdom?

I would also ask a student who wanted to go to Mississippi: What have you been doing at home in your own town, your own school or university? What have you done about removing the mote in your own eye before going down to take the beam out of the eyes of your fellow citizens in a state much poorer and much less fortunate than your own? Invasion of another community in the name of a different set of values from those held by its members requires a particular set of self-denying ordinances, for the reforming group is also tempting the group to be reformed to resort to defensive violence.

It is splendid that we have young people who are willing to take risks to accomplish tasks they believe in. It is sad that so much of the "unfinished business of democracy" remains to be done, because we have known for so long what ought to be done. If the citizens of the United States had been sufficiently alert to the educational and economic conditions existing in the old Southeast, much of this particular need for dangerous self-sacrifice could have been averted.

My children seem to be doing five times as much homework as I did when I was in school. Do you feel that such a large amount of work for children is desirable? JUNE 1965

The amount of homework you did is a useful measure only

if the school you attended resembles closely the one your child is in now and if you were taught by similar methods of instruction. It is also necessary to ask whether, at the same age and in the same class, you were equally well, less well or better prepared—whether your position in your class was the same as your child's is now. Whenever a child's school experience is quite unlike that of his parents, it is difficult to compare single aspects of these different total experiences in a meaningful way.

My mother learned Greek as well as Latin in a Chicago public high school, and every student in her class had a microscope. In contrast, I went to a school where the teacher had not managed to finish elementary Latin and no one had a microscope. In that school I had little homework. Later, when we moved, I went to a better high school, and I had a great deal more homework.

Sometimes children must do much more homework in the higher grades because they have been badly taught in the lower grades. And, looking back, many parents will realize that they went to school in a slack period when it was considered more important to carry a child along with the class than to insist on conformance to any standard of excellence. But their children who are going to school in the post-sputnik period are affected by the greater efforts of American schools to raise students' level of achievement. Some children are studying the new mathematics or science courses that seem unbelievably difficult because they are different from anything their parents learned. Many parents are correcting for this feeling by taking short courses in the new approaches to these subjects, so they will understand better what their children are learning.

"Too much homework" can be defined as homework that interferes with a child's health, his interest in learning or his opportunities to respond to the world—to explore the woods, visit a museum on his own, read books not assigned in school, look at and listen to the news of the world and spend time with his friends. But very often the "too much" really is related to time spent fussing about homework, yawning, wandering around the house, twiddling the television knobs, turning over the pages of old magazines, getting another snack from the refrigerator and calling up a friend on the pretext of discussing an assignment.

Where all the children in a school seem to have a lot of homework, this probably marks a change toward less wastefully spent school time and a better education for all children. But where particular children or children in a particular family seem to have far more homework than others, it is useful to look at the family's attitude, at the children's work habits and at the setting in which they work. For example, do the children have to wait to do their homework until the dining-room table is cleared? Do adults continually wander in and out of the room where a child is studying? Do the parents get involved in getting the work done? It is important to realize that the essential purpose of homework is to teach children how to work independently, under their own steam, at their own pace, and to keep at their work until it is done.

In a recent editorial in *Science Magazine*, "Parenthood: Right or Privilege," Garrett Hardin advocated population control through the control of female reproduction. His statement that "women want more children than the community needs" has aroused a great deal of controversy. What is your stand on this? FEBRUARY 1971

As I see it, the issue of how to stabilize the population is only beclouded by arguments about who wants children most—women or men. Those who argue that it is women's desire for children that somehow must be curbed indirectly accuse women of being responsible for the population explosion. One immediate response is an impassioned defense of women. Such arguments are self-defeating because they lead nowhere.

The real answers to the question of effective methods of contraception lie elsewhere. We should begin by asking: Which methods? Used by whom?

Mechanical devices should be made available to those—men or women—who have the most to gain by using them.

Historically in our culture, unmarried males have been more concerned with the prevention of venereal disease. Women have been concerned with the prevention of pregnancy. Males could be relied upon to use mechanical devices to protect their own health; sex in a "safe" situation does not call for such measures. Women, particularly married women who are secure in their relationship with their husbands, have wanted to have safe methods of contraception to space children, complete a family and prevent unwanted pregnancies. Married women, rather than married men, can be relied on to use the mechanical methods available to them.

The problem is a different one when it comes to the use of the newer chemicobiological contraceptives. The pill in its various forms still places the burden of contraception on women. It is the traditional way, but is it really desirable?

We are only beginning to learn what the side effects may be. We shall certainly learn to control the more obvious side effects that may endanger some users. But it would be better, even so, to have a male pill. After conception has taken place, the father's bodily state is not intimately and intricately related to the well-being of the unborn child. But anything that has affected the internal balance of the mother's body may affect the well-being of the child and that child's child in turn. We know now that a child carried by a malnourished or starving mother suffers in its growth and development. We cannot know as yet what effects the use of the pill may have on another generation.

There is no single answer to the question of who best can carry the necessary burden of contraception. We shall arrive at better answers when we begin to think more flexibly about the total problem.

ॐ

Would you say that men have a fathering instinct?
FEBRUARY 1971

No, I would say that men have an innate response to the helplessness of very young human beings. The father who sees a great deal of his child—or any child—during its early weeks of life seems to respond with a deep and continuing tender interest. In contrast, the father who has only superficial contact is likely to develop concern for his child as a person only later, when it is safely on its feet and is beginning to talk.

A new style of fatherhood developed in this country in the years after World War II, particularly among students on crowded college campuses. Living in rooms that were combination studies and nurseries, young men discovered the delight of intimate companionship with very little children.

Later the style was perpetuated by the necessities of suburban living. Overworked and often isolated in a strange community, young mothers desperately needed their husbands' help with the children at night and on weekends. Today, helping to care for young children has become expected behavior for middle-class young men.

Fathering is not an instinct. Whole societies have been able to ignore the potentialities of male tenderness for the very young. But it is a potentiality that can be developed. Prospective fathers who accompany their wives to classes in natural childbirth and baby care, who are present during the babies' birth and who are given a chance from time to time to take fully responsible care of their infants develop a great delight in fatherhood.

The real question is what we will make of the new style that has been in existence now for a generation.

In the 1950s it was the fascination of babies as individuals that captivated fathers, and millions of young men wanted another and still another young infant at home—a desire that contributed to the baby boom.

But care for an individual child's development and delight in companionship can also carry over into a new, responsible concern for that child's—and other children's—growing up. What we urgently need now is the development of a style in which men, beginning as parents, can move with children toward the discovery of new cross-generation relations. A beginning has been made by the young men who have become teachers of young children. But it is only a beginning.

More and more unmarried women are considering the option of having children and raising them in fatherless homes. How do you feel about this? NOVEMBER 1977

The idea that every woman has an inherent right to have a child, regardless of other considerations, recurs in every upsurge of feminism.

I do not consider this a viable option. But at the same time, any woman who marries may face the need to raise her children alone. There are now in our own country some 9 million single-parent families; the household head in almost all of them is a woman. Certainly, today a woman who chooses to have a child must be prepared to take on the whole task; she must be competent and able to earn a living for herself and her child. But surely this is not something to choose.

It does not seem reasonable to me to choose *deliberately* to deprive one's children of a father. The various devices we are trying to elaborate—communes, organizations like Parents Without Partners and single-parent homes—are necessary, but very poor substitutes for two adults who share fully in caring for and loving their children. In a warm, lively community where friends and neighbors are closely related to one another and share their concerns, it is often possible to find a surrogate parent for the girl or boy who is growing up in a single-parent family. But this takes a great deal of time and effort in our kind of world.

Children—girls *and* boys—need to know what it is like to be a woman and to be a man and to experience realistically the kind of relationship that grows between a woman and a man who live together every day and share their parenthood. And I believe that we should come to recognize the fact that the bond established through parenting is one that cannot be legislated away, whatever may be the fate of a particular marriage. Children have a right to their two parents and it is our responsibility, as women—and as men too—to ensure that children's needs are met.

**Are female role models essential in the rearing of profes-
sional women, or is it enough for both parents to treat the
female child as a person?** AUGUST 1975

I would say that successful adaptation is much easier for
both girls and boys who have role models of their own sex in
whatever fields they choose to enter.

Being treated with respect, regardless of sex, is of course a
great help. But sex membership is so conspicuous that it is
difficult to prevent children from associating roles and occupations with men—or women—if they see only members of
one sex performing a role or engaging in an occupation. It is
hard enough for children reared in one kind of family to acquire and live out quite different occupational identities—to
value book learning rather than the skills involved in sports
or to value musical performance rather than book learning. If
one adds to this the expectation that only members of one sex
perform a particular role, it is even less likely that members
of either sex can live out an unfamiliar role without conflict.

We have reason to believe, from studies of other societies,
that strict sex typing of any career that involves special
talents—the idea that ballet dancers are women or effeminate
men, or that airplane pilots are men or masculine women—
may be a potent source of disturbance in sex identity.

Equally difficult may be the situation of a daughter whose
mind is like her father's or a son who inherits his mother's
talent. Where role models other than the parents are not
available to such children while they are growing up, they
may be faced with the choice of denying their special ability
or denying their sex membership. In either case they are
damaged as persons.

I had my father's mind, but he had his mother's mind. Fortunately, his mother lived with us and so I early realized that
intellectual abilities of the kind I shared with my father and
grandmother were not sex-linked.

Learning about a variety of roles and finding role models
for a girl or a boy means knowing a lot of different kinds of
people—men and women—at home, in school and in the

community. It certainly isn't easy always to match up a budding with a mature talent, but parents and teachers can help children to meet and enjoy both men and women in many occupations—and this in itself is a help.

ॐ

Do children owe their parents anything in the way of concern and consideration—to say nothing of understanding that the parents need to feel the children care about them? JULY 1974

We are moving away from the belief that the mere existence of a biological relationship permits anyone to have an absolute and unqualified claim on the love and concern of another person.

It is reasonable to demand that individuals, whether children or adults, should behave responsibly and considerately toward the people with whom they live or with whom they are associated. I believe this expectation is slowly coming to replace the idea that one owes a certain kind of behavior to relatives simply because they are relatives. Particularly the idea that children are indebted to their parents and must show gratitude is not easily tolerated by young people who value greater spontaneity in expressing feeling.

We can bring up our children to be courteous and considerate of others. By our own attentiveness we can help them learn to be attentive to the needs, the fears and the anxieties of others. By our efforts to understand the world our children are growing up in we can help them realize that their parents grew up in a different world and can be deeply hurt by inappropriate behavior. We can bring up children with a willingness to listen to their elders as a way of knowing and understanding them better. But parents can succeed in this only if they do not exercise capricious, trivial and irksome authority in the name of parenthood.

At the same time I do not feel it is a contradiction to ask oneself: Are there ways in which I may please—or can hurt—someone just because I am a daughter or a sister or a niece? Attentiveness to others means a concern for their feelings. Forgetting a birthday or refusing to take part in a family

171

celebration may have nothing to do with my feelings as an individual, but for someone who responds primarily as a relative, such behavior may be a bitter blow.

The small formalities can be much more of a help than a hindrance in relationships that matter. If one's parents believe there are certain things a child should do, how easy it is to please them just by doing those things! We are moving into a world in which so much sincerity and spontaneity is demanded of everyone that many people feel they can never meet or reciprocate the love someone else bears them. Then, how easy it is to make a long-distance telephone call on Mother's Day, just because it is Mother's Day and your mother is your mother!

I remember learning very early that you couldn't possibly like—let alone love—all your relatives, but you could accord them a certain amount of warmth because, after all, they were aunts or uncles or cousins. And I believe parents can learn to treat children, and children can learn to treat parents, as persons.

ટ✦

As an anthropologist as well as a mother and a grandmother, what would you say are the most valuable qualities a mother can develop in order to help children toward maturity?
JULY 1974

In every society I know of, mothers need to develop particular qualities to help their children grow up to become mature and effective members of society. Looking at the world in which we live today, it seems to me that these are some of the capacities it is valuable for a mother to have:

To treat each child as an individual person; to realize that children are not adjuncts of their parents, but are individuals in their own right.

To set a child's feet on her own path and allow her to follow it; yet to be there when that path seems hard to follow.

To be willing to listen, and listen, and listen.

To be brave enough to show disapproval when one feels that

something is wrong, even though by doing so one may be risking rejection by the child.

To stand up for one's own beliefs and so make one's respect for a child worth having and keeping.

ও 7 ছ
RELIGION

Are you in favor of amending the Constitution to permit prayer in the public schools? AUGUST 1964

No. The separation of church and state is a necessary, basic principle for a democratic society whose members belong to many different religious groups or have no formal religious affiliation.

But we can, if we wish, preserve a sense of the importance of religion and make it possible for each child who wants to pray in school to do so without infringing on the Constitution. We already have the national custom of a short period of silence on Veterans Day. A similar period of silence could be incorporated into our school system as a way of beginning every day and every public ceremony. Instead of increasing the religious indifferentism that can develop when children have to repeat perfunctory or meaningless prayers far from their own faith, each child would in this way be given a sense of reverence for religious observances. And since each child would fill the silence according to the faith of his parents, this would give all parents the opportunity to teach their own faith. Every child, confronted by a period of solemn silence, would come face to face with the fact of prayer. Parents who did not believe in formal prayer would have to set forth their reasons to their children. But parents whose attitudes toward prayer were merely casual or negligent might be moved to question, to look for a book of prayers—or to seek advice.

No matter how divergent the religious beliefs represented in our schools, all could be included within the shelter of a shared and reverent silence.

Do you believe in God? MAY 1963
Yes.

What advice would you give to parents who are agnostic but want their children to have the best possible spiritual and educational background from which to make their own decisions about religion? MARCH 1966

I think parents should be very sure that they really *do* wish their children to make their own decisions about religion. Before they make plans, therefore, parents with agnostic beliefs should ask themselves several questions.

Would both parents be willing to have their child develop an interest in an unfamiliar religion like Buddhism, or would they want him to confine his explorations to religions within our own traditions? And among the more familiar religious groups would they try to limit their child to the so-called liberal denominations? Would they be willing to accept exacting and perhaps unfamiliar religious practices, such as fasting or prayers at meals, if the child asked for them? Would they be able to listen patiently to a variety of somewhat extreme arguments? A ten-year-old, whether he is quoting from a pamphlet on "self-contradictions in the Bible" or from a tract on "evidence for the original creation of Man," can be very trying for someone who does not share the viewpoint being argued. These are serious questions, and parents need to work out answers to them before they embark on any course that will involve the child's own later decision.

Once parents have defined the perimeter of their own tolerance, they must plan their child's religious education with as much care, thought and attention as they give to his intellectual education. If they have devout friends whom they respect for their convictions, they can ask these friends to take their child with them—or with their children—on religious occasions. In this company the child may begin to experience what religious participation means. Faith is a matter

176

of feeling, and only through contact with those who *have* faith can its nature be conveyed to young children. But this will work only if those devout friends are respected—not only for their other attainments but also for their religious beliefs and practices. Sending a child to Sunday school with the children of "some of our simpler neighbors" or letting a child attend church with a servant who is tacitly regarded as less educated automatically categorizes religion as the concern of "less-educated people." Conversely, religions that do not have a place for every kind of human being—for people of both sexes, of all ages and races, of all degrees of intelligence and all levels of civilization—are not really religions but sects. And there is a great difference, for the child, between a sectarian experience and the full experience of religious participation.

A child without religious experience shared with trusted persons who are religious may grow to adulthood either incapable of religious faith or uncritically susceptible to intemperate religious appeals. Agnostic parents who wish their children to share in the wholeness of human experience, including religious experience, will find ways of helping them to avoid both these incapacitating alternatives.

During an interview with New York newspaper reporters, Harry Truman said that he did not believe in racial intermarriage and that it ran counter to the teachings of the Bible. What is your feeling about this? FEBRUARY 1964

I myself have not heard this statement attributed to Mr. Truman, but it is my understanding that the Bible neither condemns nor approves of "interracial" marriage as we use that word today. In the Old Testament there are instances of objections to marriage with members of other tribes. In the New Testament ancient tribal laws of exclusiveness and revenge are replaced by admonitions to include all people within a circle of protectiveness and love.

While I do not believe that the only appropriate way of solving the "race problem" is by the intermingling and blending of all stocks and physical types (differences, after all, are valuable), I do look forward to the day when every human being will be free to marry as he or she pleases, and when all the peoples of the world, of whatever shade of complexion and complexity of ancestry, will be treated on their merits as human beings. Most individuals, most of the time, will choose as marriage partners people who resemble their own parents and brothers or sisters—on whom their earliest notions of possible mates are based. But members of each racial group will be proud of their own appearance and will value equally the pride that others also feel.

It is often suggested that what ails America is that our people have forgotten about God and religion. Are there correlations between religious belief and ethical standards?
FEBRUARY 1971

The association of customary morality and transitory moral standards with religious belief almost always has negative effects. It may produce exemplary behavior in the members of a particular religious group coupled with hostility to all those outside the group. Very often people who make the kind of comment you speak of are talking about morals, not about ethics.

However, all the great religions of the world are concerned with ethical standards. Many primitive religions and local cults are not. Over time there has been considerable variation in the extent to which any one of the great religions has expressed concern for ethical issues in contrast to strictly religious ones. At some periods an established religion may become stereotyped and formal in carrying out its tasks, and its members may give only lip service to spiritual and ethical problems. This happened in many American churches in their treatment of race issues.

At other times the men leading a new, vigorous religious movement—such as the Reformation or, today, the ecumenical movement—are deeply concerned with problems of ethics, and attempt to revitalize men's relationship to God by improving their relations with their fellow men.

Sometimes a religion may emphasize negative goodness. For example, there is the Christian belief in hell. The intention to abstain from sin for fear of suffering the pangs of hell may prevent men from committing unethical acts. But only in the most negative sense can this be regarded as "good" behavior. It is an open question whether any behavior based on fear of eternal punishment can be regarded as ethical or should be regarded as merely cowardly.

In contrast, the sense of obligation to all humankind—which arises from the belief that all human beings were created by God, that *all* are related as brothers and sisters and as the children of God—can give a very strong impetus to ethical decisions and positively motivated behavior.

Do you believe that in fifty years' time organized religion, the Church as an institution, will still be with us? If so, in what form? What influence will it have? APRIL 1971
The institutions of organized religions, like the formal institutions of government, tend to persist once they have been invented. This is true even though their formal structures may be modified and their aims may change over time.

In the United States in the 1920s it was predicted that the rural church was finished and that we would build very few new churches anywhere. Instead, in the 1950s new churches sprang up all over the country—in rural areas as well as in small towns, in the suburbs and in cities.

In the 1930s it was predicted that once the descendants of immigrants moved out of their urban enclaves and scattered in the suburbs, their religious affiliations—which had been part of their ethnic identity as Roman Catholics from Italy, Protestants from Czechoslovakia, Jews from Eastern Europe, and so on—would weaken. This did not happen either. Instead, in the vast new suburbs membership in church and temple provided newcomers with a much-needed basis for finding congenial friends and a Scout troop or a dancing class for the children.

In the same years migrants who came into the cities from the countryside and, for example, from Puerto Rico and the West Indies, many of whom were too poor to build new buildings, found temporary shelter in storefront churches.

For many years the principal emphasis appeared to be on traditional and conventional religious forms and on the social rewards of group affiliation. But at the same time there was a ground swell of religious concern, a deepening sense of the importance of religious experience, a growing insistence on asking new questions about old problems. In the 1960s this culminated in Vatican II, the beginning of the ecumenical movement, the search for new liturgical forms, the development of the underground church movement and the very active involvement of religious groups in contemporary social problems.

There has been a tremendous shake-up within the Roman Catholic Church as nuns have donned new, more modern habits as one way of relating themselves to the modern world and as priests who entered the ministry without doubt have re-examined their reasons for being there. Protestant churches that had had difficulty in recruiting for their seminaries suddenly were receiving new applicants at the very time when some of the richest patrons of the churches were withdrawing their support. In the eyes of these donors, the views of the young enthusiasts who were working for civil rights or migrant workers, for example, appeared too radical. Churches are having to learn to support their new activities in new ways.

The religious world is astir. There are new litanies, new ceremonies, all-night vigils and marathon prayer meetings, encounter groups and groups gathered for sensitivity training. Congregations are asking how they can open up their buildings, idle so much of the time, by locating in them crisis clinics and suicide services, Head Start classes and libraries. One library I visited, in the very forward-looking temple of the Congregation Solel, in Highland Park, Illinois, has opened its doors to all comers and allows readers to keep books as long as they need them.

No one can say now just what the religious institutions of the future will be like. But I do not doubt that the ferment that is transforming our thinking and feeling about traditional religion will result in new forms through which like-minded people can share common rituals and precious experience.

Does the recent popularity of fundamentalist forms of religion indicate that society in general is becoming more conservative? JULY 1974

No, I do not think so.

A great many people who think of themselves as liberals associate liberalism with religious indifference. It has been very strange to observe parents who have rather boasted that their adolescent children have taken up Zen or have gone off to India to find a guru, but who have been horrified when instead their children have begun to take Christianity or Judaism very seriously.

Contemporary liberals in our country have tended to disavow any serious concern with religion except as a framework for the fight for social justice and the rights of minorities and the disadvantaged. Complementary to this is the stance of those who, within the framework of a rather old-fashioned, literal approach to religion, oppose everything that liberals stand for and see Communists wherever they look. But these two extreme positions are simply accidents of the way we have treated religion in our culture.

Elsewhere the situation is quite different. Looking at several contemporary Catholic countries, for example, one finds that in one country the devout are very conservative and in another they are radical revolutionaries. Or in the same country the devout may include both radicals and conservatives. In some parts of the world today Christians are adopting a Marxist philosophy, while in other parts Communists are taking a new interest in Christianity. Many of these associations between religion and social viewpoint are fortuitous.

However, there is a certain absolute incompatibility between irresponsible affluence and the confession of any serious religious faith. For all the great religions of the world have emphasized that each believer has a responsibility for his brothers—and sisters. And in a world in which more than half the population are often hungry and a very large proportion live constantly on the edge of starvation, the quality and effectiveness of both liberalism and religious faith, whatever their association, is an open question.

~ 8 ~
OUR QUIRKS AND CROTCHETS

Americans seem to be even more fascinated by the British royal family than the British themselves. What do you think is the reason for this? MAY 1964

For the British mass audience the British royal family is *the* family. But for a long time, until the Kennedy family entered the White House, the American people as a whole did not have one special family on whose lives they could focus interest and attention. The private lives of film stars, athletic heroes and even men we have called "tycoons of industry" are not a very satisfactory substitute.

In American eyes, regardless of the country from which our ancestors have come, the king and queen of England are *the* king and *the* queen, to be enjoyed, resented, admired or repudiated. The British royal family has gratified both our search for a family to set and carry out a style of family living and our affection for a kind of fairy-tale pageantry and royal presence. Furthermore, in the British royal family there are always royal *children*. In contrast, the presence of young children in the White House is a rarity.

Today in Britain it is fashionable for intellectuals to play down the ceremonial and conspicuous aspects of royalty, but we Americans can enjoy royalty without taking responsibility for either praise or attack.

~

What annoys you most about traveling? JULY 1964

Airports without carts for moving heavy luggage, babies, coats and so on. When you complain to an airline their employees say: "We do so agree, but it's really the fault of the city of Los Angeles (or Chicago or New York). . . ."

Do you share many people's indignation about the telephone company's new system of substituting numbers for letters in telephone exchanges? SEPTEMBER 1964

My main feeling is that the telephone company has missed the boat in its public relations. If the emphasis had been laid on how much easier it was going to be to dial numbers than to have to get the operator for long-distance calls, we would have had less trouble. But instead of telling us that we have a better, more workable system than one in which people had to say A for Adam, B for Boston, P for Peter, T for Thomas— taking up endless time and trouble—somehow the other side of the picture has been allowed to intrude. People worry because they can't remember that many *numbers* and are inconvenienced by having to look up area codes, instead of realizing the freedom and accuracy that a number system gives. And it would have been so easy for the telephone companies to get out a gadget—a dial, perhaps—that would quickly convert the old letters to numbers and also indicate the code for any area. They could have been made of all colors and all materials, plain and tweedy for men, dainty for women, sturdy for children, and the whole country would have enjoyed it, the way we always enjoy something new if it is presented properly.

What opinion do you have about the theory that Shakespeare was not the real author of the works attributed to him? NOVEMBER 1964

I think theories of this kind go back to the fantasy world of early childhood, in which children like to claim that their parents are not their "real" parents—a kind of denial that those who seem to be so great and powerful really are great and powerful. Many people can live through this childlike and essentially harmless theme by proving that the great man was not the author—it was someone else instead. An over-preoccupation with the parent rather than the self (the child he produced) can lead to this kind of fantasy.

How do you explain the almost fanatical interest so many American men have in baseball? NOVEMBER 1964

In every society it is important for boys and girls to learn to feel that they are members of their own sex group. Where daily occupations are clearly and sharply divided—where the men fish and the women spin, where men plow and sow and women weed and gather in the harvest, where men work in the factory and women stay at home—there is less need for symbolic ways of establishing and expressing sex differences. But where there is a great deal of overlap in the real activities concerned with making a living, there is a greater need for men—and women—to have other ways of asserting their membership in their own sex group.

Games are a favorite way for boys and men to create a world of their own, a world from which girls—and, later, women—can be excluded. In American society, women are free to take jobs and have careers and earn money, to drive cars, to wear slacks, to go anywhere and everywhere, and men no longer feel demeaned by helping with the kinds of household chores that once constituted women's daily work. In this situation, where it is difficult for children to grasp the important differences between the life-style of a man and that of a woman, symbols become more important.

Baseball is to American boys what dressing and self-adornment are to American girls. Both are games, carried far beyond the necessities of life. Spending hours doing her hair, putting it in rollers and sitting under a mechanical dryer convinces the teen-aged girl that she is indeed a girl. Spending endless hours playing baseball, talking about baseball, reading about baseball, watching baseball and memorizing items about baseball is one way for American boys to convince themselves that they are boys.

Have you ever had your horoscope done? Was it helpful or accurate in anyway? JANUARY 1965

When I was a child I learned the horoscope rhymes about birth on a day of the week or in a given month. I was "Monday's child"—said to be "fair of face"—and it seemed to me that the prediction for some other day would have been more accurate. Then I learned: "December's child shall live to bless/The turquoise that ensures success." This seemed to me a good fortune to have.

Later we had as friends a family who always talked in terms of horoscopes. The father was a mathematician and an instrument maker. A typical comment would be: "Oh, she's a Leo person; Father wouldn't like her!" Or someone would explain: "But, you see, he's Aries . . ." I was impressed then with the way a whole constellation of personality traits could be expressed in these astrological terms and how they became a language in which people could think about their own and other people's lives.

I believe that all predictions made with authority are likely to affect the lives of those about whom they are made. When I was told that in addition to being December's child I belonged to Sagittarius, whose sign was the archer who could "run as far as anyone and shoot a little bit farther," this gave me, I think, a sense of confidence. And when I was told that Sagittarians had just had three good years and had three bad years coming up, this undoubtedly made me contrast more sharply those "good" and "bad" years.

Whether there is anything further than this in horoscopes, we do not know. The scientific attitude is always to keep an open mind.

Why do you think people are so universally fascinated with horror stories, ghost stories, etc.; in other words, why do people like to have their hair stand on end? MARCH 1965

The capacity to live out in imagination experiences one has

never had is a very important human characteristic through which all of life may be greatly enriched. For however humdrum the events of one's own life may be, it is possible to be drawn imaginatively into an enormous range of experiences—including those that inspire terror. But terror has a very different quality for adults and children. All children at some time experience fear of loss and abandonment, fear of physical suffering, fear of the dark, fear of water and fire and fear of the strange and the unknown; if they are to grow up, they must somehow learn to master these fears.

In old, stable societies there were standardized ways for children to learn how to deal with their fears. They played games in which pursuit and capture were enacted and re-enacted, and they listened to tales in which the same themes and plots were endlessly repeated. Tales about people who lived after their heads had been cut off, tales about animated body parts, tales about sticks and stones that had a life of their own, tales about giants and monsters, tales about magical animals—any of these might be part of a folklore that was shared by children and adults alike.

Stories like these, told and retold by generations of the same people, acquire a very definite style, and the listening children learned to expect the climax—learned who would die and who would be saved; how the youngest brother would certainly triumph where all the older brothers failed; and how the old witch, in furious pursuit of her fleeing daughter and her lover, would in the end be trapped and defeated. Each time a story was told, children could respond to the terror and still feel reassured that safety and victory were possible. The thrill of danger was tamed without being removed. The presence of the elders, men and women who had grown up with the stories and knew their outcome, calmed the children as they waited, tingling with excitement and fear, for the climax.

Today we do not have a single stock of old tales from which to draw—the stories our children read come from all around the world. The horrors described in modern stories may be related to aspects of the natural world (tidal waves or Arctic blizzards) or to forms of social life (the arbitrary powers of

187

kings or rajas or caliphs) that are wholly unfamiliar to the adults who tell the stories and the children who hear them— and no one can be certain of the outcome. In modern writing, the emphasis in any story is upon the inventiveness of the individual author. Each author can draw on his own individual fears—the remembered horrors of his own childhood, the fantasies related to his own experience and the possibilities for terror inherent in the events of his time.

For these reasons our modern horror stories are less close to common, shared experience; they combine the thrill of fear that is not quite real and a shuddering picture of the unusual and the unexperienced. Mild, quiet men can read every night about hairbreadth chases and escapes; strong, self-reliant women can experience vicariously the terrors of being threatened and overpowered. But even in more highly individualized tales the fundamental reassuring difference between story and reality remains. It is only a story—none of the characters is real; the grisly, ghostly steps are an invention—and the author, after all, not only knows the end but also has made up the plot. So the modern reader or the listener too can experience fear and conquer terror again and again.

In the end, however, these fears, which are less closely related to shared experience, lose their punch. A stronger dose of horror is needed to produce the old thrill of horror and the triumphant sense of danger overcome. Today especially, with mass communications, fashions in plot and suspense and horror themes spread rapidly, and the demand for new and more formidable horrors is strongly developed. For those who merely want to experience a familiar fear and know the joy and relief of conquering it, this continual change of plot is disconcerting. But for those who need continual stimulation to live out their fears of themselves and others, the escalating horrors have effects like those of larger and larger doses of addictive drugs.

Do you think the trend toward long hair and bright-colored clothes for young men is ominous? OCTOBER 1966

No, I think it is interesting. For well over a century, Western societies have insisted that the only correct way for men and boys to appear was with shorn hair and drab dress. In the same period men have used jewels and colorful materials lavishly in the adornment of women; they have used elaborate decoration in their homes and in such public buildings as theaters, opera houses, hotels and gambling casinos. But the mark of the modern, civilized man was his somber dress. Anything else was considered outlandish and exotic, even barbarian. Rajas in European capitals donned business suits, and peasants exchanged their colorful garments for dark workclothes when they moved into cities.

Yet this retreat from color and fine ornament, a characteristic of male dress in past societies, has never been quite complete. Occasionally the men who were style-setters created some special form of adornment for males, like the brocade vest of the Edwardian dandy or the shimmering black-and-white silhouette of the man in full evening dress. And monarchs and prelates, officers in dress uniform and lord mayors, hunters and jockeys, members of mens' societies like the Shriners, and even academics in their robes, still appear in elaborate and brilliant-colored garments and headdresses. We only put them out of mind by saying that these are the costumes of men who are acting out old, historic roles.

It is difficult for us to recall that short hair and dark, unadorned clothing for men in some periods of history identified the rebel and the dissenter. Cromwell's Roundheads cropped their hair and discarded ornamented dress to distinguish themselves from the loyal partisans of the Stuart kings. Revolutionaries in France put on dark clothes to cast derision on the irresponsible fripperies of the Royalist courtiers in the dying days of the French court. Utopians in their many versions adopted dark, plain clothes to set themselves still further apart from other men in ordinary American communities.

And now, since World War II, there has been a gradual revo-

189

lution in male dress. Grown men have adopted color for their leisure hours, and we can no longer look at a high school or a college crowd and calculate the proportion of boys to girls by watching the color pattern, dark and bright. The interesting thing is that boys and girls alike, not in any one country but all over the Western world, are experimenting with extravagant play on hair styles, dress and physical adornment of different kinds, now emphasizing the extreme contrast of beards with beehive hairdos and now merging their male and female identities in twinlike styles. With our great affluence, more money is available to serve the rapidly shifting demands of fashion; and with rapid world-wide communication, young people on distant continents can proclaim their closeness to one another and their remoteness from their elders.

We are experiencing rapid social change everywhere. Older people sometimes fix their attention upon just one small aspect of change, like long hair or bright clothes. They miss the synchronization of changing detail which announces, the world around, that a whole generation is in search of a new identity.

Can you explain the enormous fascination that horses seem to have for young girls—in the United States, at least?
MAY 1977

In thinking about the fascination that horses and riding have for some young girls, there are several things to keep in mind. Throughout human history the strongest and swiftest means of transportation have belonged to men, and usually as larger and faster beasts of burden and travel were domesticated, the slower and smaller ones were relegated to women. Where men rode and drove camels, women tended the "little stock" of sheep and goats; in some parts of the world where men rode spirited horses, women rode donkeys. In Victorian England where the well-to-do prized handsome, thoroughbred horses, ladies were permitted to drive pony carts. When automobiles were invented they were at first driven only by men, and horses, in the more built-up parts of the country, became an interest of women, especially adolescent girls.

Enid Bagnold's novel *National Velvet* told the story of a girl who won England's Grand National Steeplechase, financed by the money her mother had won as a Channel swimmer. It was a story dramatizing the possibilities of horse racing for girls.

In fact, boys were once equally—or even more passionately—fascinated by horses. But boys abandoned horses for cars—big cars, small cars, old cars, racing cars, rebuilt cars; every boy, almost as soon as he can hold anything in his hand, is given models of cars to play with. Even today, in spite of the changed attitudes that have accompanied the Women's Liberation Movement, relatively few girls are given miniature cars as suitable toys.

If one discounts the history of horsemanship in the wider world, it might appear that horses have a special sex-linked fascination for girls. In fact, girls are drawn into the horse cult through other girls, and riding and everything that goes with the cult can become the focus of adolescent clique loyalty. Some girls are more susceptible to a horse fad than others— for example, the only girl in a family of boys, or the girl who is her father's favorite or, sometimes, city girls who have little chance to live an outdoor life.

Riding a horse can give a girl a sense of mastery that is very appealing at times to one who has grown up in a society in which dominance is frowned upon in a woman. Riding a horse also can enhance a young girl's sense of independence and individuality as, seated in the saddle, she is raised above the common level of the ground.

Some girls who have a passion for horses in adolescence stay with it. They become horse breeders and trainers and jockeys, or try for the Olympics or ride show horses professionally. And they assert their independence by doing all these things without the help of men. More often, however, the attachment of a girl to her horse crumbles in the face of new demands on her time and energy. Her school or her parents insist that she personally must groom and feed the horse as well as exercise it daily. Then as new interests take

191

up more time the charm is broken. She parts with her horse and gives away her spurs and riding crop, as earlier she gave away toys, to a younger child.

Could a place be made for a jester in the executive branch of our government? Do you think such a person would be of any use to us? AUGUST 1977

Historically the role of the court jester was to say to a sovereign things that no one else dared to say. Known as a "fool," he was exempt from the kinds of penalties that were too likely to be the lot of ordinary men who dared to criticize a sovereign invested with great and arbitrary powers.

I don't think a jester could be incorporated into our system of government. But jesters have their modern descendants who write or talk or frolic on the stage or on television. People like columnists Russell Baker and Art Buchwald or TV personality Johnny Carson can make very pointed comments which, if they were not set within a humorous frame, would get them into trouble not only with presidents and cabinet members, members of congress and the judiciary, governors and mayors, but also with their fellow citizens who would often feel they had "gone too far." And just how far a critic *can* go depends on how distant people feel he is from the ordinary requirements of good manners and appropriate behavior—and on whether his material contributes to hate rather than to cathartic laughter.

In our society, jesters of many kinds probe our own feelings about the world we live in. As in the past the sovereign felt safe, whatever the jester said, because of his unchallenged power, so do we today feel safe because we believe we are merely the enjoying audience, not—what we are, in fact—the principal object of our jesters' wit.

You have been quoted as saying that you like to have Southern girls work for you because they have such good manners

and never forget they are women. Do you think Northern women have less good manners? DECEMBER 1963

Northerners have a different kind of manners from Southerners. A Northern girl with good manners treats everyone much alike—says thank you and please and avoids being abrupt and impertinent. But Southern children are reared to keep in mind the special attributes of everyone they speak to. When they address another person, their voices show respect for age and acknowledge the sex of that person. A man speaking to a two-year-old girl accords her a kind of respect as he says, "I'm going to walk with Miss Alice," and bends down to take her hand. A woman who drops her handkerchief waits, as a matter of course, for a five-year-old boy to pick it up for her.

Northern courtesy, on the other hand, demands that one ignore particular attributes and treat men and women, adults and children and members of all classes with exactly the same tone of voice. Old-fashioned manners in the Northeast include some respect for age. But elsewhere in the country, except in those areas influenced by the Southeast, the current style is to show respect for other people by ignoring whatever may be special about them—addressing graybeards by their first name and slapping doormen on the back.

In my office it is necessary to establish relationships over the telephone at great distances in space with many kinds of people—other Americans, English people, Continental Europeans, Africans and Asians. In this situation the hail-fellow-well-met voice is often inappropriate, and Southerners automatically make easier adjustments. I enjoy having in my office at least one Southerner who in addition to thinking that race is irrelevant also knows how to be genuinely courteous to members of races and cultures different from her own.

~२ 9 ~

EDUCATION

In your opinion, what are the characteristics of a good teacher? SEPTEMBER 1972

In our complex civilization, teaching draws on an immense diversity of talents and skills. The teacher who can hold the attention of active and inquiring ten-year-olds is a very different kind of person from the teacher who opens the world for little children, or the teacher who can carry gifted students through the known to the uncertainties of our newest thinking in a specialized field, or the teacher who can give courage and a renewed sense of purpose to the dropouts and those who have been branded as failures.

Nevertheless, I believe all good teachers have some characteristics in common. The most extraordinary thing about a really good teacher is that he or she transcends accepted educational methods. Such methods are designed to help average teachers approximate the performance of good teachers.

I think, too, that good teachers want their pupils, at whatever stage, to learn what it is their task to teach. They are willing to put up with those who are brighter than they are—and there will be some; they are also patient with those who are slower. Their enjoyment of teaching affects those who are taught, so that they feel some *positive* emotion—joy, delight, achievement, relief—when they learn what their teachers teach.

Good teachers are glad when a term begins and a little sad when it ends. They remember some of their students for many years, and their students remember them. They never make assumptions about what their pupils know; they take the trouble to find out, and they are tireless in finding new ways of repeating where repetition is necessary. In a sense, good teachers always suffer fools gladly.

Do you agree with Dr. James B. Conant that the standards in our teachers colleges are deplorably low? MAY 1964

I agree that we have treated the whole profession of teaching badly, and a profession so treated deteriorates and becomes destructively self-protective. Because of our contempt for teaching, teachers colleges have recruited fewer good students and more poor ones, and teaching in a teachers college, whatever its eminence, has become a lower-status activity than teaching in a liberal arts college. And teachers colleges have suffered also from the defensive maneuvers of the teachers whose emphasis on methods, weighing down the curriculum, was designed to keep out of the profession those who insisted on the importance of content alone.

But I do not agree that we will solve the problem by our current attempts to resolve these difficulties. We will change but not improve the situation by building national curriculums without consulting the teachers themselves, by turning teachers colleges into liberal arts colleges in which there is no interest in the special needs and problems and potentialities of teachers, or by insisting that learning to teach is of no real importance. If we are not careful we shall throw the baby out with the bathwater–as we have done so often.

How do you feel about school boycotts as a way of solving school integration problems in Northern cities? JULY 1964

Boycotts do not solve problems. They encourage those who are trying to get problems solved, and they put pressure on those who have the power–but not always the inclination–to solve them. Americans seldom act until they feel they are facing a crisis in which action is imperative. Many of the schools in Northern cities are a disgrace, not only because they reflect other parts of a disgraceful pattern–segregated, substandard housing; poverty; poor policing; lack of recreation; graft and lack of representation–but also because they provide so little leadership and are given so little support in the effort to alter these conditions.

If the citizens of American cities continue to refuse to take action until fire or mass disaster or threats of terrible violence focus their attention, we shall continue to have more troubles, of which peaceful, well-organized boycotts may be the least. Where the citizens and elected officials of cities have abdicated their responsibility, protest takes the place of planning–and everyone suffers.

Hasn't the need for a college education been overemphasized? Aren't too many people going to college—people who do not have the will or the aptitude for it? JULY 1964

No, to the first question. To live and work in an increasingly complex world and to understand its complexities, people need more and more education not only in their teens but throughout life.

Instead of the second question, there are other questions it would be more useful to ask. Are colleges giving the kinds of education that are needed? Should students go to college immediately after high school? Should college be available primarily to those whose parents can pay for it and to young people who work so hard that they only half benefit from their studies? Or should all those who can benefit by studying be paid while they learn?

I have always been disturbed by our practice in grade schools of idealizing figures in American history (George Washington

and the cherry tree, Abraham Lincoln returning a penny, etc.). Wouldn't it be better to give children a more realistic picture of these great men? JUNE 1965

The basic trouble is not the idealization of historical figures but the fact that adults feel the idealization to be false. Stories about heroism and virtue and cautionary tales about the consequences of some failure to obey, tell the truth, play fair or respect the rights of others are a necessary part of children's education.

I feel that stripped of such stories, my childhood would have been less rich. I should not like to have missed the story of the boy who stopped the hole in the dike with his finger, or the story of the old man who said, "I do not object to my ears being cut off, but I do object to their being cut off against the laws of England," or the last words attributed to Nathan Hale, "I only regret that I have but one life to lose for my country."

But sometimes an old story is told too often. Telling a story over and over until it has lost its meaning and is reduced to empty moralizing may in the end lead children to question both morality and the greatness of all great men. We need crisp, clear stories, enlivened by the storyteller's art, about present-day heroes as well as heroes of the past. Telling stories only about the Founding Fathers and Presidents who lived long ago separates children from their own world, the world of today and tomorrow. Understanding of the courage with which Franklin D. Roosevelt and John F. Kennedy fought long battles with pain and of the intrepidity of astronaut John Glenn can help children extend their sense of realism to men of other times as well. In a world in which we are creating new values, each generation needs to discover its own heroes and its own sources and forms of idealization.

In recent years there has been a great deal of psychological testing of school children. Many parents feel that inquiries into their children's personalities constitute an invasion of privacy. What is your attitude toward this question? NOVEMBER 1965

Greater awareness of the reasons for giving children psychological tests should help to clear up the problem. And one must ask whose privacy parents believe is being invaded.

There are, in fact, many kinds of psychological tests, and parents sometimes mix them up. One group of tests can help an experienced person form a better judgment about a child's abilities and present achievement than is possible on the basis of the child's school performance alone. Such tests indicate, for example, whether a child can do better than he is doing or whether he is struggling along in a class that is as yet too hard for him. Properly used, these tests can prevent a child from becoming discouraged and unsure because he is asked to work above his ability or from becoming bored and cynical because he is allowed to work far below his ability. Of course, when a child is moved to a different class because test results have suggested that he will be better off in a faster or a slower group, other people will know about the change. When this happens, some parents may feel exposed because other people find out what is usually well-known in any small community—that some children are quicker to learn than others and some just don't take to schoolwork. Tests are intended primarily to help children and their parents. But parents who have a possessive attitude toward their children's abilities may lose sight of this in their resentment against anything that may expose them, as they see it, through their children.

A second category of tests is known technically as projective tests. In these tests a person is asked to project his whole personality into partly structured materials, such as ink blots, or vague, ambiguous pictures or unfinished stories. Using projective materials, an experienced person can find out a great deal (though often not nearly as much as may be needed) about a child's hopes and fears, his emotional development and his capacity, at a given time, for coping with life and meeting situations of unusual strain. How well would he be able to master the difficulties that might arise when the family moved to a new town, when a parent or a brother or sister became seriously ill or died or when the child accidentally or purposely injured another child? Projective tests give some indication of what a child's emotional resources are. Sometimes they reveal very deep trouble.

Parents whose first concern is for their children will welcome the information that a child needs help. But just as adults may hide their own excessive, morbid fears and obsessions because someone may call them "crazy," or may refuse to have a physical examination because they fear it may turn up some symptom of illness, so also they may have great reluctance to face the knowledge that their children are in difficulties. They forget two things. Physical examinations and psychological tests may show that the person is, in fact, in good physical and mental health. And where trouble shows up, knowing what it is, is the first step toward improvement.

Children need all the help they can be given to make the most out of school. Disturbed children need support so that they will not be overwhelmed by their troubles, and all children who are encouraged to build on their actual strengths move ahead more comfortably and with greater enjoyment. Used responsibly by those who are trained and eager to help children and their parents, tests are not invasions of privacy. But parents' anxieties and inability to think of their children as individuals in their own right may make them suspicious of tests given in school. Yet, looked at with understanding, tests can help to set people—children and adults—free from fear, free to use their full capacities in ways best suited to each of them as an individual.

Do you agree that colleges should be open to all? Wouldn't such a policy make it impossible to provide a proper education for those who are academically prepared? JULY 1971

I believe that every person should have access to as much higher education as he or she can make something of at any stage of life. Students who are not prepared to go ahead, as well as those who fail or who drop out through lack of interest or for some other reason, should know that this is not the end. Those who leave school early should be assured that they can return in a year or after five years or ten years—whenever they know what they want to do and can settle down to work for it.

This means making very basic changes in our thinking and planning for higher education. Otherwise there is a real danger that we may develop a kind of pseudo education in which we pretend that students are doing academic work that they are neither prepared nor motivated to do. The outcome of this would be damaging to everyone, but most of all, I think, to those whose potentialities would remain untapped and who in the end would revolt against the pretense. Far from broadening our educational base, the result would be disastrous in a world that depends increasingly on trained skills and responsible learning.

First, I think, we must give up the present overemphasis on degrees and on education as essentially a one-track system of preparation that must be completed at an early stage of life. Instead we must come to realize that learning is a lifetime process. Then we can develop alternative routes to higher education, and open the doors to all students whenever they are ready.

But this in turn means that we must change our thinking about students. As long as we think of all students as young and as yet unprepared for "life," we can go on treating them as essentially dependent and irresponsible. But if academic institutions are redesigned to include men and women of all ages, then all students will have to be treated as adults—as people working with a seriousness of purpose.

This is the direction in which I believe we must move in order to make education relevant and open to all.

In 1831 Emerson wrote in his journal: "The things taught in colleges and schools are not an education but the means of an education." Do you think this is true today? FEBRUARY 1972

It is even more true today.

In Emerson's day it still was possible to pass on to students a fairly coherent body of knowledge and to set a style for using it. When teaching was thought of as imparting a tradition, it was reasonable to demand that students sit attentively and listen until they in turn had acquired it. Moreover it was customary—and possible—to teach most complex skills as a part of the tradition itself.

Emerson claimed that this did not yet constitute true education. Although teachers could tell their students what to read and how to think about it, an essential part of the process was the later experience of putting to use what had been learned and of discovering how traditional knowledge both shaped and was shaped by ongoing life.

Today our stores of information are so great that teaching of almost any informational material, except by way of illustration, is wasteful. We no longer can educate our children by handing on to them a well-constructed parcel of the best that has been thought or said in the past. Instead, teaching is becoming more and more instrumental and related to the future.

What we have to teach students are skills and ways of approaching problems—how to recognize the kinds of materials that are needed to work on different categories of problems and how to go about finding materials when they are needed. Indeed, we cannot even concentrate on teaching given sets of skills. They too may be out of date by the time the student begins to put them to use. What students most need to learn is how to go about acquiring new skills to meet contemporary problems or older problems seen from a new point of view.

In our rapidly changing world, students and teachers together—with the teacher acting not as someone who has mastered knowledge but as a well-informed guide—have constantly to be learning *how* to learn new things in an educational process that truly will continue throughout life.

If, as you have said, coeducation intensifies the self-depreciation of the female and the hostility and competitiveness of boys toward girls, are you opposed to coeducation?
JANUARY 1976

Coeducation is here to stay. It is consistent with our general attitudes toward the relationships of males and females. The demand for it in the 19th century was one of the earliest expressions of the women's rights movement.

But because of the way our total educational system is organized, coeducation also involves certain difficulties. For example, at present we do not take into account the discrepancies in the pace of male and female maturation or, at different ages, the necessary processes of identification between teachers and pupils.

When American boys and girls enter school, the girls are ahead, verbally and socially, in those skills that most tend to please a teacher, particularly a female teacher. The boys are more active and restless; they may have more difficulty in mastering reading and writing; and more of them may display difficulties arising from imperfect eye and hand coordination. And as most teachers in the early elementary years are women, girls have an advantage.

Again, as children approach puberty girls begin to mature earlier and more rapidly than the boys who are their classmates. Soon there are a good many girls in the class who are much bigger than the boys. A friend once commented about her son's sixth-grade class, "You'd think you were in a group of very young women and little boys."

This difference is exacerbated in junior high school, where many of the boys have not yet started their pubertal growth spurt. The girls despise the boys, who seem so far behind them in sexual development, and the boys dislike the demanding girls. And except perhaps for the principal, the science teacher and the athletic coach, most of the faculty are still women.

In coeducational colleges the scene changes again. The boys have been catching up with the girls in their physical development and are becoming intellectually as mature as the girls. But now most of the teachers are men. And the male teachers now discourage the girls, as in elementary school the female teachers were hard on the restless little boys who found it so difficult to learn to sit still and to write legibly. A male professor approached by a female student is all too likely to say, "Why does a pretty girl like you want to study geology?"—or physics or mathematics or engineering or any of the other subjects he still tends to think of as male occupations.

What are the remedies? I do not think we shall give up coeducation. It is too much a part of our egalitarian ethic. The best one can suggest is palliatives:

I believe we should do away with the junior high school or at the very least give up the isolated junior high school in which children at such very different stages of development are forced into too-close association with one another. The kinds of hostility between girls and boys that develop in this very critical stage in their growing years are not easily overcome as they approach maturity. Grouping students, irrespective of sex, in smaller classes in some relationship to their comparative intellectual and physical maturity and interest in a subject would help. Clustering schools so that there is a continuing climax from elementary school to college would make it more possible for girls to associate with boys a couple of years older and for boys to meet girls a couple of years younger than themselves.

It would be equally helpful, I believe, to have male and female teachers in about the same numbers all the way from kindergarten through college. In the 1960s a very few young men began teaching young children—and were delighted with the experience. But this was only a small and tentative beginning. We also need far more women teachers at higher educational levels. Students of all ages need to be taught both from a female and a male point of view. And the best teachers, I am sure, are the ones who continue to learn from their students of the opposite as well as the same sex.

Some educators say that college students today regard education primarily as a requisite for financial success. How do you feel about this? MAY 1977

This is, of course, true of a great many students. During the last twenty-five years we have raised the demand from the completion of high school to the completion of college—or at least junior college—for young people who propose to take up almost any occupation other than factory work or manual labor. No one today thinks it is objectionable to warn high-school dropouts or potential dropouts that they are jeopardizing their chances of ever getting a worthwhile job. We Americans firmly believe that going to high school provides youngsters with a kind of general education that everyone living in the modern world needs to have. But college is somewhat different.

Originally an arts degree in college was designed for those who intended to enter one of a limited number of professions and as a requisite for those who were interested in scholarly pursuits or scientific research. It is true that for a handful of very well-do-to students today, four years of college is a way of prolonging the years of irresponsible play; for a few other students an athletic scholarship is in itself a kind of job. Educators have deplored these practices, which exist at the fringes of the academic world, but on the whole they have accepted them. But the idea that a more diversified curriculum might be valuable to students who want to understand better the world around them did not seriously enter thinking about college-level education until recently.

And by and large we have done very little with this idea even now. We have come to demand more education for almost everyone, but we have not yet taken the trouble to redesign college curriculums so that the four additional years of study will be appropriate and a challenge to the many different kinds of students now entering our colleges.

Whatever students' own interests may be, they have little choice but to undertake the special kinds of training designed for those with a scholarly or scientific bent or for those heading toward particular professions. The result is that much of what many students are taught appears to them to be—and often is—irrelevant. But they have been told again and again that college is the necessary route to eligibility for a good job. And so what choice do they have?

I do not think "financial success" is all that they are aiming for. Most young people hope to do something worthwhile and interesting. But I do think that for a large number of students, college is an instrument, a way of getting somewhere. And rather than feeling privileged, as earlier generations did, often they feel aggrieved and fenced in by the demand that they endure what they see as a long and relatively meaningless initiation.

Scholars, scientists and professional men and women in all fields must have their specialized, appropriate kinds of training. But we need to broaden our conception of what a sound, advanced educational program can offer to our very diverse college students, who will enter a world quite unlike the one in which their parents came to adulthood.

What do you think about the present tendency for women's colleges to merge with "brother" institutions?
NOVEMBER 1977

The current emphasis on treating females and males exactly alike—as students—has very substantially altered our picture of a good educational setting. However, the push toward mergers has been primarily an economic one. Large universities have gobbled up women's colleges out of a desire for their hard-won assets, and some women's colleges have fallen by the wayside for lack of adequate funds to carry out their educational responsibilities.

If these college mergers meant a greater evenhandedness in the employment of women and men on their faculties, coeducation would represent a gain, since students would be taught by teachers of both sexes. But this is not the case. Ever since World War II there has been a steady increase in the number of men teaching in women's colleges, a development that is harmful to the career aspirations of college women.

In the 1970s the chief advantage of the women's college is that it can provide girls with models of women scholars and scientists who reassure them about their own potentialities. Otherwise there is less necessity for the single-sex educational institution than there was in the 1950s and early 1960s, when the women's and the men's colleges provided some shelter for the girl and the boy who wanted to study—and to be relieved of the immediate pressure to find a mate and marry. Today this pressure is somewhat reduced.

But the question of faculty is still important, and unsolved. Girls need models of what they themselves can become; boys need to become acquainted with intellectual women whose attainments they will come to respect and enjoy.

ह‍ॐ

St. Augustine said that memory is the most marvelous gift human beings ever received. Yet today memory seems to be a faculty left generally undeveloped in and out of our schools. Why do you think this has happened and what do you think will be the consequences? AUGUST 1978

It all depends on what you mean by memory and memory training.

What is being left undeveloped at present in our schools is what we call "memorizing." Our forebears, who had far less access to books than we do, were required to memorize long passages from the Scriptures, political speeches by famous men, scenes from Shakespeare's plays and quite a lot of more-contemporary verse. When I was in high school we had to learn a "memory gem" each month and recite it before the whole school. It was a very mixed lot that included such lines as, "The quality of mercy is not strained," and "Did you tackle the trouble that came your way, With a resolute heart and a cheerful," and "To be or not to be" and "When lilacs last in the door-yard bloom'd."

A person's literary style—or lack of it—was formed by the passages she memorized. For generations the King James Bible in English and a very small amount of poetry in French and for those with a higher education some Latin passages from Cicero or Virgil and some lines of classical Greek, all contributed to the development of style.

Today we require very little memorizing of this kind, and except in popular music there is very little learning "by ear." But girls and boys voluntarily memorize a great variety of things, such as the make-up of sports teams and sports scores, brand names, popular songs, the names of materials and the "look" of things, near and far. In our complex, technically organized world, all of us have to train our memory to follow routes and to read maps and remember the meanings of road signs and signals.

For everyday purposes we have to commit to memory a great variety of procedures that allow us to drive cars safely and use all the different kinds of machines, large and small, in our own homes—the dishwasher, the washing machine and dryer, the floor polisher, the power mower and the power saw, the hot-water heater, the electric shaver, the blender, the microwave oven, the radio and the television set, the camera and the tape recorder, the children's electric trains and mechanized toys. These are so much part of most people's everyday living that few of us consider how important memory training is in knowing how to use and control these machines. Or how important it is to learn how to "forget," so that you can make a safe transition from the old car to the new one and from old traffic rules to new ones.

There are many kinds of memory, and each kind has to be cultivated if it is to be used with any assurance. I believe that the ability to memorize easily—in the older sense—has its place in the modern world, both as a way of building up a fund of easily accessible, accurate information and, less directly, as a way of increasing our respect for and commitment to accuracy of detail. Not long ago I suggested that the time spent traveling on school buses could well be used to acquire memory training and a memory fund of things everyone needs to know.

What do you think of the practice of separating schoolchildren into classes for the gifted, the average and the slow?
JANUARY 1979

This is much too narrow a way of classifying children.

All children are able to do some things better than others can. Sheer academic achievement, based on averaging marks in school, is too limited; it is not necessarily related to originality, artistic ability, athletic ability or even maturity.

It is often—although not always—good for academically bright children to recognize that others may be slower and less capable in school, as it is also good for the slower child to be stimulated by the presence of academically bright children.

I believe it is important to include many categories in classifying the children who will be educated together in a class or a school. This means that the physically mature and talented can take part in sports together, that those who have lovely voices can sing together, but also, at times, will have to put up with singers who can barely carry a tune, and that those who want to go racing ahead in science or mathematics will have a chance to spurt but also, from time to time, a time to rest and go slowly. In this way every child has a chance to shine and also to move along with a group. We need so many kinds of excellence and appreciation of each kind.

And I do sympathize with the teacher who wants to bring out the best in each child. I remember an incident when a teacher asked a godchild of mine, "Alice, isn't there _anything_ you can do very well?" To which Alice responded cheerfully, "I can carry books on my head!"

Teachers deserve variety in the group of children they teach at one time; they should not be stuck with a class whose members are classified on the basis of one trait alone. The richness and variety of the children stimulate the teacher's widest capacities, and this is in turn not only helps the children to learn from the teacher but also to learn and understand one another.

In your opinion, what does it mean for a person to be well educated? NOVEMBER 1978

I myself use the term "well educated" in two somewhat different ways. As I see it, a well-educated woman is someone who has had the best available education in a particular field or occupational group or in the section of the country in which she has grown up. I also use the term in relationship to an individual's understanding of the world in which she lives.

In our contemporary world, a well-educated woman is at least a high-school graduate. But whatever her formal education, she is able to build on the foundation it has provided. She has the ability to write English competently and has learned how to use the resources of libraries. She can handle a new assignment without getting confused and solve a new problem in some subject she has studied. She has some knowledge in different areas of learning and can distinguish faulty assumptions from those that are defensible and open to development.

But well-educated people, I believe, also have some sense of history, some knowledge of the place of their country in the world and some idea of time and evolutionary processes. They have some idea of how individuals develop in life, how cultures have developed through time and how our beliefs—especially our religious beliefs and our beliefs about human nature—change as new scientific discoveries are made and become part of the way we think.

Taking everything into account, a well-educated woman, whatever her level of formal education may have been, has gained the ability to grow and to integrate her experience into her understanding of our living world.

~ 10 ~
THE HUMAN CONDITION

Is there any one society that you have observed in which the people seem considerably happier than those in other societies? FEBRUARY 1963

In the first place we must remember that "happiness" is not a universal ideal. Is it fair to compare people who recognize and believe in "happiness" with people who think only of fate, or of fulfilling one's duty to one's children, or of living out a life that was determined by the activities of one's reincarnated soul in a previous incarnation?

If we try to define happiness in a way that would be valid for any society, civilized or primitive, traditional or rapidly changing, the definition must be based on each people's recognition of happiness or unhappiness (and some have none), or we must invent a definition which can be applied to any society. For example, happiness might be defined as getting those good things in life that one has been led to expect. Then a happy society would be one like Samoa, where children grow up wanting very simple things—enough food, water, sleep, sex and mild amusement—and usually obtain them. Conversely, an unhappy society would be one in which people expect more than they are likely to receive. By such a definition, people are most likely to be happy in those societies that promise little and deliver the little that is promised. They are societies in which, in fact, the level of aspiration is very low. Societies whose members have very high aspirations would inevitably produce more "unhappy" people.

211

It is on such societies, however, that the growth and change of civilization depend. For it is only when people are unhappy about the discrepancy between their situation and their aspirations that they seek something that is different, better and more desirable.

ॐ

Has it ever been demonstrated that any one racial group is innately more or less intelligent than others? FEBRUARY 1963

No. At present our only method of assaying innate intelligence is to study identical twins reared in similar and dissimilar environments. While such a method can demonstrate that some of the factors of intelligence are inherited, there is no reason to believe that they are correlated with, or limited to, any racial group.

The most powerful influence on mental achievement appears to be culture. Human beings are so constructed that individuals of very different mental gifts, born into a certain culture, can function within that culture—speak its language and follow its customs. Rather than reflecting the general level of intelligence, human cultures can serve to raise or lower the level of achievement of all their members. In a culture in which counting does not go beyond twenty, for example, the brightest individual will count no further. But in a culture in which the number system is highly developed, even a very stupid individual can learn to handle quite complex numerical ideas.

The adoption of individuals from groups with technically simple cultures into groups with modern technical cultures has demonstrated that a person from a technically backward group can master the more advanced technology. Similarly, a child from a complex culture who is adopted by parents living in a simpler civilization is not likely to rise above the culture of his or her adoptive parents.

Scientists cannot say that there are no racial differences in intelligence. But we *can* say that although students have looked for such differences with great energy and enthusiasm, none has so far been demonstrated.

212

ह~

Do you agree with the theory expounded by Robert Ardrey in his book *African Genesis* that man is by nature a killer?
MAY 1963

Robert Ardrey has made a vivid detective story out of the struggles of certain anthropologists, particularly Robert Dart, to convince their fellow anthropologists that making weapons for killing is a primary instinctive urge of modern man, *Homo sapiens*. Mr. Ardrey argues that a creature called *Australopithecus*, classified by some as a precursor of man, used hunting weapons, killed other mammals, and in one case possibly a young member of its own species, and that therefore, contrary to formerly held beliefs, the urge to kill in modern man arises not out of necessity or the instinct for self-preservation but is in itself an instinct.

If the argument were phrased simply "Early man was a hunter," the story would not sound so shocking. If it were not mixed up, quite gratuitously, with illustrations of the firmness of instinct in other creatures, it would not sound so shocking. If it weren't interlarded, illogically, with remarks about juvenile delinquents in our great cities, the delight taken by modern readers in murder stories and the pleasure little boys take in things that go *bang* (Mr. Ardrey makes an easy connection between the delight taken in a loud noise and an instinctive desire to kill), it would have less popular impact.

Some human precursors were undoubtedly hunters, capable of stalking their prey, delivering a lethal blow and defending themselves against dangerous neighbors, some of whom may have been creatures like themselves. They also had other skills: how to make tools, how to talk with one another. None of these behaviors is instinctive. Men learn to make weapons, or tools, to kindle a fire or to talk to one another from being born in a group of human beings who have invented these skills. History has amply demonstrated that members of every one of the races into which human beings have been grouped are capable of the greatest violence and cruelty, and of the greatest gentleness and self-

213

sacrifice. Men of all existing races can learn to be hunters or shepherds, or both, to risk their lives daily as lifeguards or firemen or to become torturers at the command of a totalitarian state. Furthermore, modern dynamic psychology has revealed the welter of tendencies toward violence and self-sacrifice that can be re-aroused in the gentlest adults, under certain circumstances.

At birth, however, human beings carry only the *potentialities* for different kinds of behavior. It depends upon the society into which individuals are born, and upon the way they are specifically reared, which will be developed.

One feature of Ardrey's thesis that has impressed readers is his discussion of juvenile gangs who defend their territories with lethal weapons they manufacture themselves. We do not have to invoke an instinctive weapon-making urge originating in the time of *Australo-pithecus*, however, to explain their behavior. Human beings—like many other living creatures—when deprived, frightened, brutalized by external conditions, will fight and kill. The behavior of the juvenile deliquent, like the behavior of the policeman who tries to prevent it, the juvenile court that attempts to reform the offender, the street youth worker who risks his life to help redeem him—all these are human styles of behavior, learned after birth in human society, built upon the primary urges of mammals to experiment, to mate, to defend that which they hold dear, and to destroy something that threatens their existence or the existence of their young.

It is my feeling that as many people have been hurt as have been helped by psychiatry. How do you feel about this? Have you ever been psychoanalyzed? DECEMBER 1964

This is a little like saying that as many people with a broken leg have been harmed as have been helped by orthopedic surgery. People do not turn to psychiatry unless they are in some kind of trouble. And, of course, psychiatry is only one of the different kinds of help to which people in trouble turn. Some are helped by prayer, others by a change

214

of scene or job or a long rest, still others by finding a real friend or by joining Alcoholics Anonymous.

But most remedies for trouble are prescribed too indiscriminately. In one society the standard remedy may be to make an offering to the gods; in another it may be to go on a pilgrimage. In our society, whatever the complaint may be—barrenness, apathy, fear of examinations, a broken heart or some symptom like a tic—the prescribed remedy is likely to be a set of sessions with a psychiatrist. In general, a great many difficulties could be avoided if other professional people—teachers, physicians, counselors, pastors—were more alert to early signs of trouble so that remedial steps could be taken before psychiatric treatment became neccssary. But there are also difficulties that result from terrible mishaps in upbringing or that represent an extreme response to stress; for these, skillful psychiatric care is necessary.

I have never been psychoanalyzed. The close study of primitive people is another way of arriving at insight, and I do not wish to add therapeutic skills to my task of understanding a culture through observing and listening to all the members of a society—men, women and children.

What was your reaction to Jean-Paul Sartre's being awarded the Nobel Prize in Literature and then refusing it?
MARCH 1965

Sartre himself gave the best answer in his literary autobiography *The Words*. In this book he describes how as a child he learned to play roles too well, and as a result came to distrust all role-playing.

The role of the Nobel Prize winner is one that has international public significance. His words are listened to even when he speaks on subjects outside the sphere of his special competence, and he is asked to join with others in signing manifestoes to which the highest authorities must pay attention.

In *The Words* Sartre reports how as a spoiled and petted

fatherless child he was given almost unlimited freedom in his "insincere" play-acting to win praise and adulation from his family. Vehemently rejecting this discrepancy between what he really was and what he was tempted to pretend he was, he also has rejected the role of the Nobel Prize winner. His fight is to remain himself. Those who find this puzzling should read *The Words*.

In contrast, it is useful to think what winning the Nobel Peace Prize meant to Dr. Martin Luther King, Jr. For in his case, man and role matched in a sincerity that has moved millions. Both Martin Luther King, Jr., and Jean-Paul Sartre are personally concerned with the same problem—the problem of being the person each of them really is. But their life experience is different. The Nobel Prize was one more perfect and seamless garment for Dr. King. For Sartre it would be one more costume for a masked ball.

Would you say that the more "civilized" a society becomes, the more neurotics it produces? OCTOBER 1965

A neurotic person can be most simply described as someone who, while he was growing up, learned ways of behaving that are self-defeating in his society. The neurotic individual may have had some special vulnerability as an infant. Perhaps he was ill a great deal and was given care that singled him out from other children. Perhaps he walked or talked much later—or earlier—than children were expected to, and this evoked unusual treatment. The child whose misshapen feet must be put in casts or the sickly little boy who never can play ball may get out of step with his age mates and with the expectations parents and other adults have about children. Or a child may be very unusually placed in his family. He may be the only boy with six sisters, or a tiny child born between two lusty sets of twins. Or the source of the child's difficulties may be a series of events that deeply affected his relations to people—the death of his mother at the birth of the next child or the prolonged illness or absence of his father. Or a series of coincidences—an accident to a parent, moving to a new town and a severe fright—taken together may alter the child's relationship to the world.

Whatever the nature of the discrepancy, the young child may have learned ways of dealing with life that are inappropriate. And later these small patterns of maladjustment may be transformed into deepset forms of inappropriate behavior and ways of relating oneself to the world. A man may treat every challenge as a threat. A woman may break off every love relationship at the moment it appears to be successful. A man may quit a job every time he fears he may be promoted. Usually we think of individuals developing these neurotic traits within the family, in conflicts between parents and children or as the effects of contrasts and discrepancies among brothers and sisters. But where the family and the society correspond generally in their forms, ways and values, no one form of family life is more or less likely to produce neuroticism.

In a society where small boys of five are expected to be brave enough to defy their fathers and also brave enough to be sent to live as temporary hostages in another tribe, it is not this requirement that starts off a neurotic train of behavior. Here the child who is endangered is the one whose father is too mild to be defied or whose mother refuses to let her little son be sent as a hostage. In a society where all the members of a three-generation family sleep in one room, rolled in quilts on one heated platform, it is not the child who is crowded in (as might happen in our society), but the child who is separated from the others, who may become neurotic.

Becoming neurotic is not a question of the intrinsic harshness or gentleness of the environment. What matters is the fit between the growing individual and the kind of treatment he evokes in those around him. A harsh society has devices to ensure that the growing children will learn to be harsh and to accept harshness. A mild society has devices to ensure that the growing children will learn to be mild and to expect mildness from others. An incapacity to adapt to harshness—whether because of temperament, physique, illness or some unusual circumstance—will spell neuroticism for the child living in the harsh society. Very different characteristics or experiences will lead to neuroticism in a mild society.

There are some neurotic individuals even in the smallest, simplest societies. Where food is plentiful, some individuals may still hoard food. Where people are used to living in crowds, some individuals may still shrink from them. Where people move in relaxed, easy ways, some individuals may be rigid and preoccupied with every detail of carrying out every activity. In a society where stealing is not a serious problem, one may find the lonely thief who steals because somehow he feels this is a way of claiming affection that is his due, or the man who steals other things after he has stolen his brother's wife.

Simple societies are also small societies. Because there are fewer people, there are, of course, numerically fewer neurotics. But simple societies also are likely to be relatively homogeneous. Families differ in fewer ways and there are many ways in which close kin can make up for the odd behavior of a parent or the absence of a parent from the home. And a small society often can afford to tolerate an individual who becomes very neurotic—frightened or compulsive or "cranky." Everybody knows him and is used to his idiosyncrasies. People make allowances for him, and even when his behavior gets worse he does not disrupt social life.

Furthermore, in small, simple societies people usually have to be concerned with the everyday realities of making a living, keeping their chidren safe and protecting their homes from storms and natural disasters. The neurotic individual is the victim of imaginary fears. But neurotic terrors pale before actual hunger and real danger. During World War II, psychiatrists in England prepared to have many more patients—people who would break down under the stress of danger during bombings. Instead, they had fewer patients than in peacetime.

Civilizied societies are large societies. In a society that can support very large cities and can extend a system of law and trade over a very wide area, there are also greater differences among the members of the society than in a small society— differences of class or caste, differences of regional adaptation, differences related to the great complexity of living.

218

Here the experiences of one group of growing children will differ from those of another. People move around a great deal. They go up in the world or come down in the world or they adopt new, different styles of living. The upbringing of a husband and a wife may have differed greatly, and they in turn may bring up their children in a settng that is different from the ones they knew. The child's grandmother, who is very close to him, may have come from some faraway place. And the very tales that comforted her in her country child-hood may seem terrifying to a child growing up in a city. Or city parents who know nothing about animals may give their child a pet—a puppy, a parakeet or a tank of tropical fish. And then the dog runs away, the parakeet sickens or the fish de-vour their young—and no one knows how to deal with the situation, which causes the child hopeless grief.

In this sense it is possible to say that more people may become neurotic in a more complex civilization. That is, more people are likely to have disabling experiences that unfit them for living comfortably in their own society. But it may be fortunate that this is so, for the life of a great society depends on people's sense of growth and change, and very often it is the neurotics who are ridden by a feeling or respon-sibility for the woes of the world. The compulsive perfec-tionist who cannot stand the sloppy way things are done, the aggrieved neglected child who has known loneliness and grows up to champion the cause of the dispossessed—these are among the people who press for change.

By no means all who work for a better world are neurotics. But in a world where everyone fitted easily into the pattern of life as it is, where everyone could look forward to a smooth future, where everyone could predict the course of a lifetime, it is probable that most people would be too satisfied with life as they found it to keep on growing and moving from their youth to old age.

Is the medicine man or shaman in primitive society compara-ble to the psychoanalyst in our society? JUNE 1966

No. The medicine man or shaman is comparable to the faith healer. Like the faith healer, he invokes supernatural powers in which he himself and his patients believe. Whatever the nature of the ritual through which he endeavors to cure the physically or mentally sick patient, it is one that is known and trusted by all those who may be participants in it. The shaman may palm a crystal and then "extract" it from the patient's body. He may anoint the patient's body with water into which he has tempted back the soul stuff that had been stolen away. He may lure the disease out of the patient's body and into that of a sacrificial animal. He may blow life back into the patient's nostrils. When he is dealing with mental illness he may use elaborate procedures for exorcising possessing demons or for placating demanding ghosts. What all these different forms of treatment have in common is faith in the practice, trust in the practitioner and a shared desire for a cure.

Psychoanalysis, like other forms of modern scientific treatment of those who are ill or disturbed, is based on the laborious exploration of the psychodynamics of human behavior. As in all patient-therapist relationships, the element of trust is important in psychoanalysis. But the procedures used do not invoke the supernatural and do not depend on the patient's faith in them.

Has extrasensory perception been discredited in the scientific world? Or is there still a valid basis for believing that such powers may exist? OCTOBER 1967

Extrasensory perception is a scientifically inept term. By suggesting that forms of human perception exist beyond the senses, it prejudges the question. There are better ways of phrasing it. Can human communication be mediated other than through the senses we now recognize? Is mental communication possible? If so, what is the range and what are the necessary conditions? Are there barriers to distance communication as there are to sight and hearing? Is the capacity for distance communication limited to a few individuals? Does it operate only under special conditions, such as extreme fear, nearness of death or some greatly heightened emotional state? Or should it be regarded as a general human capacity, latent and undeveloped in most individuals?

Another set of related questions can be asked about the ability of an individual to "see" at a distance (clairvoyance) and to look into the past or the future (retrocognition and precognition). Phrasing questions about these abilities, of course, raises other problems. To what extent is the future determined by events now taking place? Is the ability to predict merely the ability to recognize the pattern of events already in train? Not uncommonly, a clairvoyant may predict the time and circumstances of some individual's death. Does this mean more than that the clairvoyant individual has a special sensitivity to subliminal indicators of disease? We are still largely ignorant of the processes by which sensitive, aware people organize cues.

The scientific study of ESP has taken two main forms. One is the investigation of "sensitives," persons who claim special gifts of telepathy, clairvoyance and so on. The other is the investigation of one or another of these qualities as a mode of communication. In research of this kind, the attempt is made to discover whether the necessary capacity exists in ordinary people. For example, an investigator in one building turns over cards in a deck while the subject, in another building, writes down the order in which he "senses" that the cards are falling. The results are subjected to statistical analysis. Such investigations are based on the assumption that there is another mode (or more than one other mode) of perception that is not yet recognized and explored. As the results are difficult to interpret, they have led to heated controversy and repeated attempts to discredit the investigators, the subjects and the methods of investigation. Moreover, since the arguments often turn on abstruse statistical points, these are a further source of confusion too.

But behind the arguments there is also the culturally determined prejudice of scientists and others who do not grant the question: Have we explored every sensory mode? And to add to the difficulty, there is the confusion arising from the naïve enthusiasm of equally prejudiced "believers."

I have worked among several primitive peoples among whom trance behavior is an everyday occurrence. It is assumed that the individual in trance is in communication with supernatural powers and behaves differently from others (or himself) not in trance. It is my impression that when individuals are specially chosen, they may have extraordinary capacities for exercising the special supernatural powers exhibited under trance. But where anyone may go into trance, the highly stylized trance behavior obscures rather than reveals individual capacities. I believe that the most promising line of research is the investigation of individuals to whom special capacities have been ascribed, combining systematic observation and scientific checks on the circumstances under which each individual operates.

Research is necessarily difficult. Laboratory experiments must be based on situations in which conditions can be repeated or at least controlled. However, "sensitives" are notoriously capricious. Their "powers" may leave them without warning or their display may depend on special circumstances, such as the approach of death or disaster in the life of another person. Such events are, of course, sporadic. One result is that those who want to carry on scientific investigations dislike working with individual sensitives. But at the same time, those who respect the extraordinary powers attributed to sensitives as individuals sometimes are affronted by the demand that such sensitives subject their powers to the controls necessary for scientific research.

Certainly the manifestations of what is called estrasensory perception are very varied and the alleged events take different forms in different cultures. Some forms can be explained not by a "sixth sense," but by the assumption that certain individuals use their five senses more fully; they are extremely sensitive to small cues—very fine shadings in tones of voice, almost invisible eye movements, or delicate alterations of posture and gesture. Fine discriminations of this kind are characteristic of a few highly successful fortunetellers.

They are characteristic also of diagnosticians and therapists in the many kinds of therapy in which the therapist must deduce the illness about which the patient cannot tell him. The good mother and the good nurse act "intuitively" on many of the same kinds of cues. In fact, we may postulate a continuum in sensitivity that begins with the perception of the mother in relation to the child she loves and that goes on to the perception of the individual who has listened to a stranger talking on the telephone and can predict his next actions from his present state. Telepathy, in many of its manifestations, may be explained as the capacity to "listen" intensively and to enter into and recognize the thought patterns of another person before these become conscious. Husbands and wives often are experts at communicating and interpreting each other's states of mind without words or conscious gestures.

Fashions of acceptance and rejection and of forms of research in this field come and go. As long as there is observed behavior that is unexplained, research will continue. The rejection of any field of inquiry as unscientific is itself a denial of the scientific method. But each generation of investigators must rephrase the problem so that they can take into account the failures as well as the successes of their predecessors.

Users of LSD claim that with it they have valid mystical experiences, comparable to those previously known by holy men and saints. Is there any clear difference between the two experiences? And if not, what right has society to deny anyone this new access to age-old spiritual experience?
JANUARY 1968

The question of validity has troubled every religious group that has accepted the possibility of mystical experience. As in the case of miracles, visions are subjected to the most intense and severe scrutiny. Those who claim, or have claimed for them, a unique relationship to God may be admitted to sainthood only a very long time after the event. Joan of Arc was burned at the stake as a witch in 1431 and was not canonized until 1920. In the Western Christian tradition, validity turns

223

essentially on the relationship between an individual's mystical experience and the religious beliefs of others. That is, it is the miracles, the stigmata and the visions that come to have relevance to the community of the faithful that are judged, in the end, to be valid. In this sense the question of whether or not LSD users have *valid* mystical experiences is beside the point.

The central issue is that LSD changes the state of consciousness of the user for a shorter or longer time. Puritanical Americans disapprove of all drugs of this type, even mild ones like nicotine and alcohol. Moreover, they take the stand that individuals' private lives are within the jurisdiction of public legislation. At present their zeal for total abstinence is concentrated on drugs. It is expressed also in the refusal to regard addiction as an illness instead of a crime or a sin.

The problem of LSD is further complicated by the claim that it produces a state comparable to psychosis and that controlled experimental use of this drug can give psychiatrists new access to an understanding of their patients. For many persons it is only a short step from this claim to the belief that young people, students, are being allowed to take a drug that may make them insane. Instances of disturbed individuals who have committed crimes or who have suffered irremediable injury while under the influence of LSD have strengthened this fear.

At the same time there are others who claim that certain drugs such as marijuana, mescal and now LSD open the doorways of perception and give the user an extraordinarily vivid sense of himself and his relationship to the universe. This was the viewpoint of Aldous Huxley in his book *The Doors of Perception*. In his utopian novel *The Island*, he pictures the use of psychedelic drugs in a regular form of initiation of young people to a more sensitive realization of themselves and their place in society. That is, in *The Island* Huxley attempted to construct a new religion in which these drugs play a carefully controlled part.

In his interpretation, psychedelic drugs become adjuncts to religious experience comparable to but more effective than fasting, isolation, prayer, meditation and highly controlled exercises in breathing or in taking special physical postures. The means are new, but the quest for religious experience is part of an ancient tradition in which the individual who feels a vocation makes a long, disciplined effort to attain a closer relationship to the supernatural. Even when the vision comes to an unbeliever like Saul of Tarsus, who neither sought it nor prepared for it, the experience is within a living tradition.

Certain cultures—for example, Balinese culture and the peasant version of Haitian culture—have encouraged religious-trance experience for many individuals. In these societies people take a great many precautions in selecting and ritually training those who will engage regularly in trance and in controlling where and under what circumstances trance may be induced. Individuals who go into trance at the wrong time and in the wrong place are exhorted to stop these activities or stay away from the community.

It is quite possible that the use of psychedelic drugs, whether in an old or a new religious context, may be able to facilitate mystical experience. But all that we know about religious mysticism suggests that very careful disciplines and rigorous forms of training would have to be developed on which those who used the psychedelic drugs as an adjunct to religious experience could draw. It also seems clear that in our own American tradition, one test of whether such a development was in fact a religion would be its social relevance. For unlike those Eastern religions in which mystical experience is a purely individual spiritual belief, Western religions contain the expectation that religious experience benefits not only the visionary but also others who share his faith. With this expectation the solipsistic aim of the LSD user, whose interest is wholly introspective, is out of key.

The panic roused by the widespread and uncontrolled individual experimentation with LSD is precipitating a flood of poorly conceived legislation. One unexpected by-product of these laws may be a new kind of interference with the regular religious exercises of the American Indian Church, in which peyote is used. In this situation the prohibitions become an unjustified interference with religious freedom.

It must also be recognized, however, that there is no

necessary relationship between the use of drugs and religious experience. The ordinary LSD "trip" has no more necessary relationship to mystical experience than the drinking of ten cocktails has, after which many people experience various alterations of consciousness.

From one point of view the battle between those who wish to enlarge their experience through the use of LSD and other drugs and those who are exercising all their powers to prohibit this use is a very old one in Western cultures. On the one side are those who believe that control over consciousness is crucial to human living and that loss of control inevitably leads to the emergence of dangerous, bestial impulses. On the other side are those who believe that control of consciousness is itself inimical to true spirituality.

These two views, the Apollonian and the Dionysian, represent an ancient conflict within our cultural tradition. But now, as in the past in our own society, puritanism, which is not a necessary aspect of the Apollonian conception of life, embitters many on both sides who are trying to come to grips with the deeper issues of the handling of human potentialities.

To what do you attribute the need some people feel for a belief in numerology, horoscopy (the system of casting horoscopes), astrology and other phenomena of this kind?
JANUARY 1969

Not only these quasi-magical systems, but also the world's religions, are concerned with recurrent human needs. One very basic need is expressed in questions about choice: Do human beings have freedom of choice? Where does responsibility lie? In the face of the unknown future, in what terms can you make choices? How do you interpret the consequences that flow from decisions? Is there such a thing as accident? Or luck?

One solution to this set of problems is the religious belief that the state of the universe and human destiny alike are fixed within a totally predetermined pattern. Responsibility lies outside the realm of human control, and the most anyone can do is try to find out how best to comply with the conditions of this impersonal, unchangeable pattern. In extreme contrast is the religious belief that within an ordered universe the individual, having a conscience, can make and is totally responsible for his own choices.

Looking at these two religious solutions, we can more readily understand the strength of the appeal of a quasi-magical system like horoscopy. Each individual's horoscope, cast in terms of an irreversible fact, the day and hour of his birth, provides impersonal guidance in carrying out his destiny by warning him against dangers and indicating the direction in which he may look for success. It is characteristic of all such systems that while they are based on predestination and externalized responsibility, they also permit the individual who heeds warnings and takes advantage of favorable opportunities to enjoy a sense of furthering his own best interests in the next week, month or year. And he can always try again.

Should prostitution be legalized? APRIL 1971

No, I do not think so. Were prostitution to be legalized, it would involve the passage of laws regulating the conditions under which prostitution would be legally acceptable. Invariably such laws would provide support for some of the worst features of institutionalized prostitution by underwriting the powers of pimps and madams to exploit both the women under their control and their customers. This would extend power over persons in an inadmissible way.

To me the evil thing about legalized prostitution, where it exists, is not that this makes it possible for a sailor off a ship to find a girl or a respectable man to slip away where he will only meet others bound on the same, explicit search. The evil lies in the exploitation of women who have no other form of livelihood and in the exploitation of the desires of the lonely stranger.

For many Americans the word "legalize" implies the setting of a stamp of public, social approval on a particular form of activity. For this reason, discussions of whether or not certain forms of behavior should be made legal bog down in controversies over different moral standards. Quite often our real intention is something different. It is to recognize an area of activity as one within which adults should be free to exercise choice.

So it is better, I think, to focus our attention not on legalization but on the repeal of cruel, inappropriate and restrictive laws—laws that attempt to project the morality of part of the community on the community as a whole and laws that seek to legislate personal behavior that may be harmful (if it *is* harmful) mainly to the individual who engages in it.

Prostitution is recognized, of course, in law. The point is that our laws about prostitution are cruel and barbarous and definitely discriminatory against the women involved. The laws are such that prostitutes are punished, exploited and blackmailed, while those who make their activities pay are permitted to go free or are subject only to minor penalties. For every bad law there are those who benefit from it—in graft, in the gratification of their savage desire to punish those whom they connect with their own moral failures or in the corruption of some of those who are expected to enforce the law, as vice squads are assigned to do. I believe all these laws should be repealed.

Instead we should concentrate on protective measures— the protection of minors, the protection of unconsenting adults from the harassment of solicitation on the streets (which many people feel can be an intolerable temptation) and, above all, the protection of unsophisticated, helpless and penniless young girls from exploitation by commercial interests.

The essence of prostitution is that it occurs between strangers, strangers who liquidate their indebtedness at once and without regard for each other as persons. Recently Women's Liberation groups have added prostitution to their eclectic list of grievances of women against men. As the "oldest profession," it is also the oldest form of exploitation of one person by another. But the exploitation goes both ways as women exploit men's loneliness, shame, fears and social ineptness and as men try to escape from love and responsibility through the mere payment of money in return for sex.

Must men be violent? SEPTEMBER 1972

Violence is a human capacity. But the circumstances under which men behave with violence—if they do—and the forms taken by violence depend on the kind of society in which a people live—on the culture that is handed on to them and that they in turn hand on to their children. Throughout history there have been peoples that have been peaceful and nonviolent, other peoples that have glorified some form of violence and still others that have been essentially nonviolent but that on occasion have erupted in the most terrible violence.

But societies also change very rapidly. London in 1830 was one of the most lawless and violent cities in Europe. In 1930 its citizens were among the most law-abiding and nonviolent in the world; an unarmed police force, made up of tall, patient and quiet men, was able to maintain the kind of order in which the population believed. Sweden was once a nation of violent, bellicose and conquest-minded men. Today Sweden is an eminently peaceful country.

No country that permits firearms to be widely and randomly distributed among its population—especially firearms that are capable of wounding and killing human beings—can expect to escape violence, and a great deal of violence. No country that permits the strong to oppress the weak or that permits the majority to disregard the civil rights of a minority group against the declared ethic of that society, according to which all have equal rights, can expect to escape violence. And no society that feeds its children on tales of successful violence can expect them not to believe that violence in the end is rewarded.

What are your views on euthanasia? JULY 1973

I do not believe that a society should have the power to decide that old people are useless or dispensable or no longer capable of living humanly and so end their lives. A society as such should not have this kind of power over human life, whether it is the old or the unborn, the feeble-minded or the desperately handicapped whose lives are involved. It is our responsibility, especially in a society as rich as ours, to care for those who are in need of care.

It is true that among primitive peoples living on the edge of extinction—a small band of food gatherers in a period of extreme drought, for example—it may sometimes be necessary to decide who is to survive. But even in such cases we find that most societies try to save old people as long as they can or, as among the Eskimos, let them choose when it seems best to die.

I do believe that a person who is very old or incurably ill should have that choice. But this also presents problems. At the point at which an old person no longer is able to relate in any way to his relatives and friends, he is not able to make the necessary decision. It now is advocated that the oxygen machine should be turned off when the brain is dead, even if the heart beats on; but someone must make the decision to turn off the machine.

Clearly the choice must be made long before the crisis occurs. And just as it is customary for people to make their last will and testament when they are well, in order to avoid the pressures and the forced or erratic decisions of a deathbed will, so also it is possible for persons to decide in advance and put in writing—as with a will—the circumstances under which they would want medical intervention and under what circumstances they would wish to have no further intervention.

I myself would wish to live as long as I could be a thinking and communicating person; I would not want to live as an uncommunicating body. As physicians generally respect the wishes of their patients who can make their decisions known, they also would be able to respect, with a clear conscience, the wishes their patients have set down earlier. And families would not be guilt-ridden about decisions made long before.

A further difficulty arises for the old person who does not need special medical intervention merely to keep him or her alive but who faces inevitable deterioration, pain and personality distortion. There is at present a group advocating legislation to permit a physician to give a pill, at the request of the patient, that would give release from the suffering ahead. I believe it is the right of an individual to choose not to endure destructive suffering that can end only in death.

But I also believe we should not put on practicing physicians the double burden of being honest with their patients— and their patients' families—in telling them what lies ahead *and* of assisting their patients to end their lives. In a great many early cultures the power to cure and the power to kill were lodged in the same person. It was a great step forward in the history of medicine when care and curing were separated from any other power, and I do not think we should do anything to jeopardize this dedication of the physician to the life and well-being of his individual patients.

The power of assisting the individual who elects to die with dignity should be vested in a board that is committed legally to respect the person's need and way of meeting it. Such a board would have to be made up of persons with medical training—for example, public health officials—but not men and women engaged in the medical care of the individual.

I believe individuals should have the choice of euthanasia. But such a choice must be set within a framework of ethical commitment to the value of human life.

ટ⹀

As someone who has listened to the music of many cultures, can you say what emotional value patterned sound has?
JULY 1973

In cultures in which music has become a high art with a long tradition and complex canons of style, it exists for its own sake, in a sense. Composers and performers and to a somewhat lesser extent the listening audience all are specialists whose enjoyment is dependent on lengthy and elaborate training and wide experience.

Music of this kind may touch only very lightly on the lives of many people. For others it is the most engrossing experience of their lives. Recently I talked with a young musician who had been arrested on a false charge of possessing drugs. His overriding fear was that he might be imprisoned where he could neither hear nor make music. Like any high art, music can be the source of the most intense aesthetic experience and may become the central focus of a whole way of living for an individual.

But this is not the only value music has. All peoples everywhere make music. Music (patterned sound) and dance (patterned movement) are the oldest and most persistent forms of organized symbolic behavior in the human repertoire.

A song may be no more than a single line of melody endlessly repeated and perhaps accompanied by the monotonous rhythm of clapping hands or stamping feet or sticks beaten together. A song may be a simple dialogue between two groups, or between a leader and a group, in which the melodic lines, endlessly repeated, symbolize the relationship of each to the other.

Songs may be lullabies that countless generations of mothers have sung to their children. They may be songs that comfort the dying or bewail the dead. They may be songs that hearten men for a fight or that celebrate their victories—past, present or still to come. They may be harvest songs or work songs that help men to move in unison as they plant seeds, paddle their canoes or haul a heavy beam into position.

The music people make as part of their ongoing living experience—and the dance that so often accompanies this music—is essentially a form of communication. For the actors and the audience, as well as listeners at a distance, such music sets the tone of the event and expresses the moods of human social experience.

Perhaps this is the most important function of music—to give wholeness to an event and convey a shared mood. We can see this happening today as young people travel all over the world, singing the same songs though they cannot speak the same language. Singing, they communicate to one another that they have something important in common— something that distinguishes their generation and the period in which they live. Music is the bond they share.

ॐ

Some time ago a plane crashed in South America. In order to stay alive the survivors ate the flesh of their dead companions. What is your feeling about their action? JUNE 1974

I think it is an example of how faith and the power of deeply accepted ritual can mitigate the terror and horror of an otherwise unbearable situation in such a way as to protect the humanity of the participants.

The group consisted of the members of the Old Christian rugby team—university students who with friends and relatives were flying from Montevideo, Uruguay, to Santiago, Chile, to play a series of matches. Forty-five started on the flight; sixteen survived the seventy-three-day ordeal, isolated high in the snow-covered Andean Cordillera. Eighteen, including all the women in the party, died when the plane, caught in an air pocket, slammed into a mountain peak. Nine others died when an avalanche buried the cabin they had constructed from the wreckage. One died of his injuries.

The survivors had managed to rig up a transistor radio and they listened daily to news of rescue efforts. They even saw a search plane, but could not attract its attention. Finally, on the eighth day, they heard that the search was being abandoned until the spring thaw, months away.

Faced with certain death by starvation, the group made the portentous decision to eat, carefully and ritually, the bodies of their dead companions, which were lying frozen in the snow. They made strict rules. No one was to eat from the body of a relative, the flesh was to be cut into very small pieces and each body was to last five days. Each night they prayed together. Only one of them, whom the others tried to force to eat, could not bear it and chose to die.

In the end two of the strongest young men, following a

compass setting down the rugged mountains for ten terrible days, reached an inhabited place. The others were brought down by helicopter. Some were injured; all were very emaciated. Of course the rescuers found the mutilated bodies.

The survivors admitted that they had eaten their dead comrades. One compared it to a heart transplant: "The dead sustained the living." Another said that their experience had taken them "to the very source of Christianity." In their minds what they were doing was not desecration, but a kind of communion with a human body, patterned after the ritual act of Communion in their church. It was this ritualization, I think, that saved them.

Cannibalism occurs in the modern world only under extreme conditions of starvation. Then the central fear is that the stronger of the living will kill and eat their weaker comrades. But here, I believe, the capacity of the survivors to interpret their act symbolically protected them from the fear of murder and the horror of cannibalism.

According to *Time* magazine, a Roman Catholic priest, preaching at a thanksgiving Mass for the survivors, said: "What happens to them will depend on us now, and on the love and understanding that we are capable of giving them." Their humanity, after all, is also ours.

There is a new theory that some people are "born to kill"— that they become criminals because of a faulty chromosome balance. Don't you think this leaves out a lot of other factors, particularly the individual circumstances of a person's life?
JULY 1974

A theory about human behavior that fails to take into account life experience certainly is oversimplified.

Recent theories about human beings who are said to be "born killers" are based very largely on research carried out on rats, which sometimes do display a proclivity to kill. In addition, case studies have been made of individuals who have killed in what seems to be a blind, indiscriminate way.

What it comes to, it appears to me, is that some people are more vulnerable than others to destructive experience. There is one kind of childhood experience, for example, that seems to have a predetermining effect upon some individuals who later give way to indiscriminate violence: The child tortures an animal, and this painful and ugly mishap goes unrebuked and sometimes even unnoticed by any adult.

In our culture we teach children about killing and cruelty to a living creature by teaching them how to treat and care for animals. We teach children that they must handle puppies and kittens and every kind of pet gently and care for an animal with respect for its needs. We also teach them that it is permissible to swat a fly but wrong to pull off its wings; that one may trap a mouse but that the trap must kill it instantly. When something goes gravely wrong with this kind of teaching, learning may be distorted in such a way that some who may have a genetic weakness will later react to a triggering event with pathological violence.

But this is certainly not inevitable. An incident of incipient violence may occur, but when it is treated with true concern for the child who is in trouble, the proclivity for violence may be muted for life. And one thing is clear—if we brand as a potential killer a child who has shown excessive violence, it is one way of increasing the likelihood that such a child one day may become pathologically violent.

What we should realize is that some children, particularly children who have been exposed to violence, will need more help than others in learning to live and let live.

Is jealousy innate? Do acts that trigger jealousy differ in different societies? Is it dealt with differently by different peoples? Has jealousy ever played a part in your life?
JULY 1974

I think we tend to include too many kinds of emotional responses under the heading of jealousy. Envy, cupidity, possessiveness, greed, rivalry and vulnerability to slights and self-depreciation—any of these may overlap in some way with jealousy, but they are not quite the same thing.

There are societies that make a great deal of jealousy—anger and hurt when a person one cares for, especially a spouse, lover or intimate friend, seems even for a minute to prefer someone else. But the recognized situations in which jealousy is an appropriate response may be very different. A man may become jealous on discovering that his bride is not a virgin or on realizing that he has failed to satisfy a mistress who has received another lover on the same night. Or a man may be jealous, not of another man, but of his own honor or of the honor of his family. In such a case jealousy may lead a man to kill his wife because she has been compromised by the behavior of another person, even though he knows that she is entirely innocent.

I believe that a jealous response is much stronger in persons of some temperaments than others.

Some societies institutionalize jealousy so that all husbands or all wives have learned a set of conventional responses that signify that emotion. Other societies have institutionalized wife-lending or periods of saturnalia during which jealousy is outlawed. In the one kind of society some individuals will have to act out jealousy that they personally do not feel in order not to be branded as persons lacking in feeling, in manhood or in womanhood. In the other kind of society, in which sexual jealousy is interdicted and access of other men to one's wife or other women to one's husband is explicitly permitted under specified circumstances, the situation may be unbearable.

My normal response to the kind of situation that arouses jealousy in persons of some temperaments is to identify with the affection for another person that is felt by someone I love. I include the one who is loved within the circle of those for whom I feel concern. But if this in turn leads to a real conflict, I leave.

There are as many kinds of response to jealousy and to the situations that are defined as appropriately met by feeling jealous as there are human beings of different innate temperament. And these responses are very differently expressed in different cultures. Suicide, homicide, fierce possessiveness and refusal to let go, or studied indifference—any of these may be the expected response, a kind of response to which some can conform and others cannot at all.

Do you think every human being should have the right to decide that he does not want to live? OCTOBER 1974

I do think so. But there are problems that involve the whole context of suicide.

As long as we maintain, as many people do and as the law does, that a person's life is not his own, that he merely holds in trust a life that belongs to God or to society or to the family, we will continue to take the position that suicide is, in effect, a sin or a crime. Today it is a crime for which the failed suicide may be committed to a mental hospital instead of being condemned to prison, but it is still a crime. However, even if we come to believe, as I think we should, that each person has the right to decide how long his life should be and when he is ready to end it, there remain thorny problems.

We may agree that individuals who are in full possession of their senses and are conscious of the implications of what they are about to do should have the right to terminate their lives. But how do we deal with the widely held belief that anyone who attempts suicide is not in full possession of his senses—that he is, in fact, at least temporarily insane? In effect, what we are saying is that suicide is an involuntary act. Under these circumstances we have little doubt that it becomes the duty of society to protect the would-be suicide, bereft of the normal ability to make choices, from himself.

Some societies deal with the problem of voluntary and involuntary suicide by specifying the conditions under which suicide is a rational and acceptable act. In our own society, lacking any such ordered and agreed-upon alternatives, the most we can do is to introduce the test of help.

In various parts of the country organizations have been formed whose aim is to give help of some kind to desperate people who are contemplating suicide but who, if they are given help and support, may change their minds. Unfortu-

237

nately, this is only a small beginning. If every person who was desperate, lonely, frantic and despairing knew that there were resources to which she or he could turn for help, we could be reasonably sure that those who did not ask for help did not want it. But as long as we leave young and old people, and even children, in unprotected situations of extreme despair, we canot be sure what their intention is. An attempt at suicide may express a passionate wish to live.

Do adolescents in other societies put such a great value on popularity as our adolescents do? JUNE 1976

Popularity as an adolescent goal is a distinctly American phenomenon.

In many European countries an adolescent girl or boy will form an intensely private and idealistic relationship with a friend of the same sex. Or like-minded young people may join together to form a small, very exclusive group around some common interest. Such adolescent friendships, in which self-discovery and exploration of the world are intimately shared, may evoke a lifelong loyalty in spite of every kind of change.

In the United States winning popularity in some adolescent group is a way of reassuring parents who want their children to succeed in a world of which they themselves may know very little and of giving confidence to adolescent girls and boys who are taking on the styles of their peers as a way of breaking the bonds of parental affection as well as parental restrictions. The dating styles of the 1930s and 1940s were an extreme form of popularity contest in which personal choice was subordinated to the excitement of being seen out on a date with a popular member of the other sex. Fortunately, this is a style that has all but vanished.

But adolescents in all societies of which we have any record do seek the comfort and support of their own age group. This is particularly emphasized where immigration, differences in education and very rapid social change have widened the generation gap between parents and children. The fact that other adolescents value who you are—the kind of person you are becoming—may be crucial to a young person's growth and development.

꿈

How do you define privacy? How important is individual privacy to members of a family? AUGUST 1977

Privacy is important to every human being. Recognition of the right to privacy, however it is expressed, is the world's way—and the family's way too—of recognizing the fact that each individual is in some sense unique and must have some freedom to be herself for herself alone. Privacy protects the inner core of the individual's being.

But if one looks around the world, it is clear that respect for the privacy of another person can be expressed in very different—and, to us, quite unexpected—ways: by never touching another person without express permission, by leaving a space around a person, by assigning to each person a house, a room or even a special place within a room that others may not enter without invitation, by never looking someone directly in the eye, even by never calling a person by her or his given name.

I know of no society without rules that protect personal privacy. But in most societies privacy is also a privilege that is unevenly accorded—more to adults than to children, more to women or to men, more to the well than to the sick, more to the rich than to the poor and, very often, more to those of high rank than of low rank. However, the rules also may be reversed, so that kings and all persons in important public positions may be almost totally deprived of real privacy.

Whatever the standards of privacy are, they must be observed; otherwise the person whose privacy has been invaded is almost certain to feel insulted, outraged and denigrated. Invasions of privacy affect very different aspects of living. In our own society, for example, almost every one of us would feel violated if there were no privacy for sexual relations, if we had to bathe or excrete in public, if we were forced to reveal details of our income, if we were made to admit irregularities in our private life or if we found that someone—anyone—had opened and read a private letter.

Respect for the privacy of all those who live together in a home is one way in which each one of us learns and expresses a basic concern for the individuality of other people. As part of her learning, a child comes to value both what she keeps to herself as an individual and what, by her own choice, she shares with others. The rules for the protection of privacy may change radically over a lifetime, as they have in our own and most other societies. But having learned at home within the intimacy of one's own family how valuable privacy is, one can learn new rules and live by them. And one can learn in the same way to respect the rules, different from one's own, by which another person—one's grandmother or, equally, a stranger in a strange land—protects her individuality.

Do you still adhere to the notion that it is temperament rather than sex that determines social roles and that social conditioning determines an individual's temperament? AUGUST 1977

First let's clarify the terms. By temperament I mean the constellation of traits determined by the individual's biological heritage. You are born with your own particular temperament—your way of approaching life.

Character is distinct from temperament. By character I mean the constellation of traits that are emphasized in the upbringing of individuals as members of a given culture—as Americans or Eskimos or Chinese. It is our shared cultural character that helps us to understand and communicate with one another as Americans.

Personality combines the two, temperament and character. It is the outcome of the combination. The personality of an individual with a certain inborn temperament is shaped by the experience of growing up and living as a woman or a man in a particular cultural setting.

On the basis of research I have carried out, I believe that there are male and female versions of the same temperament. Temperamentally there are male as well as female introverts and extroverts, fiercely brave women as well as fiercely brave men, shy and gentle men as well as shy and gentle women.

Every society emphasizes an expected personality for each sex. Sometimes both men and women are expected to have the same kind of personality. That is, both men and women are expected to be outgoing, active people or, on the contrary, introspective, meditative people. In cultures where this is so, sex differences are reflected in the particular ways in which a woman and a man are expected to behave and the activities each is expected to engage in. In a culture in which both men and women are expected to be outgoing and active, women may be expected to take a lot of initiative in personal relations between men and women, while men may be expected to take the initiative in public, community activities.

In other cultures it is expected that the personalities of women and men will be complementary. The personality of women is based on one set of temperamental traits and that of men on another. In such a culture women may be expected to be passive, gentle and modest, while men may be expected to be active and self-assertive in whatever activities persons of either sex engage in.

Neither sex nor temperament as such "determines" social roles but in different cultures social roles may be assigned on the basis of either sex or temperament. Sex is the easiest way of making a division in assigning social rules: Women do the fishing, men the hunting; women care for the home, men run public life.

But since all temperaments are represented in both sexes, the assignment of social roles entirely on the basis of sex, rather than temperament, is likely to be very unsatisfactory to a great many individuals. What we should be aiming for, I think, is a kind of social world in which the great variety of personalities, masculine and feminine, is recognized, and in which individuals are free to choose social roles that are in keeping with their temperament as well as with their trained skills.

ह~

Do you think that Americans have a collective national character? If so, how would you describe it? AUGUST 1977

The term "national character" is used in several different ways. Sometimes it is used to refer to the stereotypical images that the people of one country have of members of other nations. These are reflected in such statements as "Scotsmen are stingy" or "Frenchmen are interested only in sex"or "Germans are orderly and obedient."

The term also may be used to refer to the stereotypical images a people have of themselves, which may be complimentary or decidedly uncomplimentary. For example, we say about ourselves that "Americans are generous and feed the world," and also, "Americans are wasteful and materialistic."

Sometimes we become conscious of "national character" only when we meet fellow nationals abroad and are repelled by behavior we recognize that we share in some way; or, on the contrary, we are delighted to meet a stranger in a faraway place whose familiar accent and manner suddenly make us feel warm and friendly.

Technically, anthropologists mean something else by "national character." We use the term to refer to the cluster of traits that members of a nation share because they have grown up and live within a shared set of social institutions: a form of government, a system of taxation, a legal system, a type of national economy, and so on. And these same people share a set of beliefs about the past and various kinds of historical experiences: wars with particular enemies, victories and defeats, periods of depression and periods of optimism and success.

Such a cluster of shared traits does not mean that all Americans are alike—that, for example, all Americans are generous. It does mean that the different ways in which they are generous and ungenerous are related to one another. So whether or not we individually give generously to those in need or grumble about paying taxes, we are more likely to trust private charity—such organizations as CARE, or Food for the World, or the Hospital Ship HOPE, or the Save the Children Federation—than "foreign aid" administered by governments.

And a phrase like "majority rule" will raise echoes in our minds, whether we firmly believe that representative democracy is the only rational and fair form of government or have decided that our form of democracy has failed. Also we may get into difficulties in trying to understand another people even though we share many of their values. For example, when the question of compromise comes up, Americans tend to feel that in any compromise the very best of each party's proposals is lost; the British feel instead that compromise is a good thing, regardless of how unequally the two sides have had to surrender their cherished goals.

National character can best be described and identified when the behavior of members of one nation is viewed in relation to the behavior of people of another nation. It is especially revealing to compare the peoples of the various English-speaking countries that were colonized from the British Isles—the United States, Canada, Australia, New Zealand, South Africa and the several English-speaking Caribbean islands. Such comparisons bring into high relief the many ways in which a people starting with the same set of national institutions can diverge as they live through generations of different and contrasting experiences.

It is possible to identify an American national character, particularly in those situations in which we are responding to a common event. However, most of the time we act not so much as "Americans" but as Georgians or Texans or Vermonters or Californians, as Harvard men or Vassar women, as artists or wives and mothers, as high-school graduates or highly trained scientists. And we always behave as individuals, on the basis of the way each of us has experienced the world. Only occasionally do we realize that we are in all this also acting as "Americans."

You speak of "we" as a historical and cultural term. But how do you help people to realize that all of us are "we"?
FEBRUARY 1978

In those rare moments of national triumph or tragedy in

243

which everyone feels united, all Americans become "we." Certainly we as a nation sorrowed when President Kennedy was shot down and we as a people triumphed on the day of the first moon walk.

At other times "we" may represent only one's own family or, very narrowly, only one's own social, religious, ethnic or racial group. The interesting thing is that most people do continually shift their stance and identify themselves with a great variety of groups, each of which becomes "we" in one context or another. The "we" classification changes as our perspective on the world changes, now expanding to include all human beings and now contracting to "thee and me."

In contrast to those with whom we identify, there are those whom we call "they"—a vague and anonymous "they" whose interests by definition are opposed to whatever "we" ourselves stand for. "They" litter the streets; "they" are against civil rights; "they" spread destructive rumors in a crisis and hoard food in times of scarcity; "they" condone bribery and corruption in high places. "They," clearly, are outsiders who all too often are to blame when "we" fail.

Children who are continually told not to behave like the So-and-so children down the block will always have a hard time finding a wider "we" group. Other people, different from themselves in appearance, speech, education, wealth or manners, have come to represent an evil and rejected part of themselves, a part against which their parents continually warned them when they appeared, inappropriately, with dirty hands and uncombed hair, used "bad" grammar or "bad" language, slouched instead of standing up straight or expressed radical or other ideas considered unacceptable.

A first requirement in bringing up children who will find it easy to share a common humanity with others who are different in their appearance, education and aspirations is never to exclude as different from our own group the child whose behavior we disapprove of. By pointing out that the child down the street who never is clean and screams dirty words is an outsider—is poor or has drug-addicted parents or belongs to a different ethnic, racial or religious group—we convey to our children the idea that "they," who are unlike ourselves, are everything "we" reject in ourselves.

In wartime, when we feel that our country's safety may be at stake, our fellow citizens become "we" because we value them as fellow citizens. But at the same time millions of people who before were only vaguely "not us" become dangerously "they"—enemies whom it is moral and patriotic to kill.

The growth of civilization has been a history of including more people, and more diverse people, in the category of "we." But the scope of the "theys" whom we cannot trust and who may want to destroy us has increased simultaneously. Our best hope is that we can come to care positively about the diversity of human beings and ally ourselves with many different groups, all of whom we think of as "we." But until we do better at accepting our own faults and failures along with our successes, I do not know whether we shall be able to recognize that "they" are also "we."

On your anthropological expeditions, what group of primitive people seemed to you the most peaceful and co-operative? What group seemed to you the fiercest? What can we learn from both? FEBRUARY 1978

The key phrase is "seemed to you" followed by superlatives: the *most* peaceful and the fierc*est*. A literal answer would be entirely dependent on the nature of the people I myself have studied—six South Seas peoples and one American Indian group.

It is rather more useful to draw on comparative studies in which we have tried to place various primitive peoples as co-operative, competitive or indivualistic in their basic approach to living. As it turns out, these characteristics do not necessarily go along with fierceness or peacefulness. A people may be very fierce but so individualistic that they are not very good organizers of group actions; they may quarrel fiercely among themselves but they do not make war.

Another people who are very co-operative in their relations with one another use their capacity for working together harmoniously in efficient war-making.

If we look back at our own Euro-American history, we discover that over time there have been very marked shifts in "fierceness"—for example, if we compare earlier Sweden with modern Sweden or the inhabitants of the little Jewish towns of Eastern Europe with their descendants in contemporary Israel. In evaluating how fierce or how peaceful, how co-operative or how competitive a people are, we have to allow for the immediate conditions in which they live, who their neighbors, friends and enemies are and how they view their own past, peaceful or warlike. Compare, for example, the self-images of two American states, Rhode Island and Texas, one of which began its known history as a refuge for the religiously or economically persecuted in earliest New England and the other, the Lone Star State, which sees itself as uniquely founded on autonomy—entirely forgetting that Vermont too was briefly an independent republic before it joined the rebelling colonies.

We can learn some things from comparative studies of single traits, but we do learn much more from studies of whole patterns of behavior, especially if these are extended over time.

Do you believe in the power of demons and evil spirits?
AUGUST 1978

No. But I know that the idea of demons and evil spirits can have devastating power over those who do believe in them.

Self-analysis (sometimes with professional help) seems to be one of the great preoccupations of Americans these days. Are we gaining anything of value from this? NOVEMBER 1978

Self-analysis has accompanied the development of the various schools of psychotherapy, from the sophisticated, long-term procedures of a Freudian psychoanalysis, which may take many years of several sessions a week, to the many kinds of "instant" therapy like Couéism, which could be taught in a few short lessons ("Day by day, in every way, I'm getting better and better"). Psychotherapy, in the sense that the individual realizes a deep personal need and the possibility of change, developed only when the idea of rapid change became a recognized aspect of social life. And if we map the acceptance of psychoanalysis, we find that it took hold in capital cities like Vienna and Berlin, London and New York, where many kinds of people meet and sophistication is born of such encounters, but that its acceptance came much more slowly elsewhere.

In capital cities where the arts flourish, talented women and men gather to argue new issues and experiment with new forms of self-expression. But for those who have no cultivated talent, practice in self-knowledge can provide an alternative route to sophistication. The childhood experience that reappears in the work of artists also can be framed in words exchanged between patient and therapist, and so be given a form that no longer need haunt one's dreams. Dreams themselves can become a form of self-expression and an aid to healing.

A willingness to look at oneself within some framework of analysis and to discover how one can escape from a nagging sense of inferiority, from a prevailing feeling of grievance against the world or from continuing to fight some childhood battle with a parent by fighting every significant man or woman one meets—all this can add immeasurably to the individual's sense of herself as a person.

The principal danger, I think, lies not in analyzing oneself but in interminably analyzing others—one's spouse, friends, parents, children, teachers, pupils, boss, co-workers and public figures—arriving at pat, facile explanations of their character and behavior and using these explanations punitively—for example, in lectures delivered to children or quarrels between lovers.

In all responsible forms of therapy, the therapist has already worked through various personal psychological difficulties that are also a source of deep distress for those who come seeking help. Psychotherapy is not an activity that can be practiced by the equally ignorant and untrained on one another. Group therapy, in the course of which equals who still lack self-knowledge may criticize one another, requires a highly skilled group therapist who is ever watchful of danger.

Self-analysis with, and later without, the help of a highly trained professional therapist can be very valuable. Among friends, however, sympathetic and nonjudgmental listening is both much safer and more rewarding. One unfortunate by-product of the availability of professional help is that friends are less willing than they once were just to listen. They sometimes feel unnecessarily burdened by confidences and drive their harassed friends, perhaps quite unnecessarily, into psychotherapy, when what was most immediately needed was a chance to think aloud with someone who was close and knew a good deal about one's life.

How do you define success? Does the meaning of success in our society today differ from its meaning in the past?
NOVEMBER 1978

I don't think we have changed our conception of success.

We define success—now as in the past—as pre-eminence within a category. The best ice skater, the richest man in town, the most popular actress, the winner of an important award—the winner of an Oscar or a Nobel prize—the most widely read author, the baseball player who commands the highest salary—all these are successful men and women, each within a particular field.

Traditionally we also have distinguished between well-earned success—achievement that is the outcome of planning and concentrated effort—and success that seems to be based on luck, where the outcome appears to be disproportionate to the effort or the just deserts of the person.

We applaud spectacular success in a field other than our own. An actress can admire the success of a baseball player or a ballet dancer. A writer can admire an acrobat or a painter who is successful. But we are very grudging in our applause for success in our own field. As we see it, one person's success detracts from another's. You can't be best or next to the top or one of the three best (whatever) without preventing someone else from having that rank.

And we do tend to rank people on a single scale, without taking into account all the complicated things that may be involved. We say, "She is good (or better or best) as an organizer"—or whatever the talent or trait we have singled out may be.

Personally, I think success is a combination of good management and good luck. I myself would rather do well in a field in which I have talent than fail gloriously in a field in which I had high aspirations but not a matching talent. The kind of aspiration that may end in glorious failure has a quality I can admire, but I do not envy it in others. And I must admit that I personally measure success in terms of the contributions an individual makes to her or his fellow human beings.

≪ 11 ≫
PERSONAL CHOICES

A columnist in a California newspaper has accused you of thinking you are an authority on everything in the world—in fact, "a polymath." You do answer a great variety of questions in Redbook and in question periods after your lectures. Will you comment on his accusation? JANUARY 1965

There are two comments I might make. First, if one puts oneself in a position to be asked questions in a public forum, one must stand up to the questions that are asked, whatever they may be. A speaker can avoid this by accepting only written questions and selecting those it is convenient to answer, or by giving a carefully prepared statement to the press instead of holding an open press conference. I like neither of these methods. As a result, I am sometimes asked questions I would not have elected to discuss, mainly because I do not feel myself well enough informed to do so.

My second comment is that the anthropologist's one special area of competence is the ability to think about a whole society and everything in it. This is what we have learned to do in our years of hard work in areas where disease is rampant, nutrition is poor and comfort is nil. Working in tiny primitive societies, we learn to think about the way a lullaby is related to a funeral dirge, a way of handling tools is related to a way of looking at the universe; and we bring this training back to our own society. We cannot know the details of each facet of our complex culture, but we can keep our eyes on the way the different facets are related one to another. In this sense an experienced anthropologist is perhaps the closest

251

thing we have to the "world's greatest authority on everything—the polymath." And in this sense I feel the responsibility at least to think seriously about questions that are proposed to me.

ट☙

At what time in history would you most like to have lived?
MARCH 1963

I am glad to be living today. In this period, in which our understanding of human behavior is expanding at an unprecedented rate and in which we are faced with greater responsibility than at any other time in history, every living person is given opportunities for significant action. Today we are faced with the need not only to preserve ourselves, our children, our country and our values, but also to preserve the whole world from the threat of possible destruction. I would not choose to have lived in a period when the horizons were narrower and the urgency to act less strong and clear.

ट☙

Why do you write for such different kinds of magazines?
JULY 1963

I write for such diverse publications as *Redbook, The American Journal of Orthopsychiatry, Foreign Affairs, The Harvard Business Review, Public Health Papers of the World Health Organization, TV Guide, Seventeen, Journal of Higher Education, Mennonite, Think* and *The American Anthropologist*. I do this because I believe that in a democracy it is essential for the layman to understand the gist of the work being done in our highly compartmentalized academic disciplines. This is particularly so in the social sciences, where it is essential that public understanding keep in step with the increased understanding of the social scientist.

I believe that almost any idea can be stated simply enough so that it is intelligible to laymen, and that if one cannot state a matter clearly enough so that even an intelligent twelve-year-old can understand it, one should remain within the

252

cloistered walls of the university and laboratory until one gets a better grasp of one's subject matter. It is notorious that recent graduate students can often teach graduate students successfully, but fail miserably with college freshmen. The ability to present material in a simple fashion improves as one gets further from the textbooks and has more experience in the real world. I have made it a practice to try to alter the climate of opinion so that new ideas may bud and flower.

In what place in the world would you like most to live?
JULY 1963

Where I do live—in New York City.

Among all the people you have met and talked with, whom have you found the most stimulating? SEPTEMBER 1963

John G. Winant, our ambassador to Great Britain during World War II. He combined an extraordinary intellectual speed, so that one never had to pause or rephrase an idea, with a tremendous sense of moral responsibility, so that all quick solutions had to be tested, turned over and examined from all sides. One could actually *see* his extraordinary mental processes at work as one of his hands moved with the speed of thought while the other almost fumbled in the effort to slow down and consider all the consequences. Every conversation with him was both stimulating and momentous.

Of all the famous people you have met, which ones impressed you the most, and why? OCTOBER 1966

When one meets a man or a woman who has become famous as an author, a musician, a statesman, a hero, an explorer or the discoverer of an important scientific truth, one hopes, I think, to find some correspondence between the quality of the person and the quality of the acts that led to fame. Often there appears to be little relationship between the two. The author's novels are fascinating; the author himself is a fussy and petulant bore. But when one feels a real congruence between the man and his work, it gives one a tremendous lift, a feeling of pride in being a human being. This is how I felt when I first heard Fritz Kreisler play the violin and when I first met Anna Freud.

What national television programs do you watch, and which do you like—if any? DECEMBER 1963

I do not watch any television program regularly. I do not lead the kind of life that fits in with fixed habits. Even reading *The New York Times* every day is sometimes difficult, and I seldom have the time to sit down and watch a newscast. Moreover, the way both television and radio jangle the human mind with continual trivial advertising interruptions makes both of them uncongenial sources of news.

What I value television for is the big live broadcasts of significant events. At the inauguration of President Kennedy, I would not have missed the fire on the podium for anything in the world—with no one worrying as to whether it might be a bomb and solemn dignitaries trying to save the broadcast wiring. I have watched with fascination the impressive telecasts of John Glenn's space flight and his meeting with the President, and such events as G. David Schine's testimony at the McCarthy hearings, and party conventions, and speeches made by losing candidates conceding victory, and the August 28th civil rights march on Washington. If I hear that foreign dignitaries are often subjected to rough treatment on a certain television program, I want to know just how terrible that treatment is. And when the press and radio report the presence of a tremendous and enthusiastic crowd at an important speech, I want to *see* that crowd—if not actually, then on the television screen.

I think you'd make a marvelous Secretary of Health, Education and Welfare. Would you accept the post if it were offered to you? FEBRUARY 1964

This is the kind of post that should be occupied by a professional person with a lifetime of experience in one of the three fields. The more complex our knowledge becomes, the more complicated its execution becomes, the less we can afford to depend upon even the most gifted amateurs. I am a research scientist, not an experienced administrator, and I would not consider myself a suitable candidate for such a position.

Who are your favorite novelists? MAY 1964

The game of favorites is an old American custom. It makes a good children's game, but it can be overdone. Favorite when? At twelve? At twenty? At forty? Now? Favorite in what connection? Because a novelist has written novels of great significance? Because a novel is a depiction of universal values? Or because I read a particular book at just the moment in my life when it had a special significance for me? One book of this kind is Virginia Woolf's *The Waves*, which I read in New Guinea in 1932 when I was developing a theory of temperament. Another is Mary Webb's *Precious Bane*, which was sent up to me in the New Guinea mountains, where for three months I had been living on three rationed pages a day of Laurence Sterne's *Tristram Shandy*. Two others are Nevil Shute's *Legacy* and D. H. Lawrence's *Kangaroo*, which together provided background when I was lecturing in Australia in 1951.

Novels serve many different purposes in life, and at different times we have quite different feelings and ideas about their authors. Some novels, like *Vanity Fair* and *David Copperfield*, can be read several times—in adolescence for their plots and their revelations about life, later for the author's style, and later still to recreate the past or to see the present in a new perspective.

What national magazines do you read regularly? JULY 1964

None. At home I read *The New York Times* every day and, when I am away, whenever I can get it. When I am traveling I read the local press with care. I buy particular issues of magazines because of special topics. Sometimes I subscribe to a magazine for a brief trial period. *Science,* with its news of the scientific world, comes every week. Now and then I look over the newsstands and pick out a magazine I have never read or have not read for a long time. When an interesting event takes place, I buy a batch of the magazines that are covering it from different points of view. For example, I looked at various picture magazines that recorded the first space flights; and when, for the first time in human history, human martyrdom—the suicide of a Buddhist monk—was recorded photographically by eyewitnesses, I followed the different ways in which European and American magazines interpreted the event.

Because I am a professional person, I subscribe to a number of professional journals and I am sent membership publications, such as the journal of the American Association of University Women and the bulletin of the Association for the United Nations. But on the whole I prefer to relate to what is going on and then to read about the particular event—a controversy about teachers' education that boils up with James Conant's book on education; the horrid experiments conducted at Yale to find out how far subjects in a psychology experiment would go when ordered, as they supposed, to inflict pain; the litigation over the right of a Negro American and a white American to enter into a common-law marriage. In order to follow up an interesting event I may first read the evening papers, then the weekly magazines and the reviews, then whatever articles may turn up in a scientific journal or a journal of affairs like *Foreign Affairs,* and I will also watch the correspondence columns of a newspaper I do not usually read, or try to see a television news roundup.

To avoid being overwhelmed by the printed torrent, one is easily tempted to read just one newspaper and settle down in the rut defined by its editorial policy, to listen to one radio news commentator or to watch one television newscast. Every household has to work out its own strategy of really keeping up with what is happening in the world, a strategy that will change as children grow older and take a larger part in following events.

Would you mind naming the three or four movies that have impressed you most in recent years? SEPTEMBER 1964

As a moviegoer I am exceedingly erratic. Once in a while, late at night, I like to go to a movie on the spur of the moment. In a city like New York there is almost always (but not invariably) some movie one has wanted to see; and whenever small theaters bring back movies of different vintages one can go to see a film made twenty years ago and compare it with another made by the same actor or with a different film on the same theme. Quite often I see on its tenth time around a movie I have wanted to see but somehow have always missed. So I may collapse time a little. But I would list, as films that have moved me, *Rashomon, High Noon, The Red Balloon, Hiroshima Mon Amour, Ballad of a Soldier,* and *Sundays and Cybèle.* It seems very important that films are enough of a cross-national language that through them we glimpse other national styles of thinking and feeling.

Among the younger generation of anthropologists, who do you think is making the most significant contribution? JANUARY 1965

I think I have mentioned in earlier columns my feeling about the American preference for rating things on a single scale—for asking about one's favorite color or favorite book. I cannot think about people—or about books or colors or flowers, for that matter—ranked in a simple hierarchy. I am often asked to place a student among the top five per cent or ten per cent of the graduate students I have taught. Usually I refuse to do so because I am conscious of the differences among them, especially the very different talents and skills and interests they have.

Anthropologists are highly individual and specialized people. Each of them is marked by the kind of work he or she prefers and has done, which in time becomes an aspect of that individual's personality. How, then, is one to choose among them?

Consider a man who has done a year's field work in New Guinea, three years' work in Mexico, two years' theoretical work in Paris, who has published one large monograph and is now back in New Guinea for another five years' field work. Or a man who has been working at establishing new styles of archeological work on primitive and historical materials, and who has developed a way of building model "sites" from specifications so that students can excavate them and in doing so learn how to work with and think about archeological problems. Or a girl who has spent three long years extracting the last living, though hidden, traces of a difficult North American Indian culture and who has developed a new theory about one of the most striking American Indian institutions, the potlatch. Or a young blind anthropologist who spent almost a year living alone in a Mexican village where most of the adults are blind, studying the effects of blindness on people's expectations. Or still another young anthropologist who has solved the mysteries surrounding the life of the African pygmies, who lived with them deep in the Ituri forest, following the hunters moving at breakneck speed along forest paths where he had to bend double to avoid the branches that were above their heads, and who has given us an inimitable record of their life. Or a man who has used his field work to organize in his own head some seventy cultures—studied by others—so he can search through all of them for new ways of formulating and working on problems, a kind of activity for which we cannot yet, because of its extreme complexity, program computers. Or a girl who has used her anthropological training to study the life of primates, from which she is bringing us fascinating accounts that are altering our understanding of the processes of learning among animals. Or still another man who has laid out ten years' work, based on his field work in a Borneo jungle, on an exploration of the problem of what special sensory experiences—color or temperature—mean in the lives of a people. Each of these men and women is a unique and exciting individual. We cannot place them in a hierarchical relation to one another. We can just be glad they are here, at work.

ॐ

Do you have any brothers and sisters? If so, how did they influence you in your formative years? JANUARY 1967

I am the eldest of five children. The next was my brother, two years and four months younger. A sister four years younger died in infancy. Then came two little sisters, seven and nine years younger than I. Because of the wide age interval, my brother and I formed one group and the "babies" another.

Having a younger brother made me look for situations away from home in which I would be the younger one, taking delight in and admiring the superior capacities of others who were older than myself. As the eldest child I sometimes was troubled by finding myself in the exposed position of doing something better just because I was older. My father always paid us for getting good marks in school. A college professor, he insisted that students who just got by with passing grades would never succeed in life. In addition, he demanded that I make better grades than my brother, because he felt that studying and making good marks are easier for a girl.

The loss of my first little sister while she was still a happy, delighted infant permanently shaped my attitudes toward life. For a long time I refused to believe that she was really gone. I daydreamed about finding her again, and these dreams merged into fantasies about a twin sister who I imagined had been stolen by the gypsies and whom I might find again someday. Then when my next little sister was born, a very gay and happy baby, I felt this was a restitution. Her coming gave me a sure expectation that losses can be recouped and that no disaster is permanently crippling.

If you had to choose another country in which to spend the rest of your life, which countries would you consider, and why? JANUARY 1967

I value cities. Cities are meeting places, points of convergence. A city also is where one expects to find a university, libraries, bookstores, theaters, art galleries, music, and excited young people coming and going. The presence of a great city with a thriving intellectual and artistic life would be important.

Another consideration would be that of language. I would prefer to live where I could make use of at least some of my existing language skills. I would not mind learning a new language. But I would prefer not to have to learn a new script, for this, I think, would tend to slow down my participation in the society.

Because I was brought up in the eastern United States, there are certain characteristics of the Temperate Zone that I find most attractive. Climate; the range of temperatures; trees, shrubs and flowers that vary with the landscape and change with the seasons; and the presence and sound of familiar, rather than exotic, birds and beasts—all these, taken together, might affect my choice. I would not want to live where it was very cold, especially where it was cold, damp and rainy most of the time; nor would I choose to live where the sun blazed down every day without respite. I think I would know enough to search for a landscape of the spirit, the kind of landscape made precious to a people by long familiarity and intensity of feeling.

In the end, however, it would be the people, the kind of life they lived and the things that needed to be done, that would determine my choice. There are two kinds of country that catch my imagination. One is the young country—Australia and Israel, for example—that is in need of trained people. The other is the very old country—Iran, for example—that is embarking on a new course involving deep and rapid change. Countries like these probably would compete successfully in my mind with nations whose ways of life have been established over the years—countries like France and England, Italy and Russia, Denmark and Norway. And perhaps if I were in a sacrificial mood and knew that my choice would allow me to exercise some distinctive skill, I might select an extremely difficult country—South Africa, Haiti or Indonesia, for example—a country torn by discord and struggle over how life is to be lived and what the future holds.

If we rule out your present profession as an anthropologist, what field would you want to enter and why? MARCH 1968

I find this a very difficult question. One way of answering it is to go back to the possibilities I considered before I chose to become an anthropologist. The three toward which I felt drawn were the arts, politics—especially politics as a way of working toward the amelioration of the conditions of life for the underdog—and social science.

I rejected the arts, first painting and then writing, because I felt I did not have the talent to pursue a career as an artist in a world that had a place only for the supremely gifted painter or poet. Politics continued to attract me because I enjoyed speaking to audiences, writing exhortatory articles, organizing activities and working directly with people. But in the end I chose anthropology.

Initially I regarded my other possible career choices as alternatives to social science, not as alternatives specifically to anthropology. Then in anthropology I saw an opportunity to be guided by my preferences and make use of the skills that had led me to formulate my original set of choices. Anthropology is not a science in which one works primarily with materials others have provided. Rather, it involves working actively with living people, using many of the talents that are also valuable in politics. It means observing and finding ways to record all the things one has observed. It means writing. And the findings of anthropology are highly relevant to our future ability to make a better world for people to live in.

Of course, I can think of ways of expanding the fields of knowledge open to me. I would like to have more training in the natural sciences, more opportunity for study of the living natural world, a broader knowledge of the history of those areas of the world in which I initially learned only to deal with primitive peoples, a firmer grasp of modern mathematics. . . . But when it comes to the choice of a profession, I am like the Englishman who said, "If I had not been born an Englishman, I would have wanted most to be born one."

Have you ever used "feminine wiles" to get what you wanted? NOVEMBER 1978

Yes, occasionally I have.

Once in a while I have allowed a man to reject me when I wished to initiate the rejection but believed it would severely injure the man's ego for me to do so. And a few times in my life I have asked for something as a concession or a privilege that was really my right to have. My father used to say that my mother was mistaken in asking for her rights; he believed that men dislike conceding rights and prefer women who say, Oh! and, Ah! in the right places. But this was not my mother's way.

On rare occasions I have used an irrational appeal to persuade a group to stop one piece of irrationality in the name of another. For example, I once persuaded a committee of my peers to admit parapsychologists to full membership in a scientific organization by pointing out to this group—many of whose members were antireligious—that the Pope had once censured Galileo for his discoveries.

I remember such instances because increasingly I have have come to think of behavior of this kind as manipulative and unethical, even though it may sometimes be necessary. It seems to me very important to continue to distinguish between two evils. It may be necessary temporarily to accept a lesser evil, but one must never label a necessary evil as good.

Do you recall daydreams you had as a child? What role do you think daydreams have played in your life?

SEPTEMBER 1968

I do remember early daydreams, and it surprised me to find that many people do not. At one time I planned an elaborate retrospective study in which I proposed to use daydreams as measures of maturity and contentment. But when I found that most people had great difficulty in remembering, I had to give up what had seemed a promising idea.

But looking at daydreams seems to me one way of approaching one's own deeper wishes, and I have used mine for this kind of understanding.

One recurrent daydream during my childhood was of finding a twin sister who, I fantasied, had been stolen at birth and who, when I found her, would be an ideal playmate. In later years this daydream was transformed into one of finding a double who would take over half the things I was asked to do, the things there never was time for one person alone to accomplish. This seemed an excellent idea until one day I realized that having a satisfactory alter ego would only make life doubly difficult, because she too would think up new things to do for which neither of us would have the necessary time or energy. Thus ended a daydream that during childhood had lightened hours of compulsory waiting and later had relieved the tedium of sleepless periods.

In another childhood daydream I fantasied that *I* was the kidnapped child. I was taken to some adventurous place, where I learned many languages and skills that were inaccessible to me at home. When at last I returned, I was identified as myself and was welcomed home as a very superior person. Part of the appeal of this daydream was that my own identity somehow withstood transformation while I lived among gypsies, or in an exotic land, or was a member of a band working for the victory of a good cause. The dream was so real that I was pleased when a cut on my wrist left a permanent scar, for this mark would help to show who I was. This is a kind of daydream that feeds a child's sense of being different from his family and still, in its outcome, reassures him that he does belong.

As I grew older I began to use the disappearance of a daydream about any special subject as a measure of my own contentment. And then, somewhat later, I began to be afraid that my own daydreaming might affect other people's lives. I think this coincided with a period when I was taking on responsibilities for students and their search for career plans. As a teacher I learned how careful I had to be not to impose my own daydream, not even one I conjured up about the expectant student earnestly looking for a problem or a project to work on. The difficulty is that the picture evoked by a teacher's imagination may leave the recipient powerless to form pictures of his own. The problem, as I see it, is to provoke the student's daydreaming capacity without interposing your own. Of course, this is a problem for parents as well as teachers—how to cultivate a child's (or a student's) own potentialities without in any way determining the direction in which he will grow and blossom.

I often use my daydreams as a way of deciding what my actual feelings are. When I am of two minds, or more, about a problem, playing out the consequences of one choice, and then another, gives me a chance to experiment. When the daydream goes dead, when I find I don't want to go on with the story, I realize this is something I don't want to do. But when the story flows along happily, I suddenly know that I have made up my mind.

In your busy life do you ever feel the need for solitude?
FEBRUARY 1971

I like to be alone to work, away from interruptions. I like to be free to write in the early morning before the news of the world comes crowding in, before the mailman brings importunate letters and the telephone begins its insistent ringing. Early morning is the time I write best.

I like to feel free to get up in the middle of the night—to record an idea, to run a bath or to move around the room preparing for a journey—without having to worry about waking up someone who needs to sleep.

I enjoy long plane trips. On them I take work along I need not do immediately and books I need not read and when there is no one I know on the plane with whom I will have to talk. I used to love long voyages for the hours during which I was free just to lie in a deck chair and look at the sea. I enjoy watching sunrise and sunset—sunrise in flight and sunset at sea—and discovering unexpected, changing cloud configurations.

It is true, this is not "solitude" as many people think of it. I don't have any real desire to get away from people. I enjoy watching others—a mother and a child playing together, children exploring an airport, couples strolling down a street. But I also enjoy, for the moment, not having to respond to the life going on around me—being free not to listen or watch purposefully.

I never think of solitude as preferable to the company of people I love except when I have work to do or a problem to think out. I would never go to a play or a concert or an art exhibition alone. I enjoy reading while someone else is also reading by the fire in the same room, or near me on a steep cliff above the sea or at the sunny edge of an autumn wood. But these are quiet pleasures I seldom have. Because I never have time to see as much of my friends as I would like, when I am with them we talk, even on a holiday.

Many people think of going to the South Seas as a kind of social solitude and visualize it as an escape from the interruptions and urgencies of the modern world. For me, of course, this isn't true. I enjoy field work because it is so completely demanding. When I am in the field I have to listen, even in my sleep, for any unusual or unexpected sound. It may signal some event to which I must pay attention—immediately.

In 1953 when I returned to Manus, in the Admiralty Islands, my life was pervaded by sound. The village houses were crowded together. Less than four feet separated my house from those of my neighbors on two sides. In each there was a large family with many children. At what ever hour of the night the fishermen left, they lighted bright lamps and shouted to one another. When they returned with the night's catch, the whole family woke up to have a meal. During that

whole stay in Peri village I never slept more than two con-
secutive hours.

Air travel, for all its conveniences, has one great drawback
for me. After an arduous field trip it used to be an enormous
pleasure to go home by ship. On a ship I could choose my
own companions or sit quietly doing nothing, and I could
sleep without being awakened.

I very much enjoy sleep from which I know I'll not be
awakened by a bell or a tap on the door. But I don't like
dreamless sleep or sleep in which one dream is monoto-
nously repeated. That seems a waste of a good night. However, there are very few nights when I do not know, before I
go to sleep, the exact hour at which the alarm will wake me
up.

But this is the way I choose to live.

**Aside from your mother and grandmother, who were your
female role models, personal as well as professional?**
MAY 1975

In my childhood there were my mother's college friends,
altogether a remarkable group of women. They gave me a
sense of the wide range of choices open to a woman who
wanted to be a person and make a contribution to the world,
but they also showed me that a gift by itself was not enough.
You had to work hard to turn a gift into some kind of accomplishment.

Then there were the two godmothers I chose for myself
when I decided to be christened. One was the charming
daughter of the minister of our little church. She smoothed
her father's way in the world and later, in the First World War,
became a YMCA secretary overseas. She was for me a model
of extended graciousness and love. The other was a massive
executive woman of great erudition and authority who built
herself a complete life, elegant, book-filled and sophisticated. She used to say that she never envied women their
husbands but she did envy them their children. She was,
among other things, a master editor. She edited my book

Male and Female with the fine objectivity possible only to a sophisticated celibate. When she was eighty I asked her to undertake an emergency editing job and ventured to tell her, "Aunt Isabel, a lot of it will be in Russian!" I knew she did not speak Russian, although she used to learn a different European language every summer. But she replied, "I'll bring my dictionaries."

In college there was the anthropologist Ruth Benedict, whose exquisite responsiveness to literature and disciplined appreciation of anthropological materials gave me a sense of how poetry and scientific work could be combined. I had been hesitating over a career in the arts, in science or in politics. Knowing Ruth Benedict, I could see how a concern for the arts and science were linked—and I chose anthropology. But I did nothing in politics until the beginning of the Second World War, when Eleanor Roosevelt, with her tremendous willingness to listen and try to understand the world around her, became a political role model for me.

ౘ☙

What seems to some people money well spent on personal pleasures seems wasted money to others. Is there something you "squander" money on—and what kind of squandering particularly exasperates you? SEPTEMBER 1976

I grew up in the days of ten-cent movies, two-cent first-class postage stamps and penny post cards, five-cent ice-cream cones and ten-cent hot dogs. Paying an enormous sum today upsets me far more when it is for something I bought for much less as a child. I am not surprised or upset by the cost of long-playing records or tape-recorder cassettes or first class airplane tickets because I have no childhood standards of comparison for things like these.

The kind of thing I mind most is knowing that someone—myself or anyone else—is spending a lot of money on mediocre food in a supposedly "four-star" restaurant or for tickets to a poor show or for a table at a nightclub with poor food, bad drinks and a dull floor show—especially as I don't much like nightclubs. I am very much annoyed by silly and expensive gifts—such things as gold pens or pencils or lighters with my initials engraved on them, so that I can't even give them away to people who enjoy silly things. I feel burdened by academic hoods and medals that are too heavy even to carry around—all the sorts of things that can't be used or sold or given away and can't in decency be thrown away.

Once I was given a solid ebony carving of a male elephant trampling a female lion, brought especially for me from the Sudan. It weighed twelve pounds. I know this because I had to carry it as excess luggage flying out of West Berlin. And then I had to keep it on a closet shelf for years in case the donor, whom I valued highly, should come to the United States and visit me at home. I think I am most infuriated by expensive presents that I do not want and cannot use and that I cannot give away, either because they have my initials or name on them or because to do so might hurt the feelings of the giver. And if I know that the giver is hard up, I am even more infuriated.

But I do enjoy being taken out to dinner by someone who is very well-to-do (or who has a liberal expense account from a fat and undeserving institution), someone who is himself a connoisseur of good restaurants and good food. I suppose this can be called squandering, but I do enjoy ordering, just this once, an expensive dish I have never eaten or asking for a very good wine. This is one reason that I occasionally accept invitations from organizations whose directors feel that a speaker should be willing to forgo payment in favor of lavish entertainment and the pleasure of speaking to that special audience. I sometimes accept such an engagement because I do want to reach that audience—and I order a particularly delicious, expensive breakfast in bed.

Some of the things I do other people may think are extravagant, but I do not. I do not hesitate to make long-distance telephone calls around the world or take taxis or charter an airplane in order to save time or energy or to fit things I believe are important into a too-tight schedule. Anything that saves anyone—myself or anyone who is working hard—time and energy for better things I regard as useful, never as money squandered or spent extravagantly.

ৡৡ

We know that as an anthropologist you have collected hundred of artifacts that help us to understand other cultures. But do you have a personal collection any kind? MAY 1977

Collecting, it seems to me, is a matter of temperament. I am not a collector. Even in my capacity as a museum curator, it is my belief that we should study our collections, publish about them and then give or lend many of the objects to other museums for further study.

In addition, museum curators are discouraged from acquiring—or are definitely not allowed to own—objects from an area in which they specialize. They may receive gifts, of course, from other parts of the world. But if an object is a genuine museum piece, I feel it should be given to a museum at once. Alternatively, it may be donated to a cause that attracts collectors who will purchase it, cherish it and eventually give it to a museum.

I have a few modern Balinese carvings, and, from New Guinea, a few modern lime spatulas that have been redesigned to be used as paper knives and a wooden bowl or two without any ethnographic value. On my desk I have various small objects given me by visitors from faraway places: a Chinese brush jar for my pencils, a miniature of a Japanese baby sitting in a rice basket, a model sputnik, a wood carving of a serious ape reading a volume of Darwin, a tiny Eskimo carving of a woman with a knife. These small objects come, stay for a while and eventually are replaced by other small, unusual bits from elsewhere in the world.

At home I love to look at a Korean bowl made by modern Koreans who have rediscovered an ancient technique of glazing, and I enjoy the way this contemporary bowl is related in color, form and glaze to some old Japanese jars in my apartment.

But I feel no urge to collect for my personal pleasure. The systematic collections of things made by the people I have studied remain where they belong—in the museum.

ৡৡ

Do you have your own methods or tricks for coping with fatigue and jet lag when you travel? NOVEMBER 1977

Fortunately, I am able to cat-nap in almost any position and at any time of the day or night. Many people don't seem to be able to do this. Any other tricks for protecting myself from the wear and tear of travel have to relate to my ability to sleep— and rest—at any time and to wake up alert and wide-awake wherever I am.

I think it is important to distinguish between a jet-lag response that is physiological and one that is psychological. Physiologically I may feel sleepy or hungry because my body tells me (inappropriately) that now is the time I usually go to sleep or have a meal. The solution is simple and obvious: I ask my hostess for a bit of food that is easily available and ready to eat and that I can take to my room, or into the car if we have to drive somewhere. And if I am sleepy, I try to take a nap.

But psychological jet lag is a very different thing. Essentially it is a stubborn refusal to adjust to the time where one is. Once I stayed awake for 36 hours. I then called the long-distance operator and asked what time it was in Australia— where I had just been. When she had given me the information, I told myself firmly that I was here in New York at ten o'clock at night on Monday, *not* in Australia at two o'clock in the afternoon on Tuesday. Once I got this into my head, I went to bed and slept straight through the night. It's not really a question of will power, I think, but of accepting reality with confidence.

When you were a little girl, who were your heroes and heroines in American history? NOVEMBER 1977

Barbara Frietchie was one of my heroines—partly, I think, because I had been told how one of my grandmother's sisters had challenged the Rebel troops in Ohio during the Civil War, as Barbara Frietchie had done in Maryland. To quote the Whittier poem: "'Shoot, if you must, this old gray head, But spare your country's flag!' she said." I liked her spunk.

My greatest hero was Abraham Lincoln, who studied by candlelight in a log cabin and became the President who gave us the Emancipation Proclamation and the Gettysburg Address.

And Nathan Hale, who said proudly before his execution, "I only regret that I have but one life to lose for my country."

And Priscilla, who asked, "Why don't you speak for yourself, John?"

Patrick Henry, who said "Give me liberty or give me death."

And Mary Garvin, the heroine of another Whittier poem, whose dying mother sent her back to the parents from whom the mother herself had been stolen by Indians when she was a child.

In my mind I mixed people in poems and people in history books and both were equally real to me. I filled in names when my mother used to recite from Longfellow's "A Psalm of Life":

Lives of great men all remind us
    We can make our lives sublime,
And, departing, leave behind us
    Footprints on the sands of time.

Very exalted sentiments. But we also used to say:

Wives of great men all remind us
    We should make our lives a serial,
And, departing, leave behind us
    Biographical material.

What one 20th-century invention do you most appreciate?
FEBRUARY 1978

I always have difficulty with a question like this one, which assumes that you can isolate things by category and say what your favorite color is, for example, without designating favorite for what—a dress, a dish or a piece of furniture, a flower or a precious stone.

The invention I most appreciate depends on the context. Speaking as a field worker I would list plastic bags, antibiotics and transistorized equipment. As a professional person I would list Manila folders—people used to tie up papers in packages and there was no way to file them or get at them easily—and also electric typewriters and duplicating machines.

Speaking as a woman, I would list materials that wash easily and do not wrinkle or shrink, and tampons and antiperspirants. Speaking as a mother, I would mention zippers, and as a grandmother, a kind of hairbrush that removes tangles painlessly from a child's long hair. And considering my accumulating slight decrepitudes, I appreciate bifocals, hearing aids and most especially my tall walking stick (not strictly a 20th-century invention, but my 20th-century adaptation of the tall thumbstick used by English countrymen in earlier days).

Who are the storytellers you like best? AUGUST 1978

I enjoy most actual *tellers* of stories, but I assume that this question has to do with the authors of *written* stories in which the emphasis is on the narrative. Then, unless the theme is a very great one indeed, I usually most enjoy the kind of fiction writer whose themes are close to popular culture, writers such as Henry Handel Richardson, who wrote *The Adventures of Richard Mahoney,* Lawrence Durrell, the author of *The Alexandria Quartet,* and William Golding, the author of *The Lord of the Flies.*

I especially enjoy storytellers who re-created the same themes in different settings, as Nevil Shute did in his novels about people caught in World War II or involved in the world of aviation, in such books as *Round the Bend, No Highway, A Town Like Alice, Death of a Wren* and *Trustee From the Tool Room;* and as C. P. Snow did in his cycle of novels, *Strangers and Brothers,* in which the characters move through time in settings connected with science, university life and politics. I like to know that I will encounter the same or a related theme, differently treated, and that I will once more meet the same cast of characters in a new context.

This kind of preference is built up early, I think, in books written for children, which often take the form of a series, such as the English set by Arthur Ransome that began with *Swallows and Amazons,* or Louisa May Alcott's unforgettable American set, *Little Women, Little Men* and *Jo's Boys,* or her charming *Eight Cousins* and *Rose in Bloom.* In my childhood there were also series of which my mother deeply disapproved (but I read them), such as the Elsie Dinsmore books or the Rover Boys, the Motor Boat Boys and many others. Series, good or bad, cater to children's love of the familiar and need for continuity. Children enjoy meeting old friends and making new acquaintances in the Babar books and the Oz books. And the preference lingers on.

Are you a cautious person or a risk taker? JUNE 1974

As it happens, in my case caution and risk-taking are not paired opposites.

I never gamble. As a matter of temperament I neither enjoy gambling nor feel I must avoid it. It simply does not interest me. And I do not believe in ever taking an unnecessary risk. But when it is essential to do so for some important purpose, such as getting to an otherwise inaccessible field site where I have work to do, I do not hesitate to fly in a small, one-motor plane with an indifferent pilot over rough terrain through which I could not walk, or to travel in a frail native canoe on the open sea.

I do not get any thrill whatsoever out of taking a risk, whatever the purpose, nor do I ever court a dangerous situation. I take every precaution to see that anything I do will turn out as I want it to. Once that has been done, I relax and accept what happens.

Both my daughter and granddaughter are cautiously daring. As a child my daughter would climb the tallest tree, cautiously testing each branch on her way up. I myself would never climb any tree unless there was something I could not accomplish without first getting to the treetop.

If you were a young woman living in the United States today, do you think you would want to have a child?
SEPTEMBER 1976

Most of the conditions that governed my decisions fifty years ago would govern them today. In choosing whether or not to have a child I would want to be sure that my husband both wanted a child and would be a good father. I would want to be certain he would welcome either a girl or a boy; we could not then and we still cannot predetermine a child's sex. Today I would want to be sure that having a child meant to my husband—as well as to me—the intention to stay married at least until the child was ready to leave home.

And I would want to be certain that having a child to care for was compatible with my husband's chosen career and fitted my own career commitments. For example, if we were committed to extended periods of field work in very undeveloped, dangerous or impoverished areas, I would not want to take a child to the field with us. There would have to be someone at home whom we both trusted to care for our child, or I would have to plan to stay home myself.

Today I would not want to have more than two children. This is a period when young people must set new standards for reducing the rate of population growth as rapidly as possible. This is particularly important in a rich country like ours where each child, simply by virtue of membership in our affluent, wasteful society, consumes a vastly disproportionate amount of the world's irreplaceable resources (forty times as much as each surviving child does in India) and produces a disproportionate amount of pollution.

I would want to have a child because I enjoy being a woman. I would enjoy—as I have enjoyed—the whole process of conception, pregnancy, birth and lactation. I would enjoy the years of watching our child—endowed with a heritage I knew and a father I loved—develop as a separate but related human being. One of life's great delights is watching how a developing child changes her appearance over the years, resembling now one parent and now the other and from time to time looking more like one and then another more remote ancestor.

I would never under any circumstances consider having a child who I knew would be fatherless after it was conceived. But if my husband were going into danger, I think I would risk a pregnancy . . . in hope.

Should it be impossible for us to have a child of our own, I would not adopt a child unknown to us. Instead I would hope to find among the circle of our relatives and friends children to whom we could give meaningful help or comfort or support, love and friendship. In this way we—my husband and I together—would strengthen our ties to the future and our ongoing sense of responsibility.

Is your over-all outlook on mankind one of optimism? If so, for what reason? FEBRUARY 1972

I am optimistic by nature. I am glad that I am alive. I am even glad that I am living at this particular very difficult, very dangerous and very crucial period in human history.

To this extent my viewpoint about the future reflects a personal temperamental bent—something that must always be taken into account. But, of course, unsupported optimism is not enough.

I support my optimism with my knowledge of how far mankind has come. Throughout the hundreds of thousands of years that human life has evolved, at first physically and later culturally, human beings have withstood tremendous changes and have adjusted to radically new demands. What we have to realize, I believe, is that human ingenuity, imagination and faith in life itself have been crucial both in initiating changes and in meeting new demands imposed by change.

As an anthropologist I also have seen how a living generation of men born into a Stone Age culture has moved into the modern world all at once, skipping the many small steps by which mankind as a whole moved from the distant past into the present.

I find these things encouraging. An earlier generation invented the idea of invention. Now we have invented the industrialization of invention—a way of meeting a recognized problem by setting hundreds of trained persons together to work out solutions and, equally important, to work out the means of putting solutions into practice.

This is what made it possible to send men to the moon and to begin the exploration of outer space. This should give us reason to believe also that we can meet the interlocking problems of runaway populations, war and the pollution of the earth on which we depend for life. None of these problems are insoluble.

What we need is the will to demand solutions and the patience to learn how to carry them out.

What is the source of your essential optimism?

NOVEMBER 1978

I believe that it was crucial for my life-long optimism that I was a very welcome and greatly loved, breast-fed baby.

At the turn of the century, when I was born, writers on infant care were beginning to warn mothers—incorrectly, as we now know—against picking up a baby just because the infant was crying. But my mother said her babies were good babies; if they cried, it was because they needed to be picked up. So I never was left alone to cry desolately. And the only time I ever suffered a feeling of unbearable homesickness was on the occasion I returned in later years to the little seaside resort of Lavallette, New Jersey, where I had spent my very first summer. There the sound of the surf awakened an intense nostalgia for those early, blissful days.

Unfortunately, we do not know to what extent optimism is an inborn genetic trait, basic to one's temperament, and to what extent it is based on prenatal, newborn and later-childhood experiences. We do not know whether a child who appears to be optimistic can be transformed into a pessimist, and vice versa.

A great deal of research has been done on the effects of childhood trauma, that is, on events that harm a child. We know that such experiences as separation from the mother in the earliest months of life, the death of a parent, severe physical injury that keeps a child bedridden for months or an accident that results in the death of a playmate or sibling—all these things, especially when one trauma follows on another, can produce a fixed expectation that even the best things in life will turn out badly.

But we do not even have a name for the kind of event that is the opposite of trauma. By this I mean events that in their happy fulfillment of promise build in the individual the expectation that life itself will be fulfilling and will turn out well. Our ignorance is partly—perhaps almost wholly— owing to the historical circumstance that much of our understanding of human behavior has come about through psychiatry and clinical psychology, professions concerned principally with troubled individuals. Had a genius like Sigmund Freud spent a lifetime working on the nature of the happy child, we might now know more about the effect of felicitous circumstances in any individual's life.

We do not even know whether the survival of a society depends on the presence of both optimists and pessimists in the general population, but there are reasons for believing that both play a necessary part. In a society with too heavy a stress on optimism, people are likely to react precipitantly and to take too few precautions to plan systematically. On the other hand, a predominance of pessimism in a society may give too much weight to conservatism and lead to avoidance of the new as too risky and unknown.

In my own life it has been important to me that almost every loss—or what seemed at first to be a loss—was later somehow followed by a restoration or else made possible a different gain. When I was five I lost a much-loved baby sister, but two years later another baby sister was born. And the one time I failed to win a coveted fellowship, it later became clear—at least to me—that it would have been disastrous had I succeeded. It is also true that pessimists, individuals who are late risers and night people and friends who suffer from depression have sought me out, as if they needed contact with my optimism and early-morning, dependable energy.

Am I by my very nature an essential optimist? Have the events of my life really been, on the whole, propitious and fortunate in their outcome? Or have I simply counted my blessings and neglected to notice other, unpropitious things? Who can say?

੨੭

What have you most wanted to do in life? What, if anything, has stopped you? JULY 1971

I have wanted to do what I have done. If I were given a chance to live my life over again, there is hardly anything I would change. I would make the same choices.

What I wanted in life was to have a career in which I would make a contribution. I wanted to do the things that needed to be done. I wanted a child. I didn't want to do things that other people could do as well as or better than I could.

Fortunately, I have always thought that I was free to make choices, so I have felt that what I have done is what I wanted to do.

AFTERWORD:
MARGARET MEAD
1901-1978

Margaret Mead died on the fifteenth of November, 1978. She was an exciting, inspiring and beloved colleague of all of us who work at *Redbook Magazine.* Some of us knew her and worked with her for all the time she was one of us—sixteen years. Some of us knew her only briefly and only enough to say hello. All of us knew, when we were in her presence, that we were in the presence of greatness.

There are a few human beings in every time and in every gathering of people who convey a sense of universality, of abiding humanity—of, one wants to say, immortality. These are the people who help us to feel that there is a connection between all peoples in all places and in all times and that the connection extends as well to the source of creation and to the beginnings and the ends of days.

Margaret Mead, it seems to us, was one of those human beings.

Her wisdom was with her from her earliest years, and she shared it universally until the end. She published her first book in 1928, when she was twenty-seven years old. It was called *Coming of Age in Samoa,* and it established her almost immediately as a major figure, not only in her field, which was anthropology, but in the world at large as well.

Since then her books, her scientific papers, her popular writings (including her columns in *Redbook*), her speeches, her prefaces, introductions and contributions to the works of others, have accumulated into a sizable monument to her genius and a treasury for those who seek ways to appreciate and understand the human condition.

Tributes like these to her life will make her sound formidable. She was not. She was accessible to everyone. She was as helpful, direct and friendly speaking to the congregations of the smallest churches or synagogues in Iowa or Maine or Georgia or to villagers in Greece as she was un-awed, forceful and wise in the White House or in the halls of Congress, where she was frequently called upon for advice and counsel.

New York cab drivers knew her and admired her. Oc-togenarians and teen-agers in the South Pacific honored and loved her and looked forward to her comings and goings. Scientific societies sought her leadership. Children visited with her in the American Museum of Natural History, where she made her office for more than fifty years. Scores of or-ganizations at home and abroad asked her to speak to them every year. In an average year she often spoke to more than one hundred groups, roughly two a week, many of them for no fee. She went everywhere. She was tireless and disre-garded time. She wanted to speak to everyone and she did.

Margaret Mead was tough and smart and vigorous. She brooked no nonsense. Her voice shouting, "Rubbish!" when she was faced with nonsensical argument and false facts was a joy to hear and a sustenance for her listeners. She worked all her life in behalf of equality and opportunity for women. And women everywhere cherished her. And so did men.

She railed and fought against those in power who used food as a weapon in international political struggles. For her, trad-ing in food while human beings starve or are in want was a criminal strategy she would not abide, and she tried to get us all to see it as an unspeakable evil.

In behalf of all of us, she worried constantly about the dangers of nuclear radiation, the piling up of nuclear weapons, the distribution of nuclear wastes, the pollution of our air, our earth, our water, and our general disregard for the safety of humanity. She sought ways for women and men to learn to live together rationally and in comfort. She was worried that our communities did not care well enough for home-less children, and the handicapped and the aged.

She spoke, as she wrote, directly, with kindness, casting no blame, leaving no guilt.

She tried to help us all to see that we share the world and must live in it and work in it together.

She cared about us all. She wanted us to care about each other in all our colors, all our ethnic and religious and national backgrounds, in all our sexes, all our moods and all our modes. She nourished those who would listen to her.

She was a woman.

—Sey Chassler
Editor-in-Chief
Redbook Magazine

INDEX